BILL LUCAS

DISCOVER YOUR HIDDEN TALENTS

The essential guide to lifelong learning

Published by
Network Educational Press Ltd
PO Box 635
Stafford
ST16 1BF
www.networkpress.co.uk

ISBN 1 85539 104 X Paperback
ISBN 1 85539 163 5 Hardback

Managing editor: Dawn Booth
Design & layout: Neil Hawkins
Illustrations: Dave Thompson
Cover design: Paul Keen
Printed in Great Britain by MPG Books Ltd, Bodmin, Cornwall

Acknowledgements

Many thanks to:
My family, especially Henrietta for her active encouragement and support. My publisher and all the editorial and design team. The expert panel who guided me throughout the process of writing and re-writing – Professor Guy Claxton, Professor Louise Stoll, Professor Elizabeth Leo, Dr Peter Honey, Mike Leibling and Octavius Black. Special thanks to Guy, without whose rigorous feedback the book might not be in the shape it finally is now!

Contents

How to use this book

Discover Your Hidden Talents is a guide to your learning.

It has been written so that you can find everything you might reasonably want to know about becoming a good learner between the covers of one book. It has been designed in such a way that you should be able to locate topics easily.

Discover Your Hidden Talents is divided into three parts.

Part One deals with the big picture. It outlines some essential facts about your mind and explains a useful model – Ready, Go, Steady – to help you plan your learning.

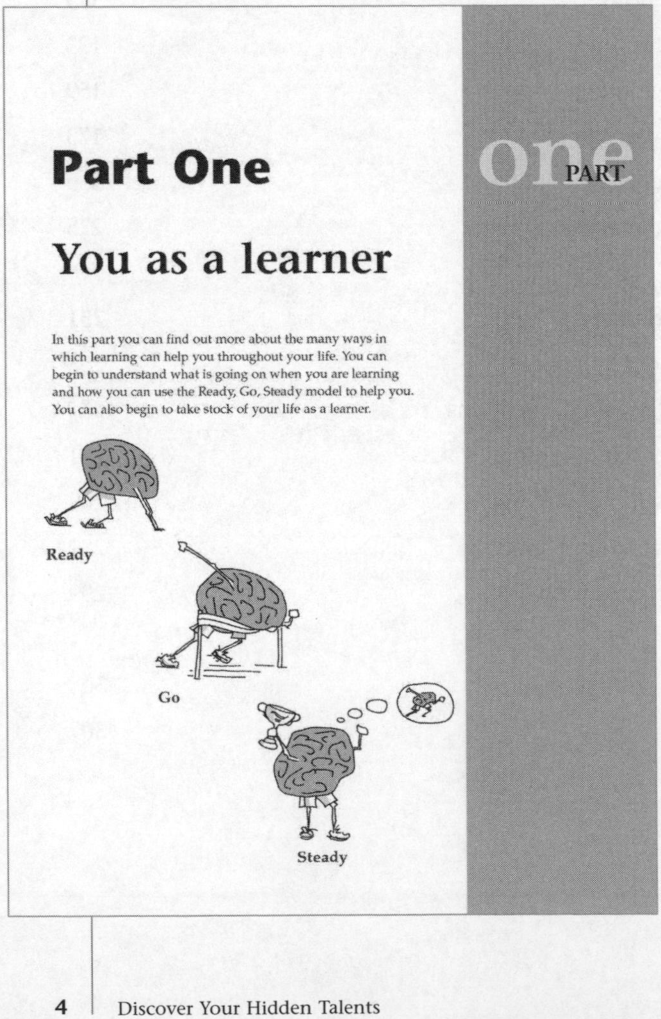

Part One

one PART

You as a learner

In this part you can find out more about the many ways in which learning can help you throughout your life. You can begin to understand what is going on when you are learning and how you can use the Ready, Go, Steady model to help you. You can also begin to take stock of your life as a learner.

Ready

Go

Steady

Part Two goes into more detail. You can:

- find out about the 5Rs of lifelong learning
- discover some of the big ideas which have excited learners over the ages
- see how to apply the most important theories in your life by trying out new techniques.

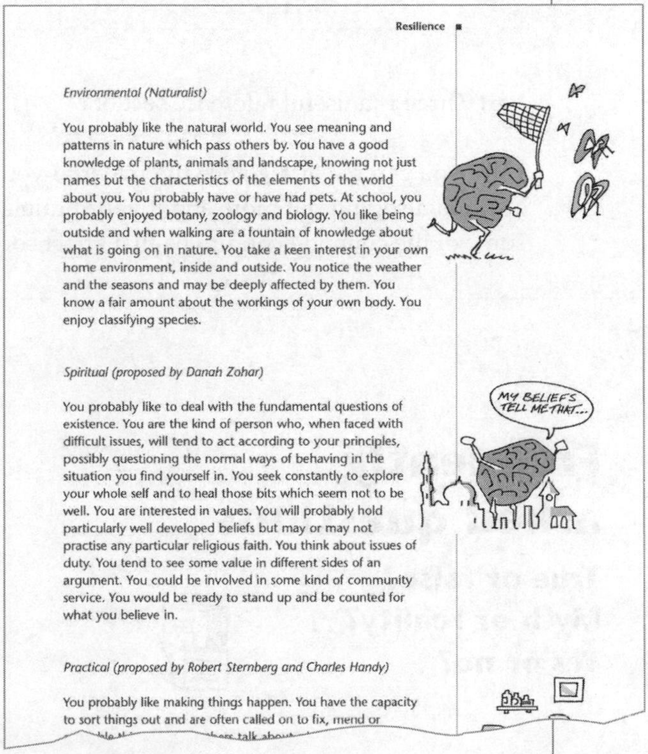

Resilience

Environmental (Naturalist)

You probably like the natural world. You see meaning and patterns in nature which pass others by. You have a good knowledge of plants, animals and landscape, knowing not just names but the characteristics of the elements of the world about you. You probably have or have had pets. At school, you probably enjoyed botany, zoology and biology. You like being outside and when walking are a fountain of knowledge about what is going on in nature. You take a keen interest in your own home environment, inside and outside. You notice the weather and the seasons and may be deeply affected by them. You know a fair amount about the workings of your own body. You enjoy classifying species.

Spiritual (proposed by Danah Zohar)

You probably like to deal with the fundamental questions of existence. You are the kind of person who, when faced with difficult issues, will tend to act according to your principles, possibly questioning the normal ways of behaving in the situation you find yourself in. You seek constantly to explore your whole self and to heal those bits which seem not to be well. You are interested in values. You will probably hold particularly well developed beliefs but may or may not practise any particular religious faith. You think about issues of duty. You tend to see some value in different sides of an argument. You could be involved in some kind of community service. You would be ready to stand up and be counted for what you believe in.

Practical (proposed by Robert Sternberg and Charles Handy)

You probably like making things happen. You have the capacity to sort things out and are often called on to fix, mend or

Everything is explained in clear, 'how-to' steps.

How to listen actively

1. Maintain eye contact.
2. Focus on what someone is saying not how they are saying it.
3. From time to time, make sure that you show your interest.
4. Be patient and check your understanding of what is being said.
5. Avoid jumping in with too many questions.
6. Try to empathize, imagining what it is like to be in the other person's shoes. Draw him/her out.
7. Pick up non-verbal cues that suggest a response from you would be helpful.
8. Try not to let your mind wander.
9. Treat listening as a challenging mental task and feel good because you are managing to achieve it.
10. Stay active by asking questions about what you are listening to.

Each technique begins with a 'Why bother … ?' so that at every stage you are clear about the purpose of what you are finding out.

Why bother learning how to revise?

Life is full of tests and examinations and revision is a key skill.
Regularly revising what you have learned is the best way of remembering it.

Part Three is a useful reference section.

Here you can see at a glance the material you have read in Part Two. You can also find out more about your brain and begin to understand some of the common conditions that affect some learners.

Chapter 14

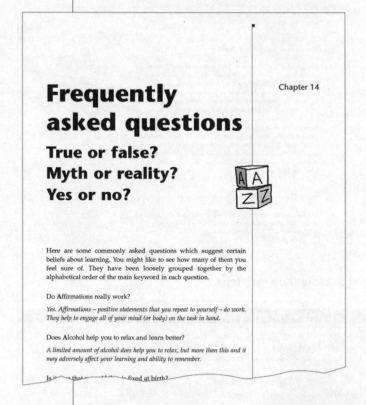

Frequently asked questions

True or false? Myth or reality? Yes or no?

Here are some commonly asked questions which suggest certain beliefs about learning. You might like to see how many of them you feel sure of. They have been loosely grouped together by the alphabetical order of the main keyword in each question.

Do Affirmations really work?

Yes. Affirmations – positive statements that you repeat to yourself – do work. They help to engage all of your mind (or body) on the task in hand.

Does Alcohol help you to relax and learn better?

A limited amount of alcohol does help you to relax, but more than this and it may adversely affect your learning and ability to remember.

Is it … that … is fixed at birth?

A comprehensive index at the end should ensure that you can find your way to anything that you might want.

The following icons are used throughout the book to help you to find your way around easily:

An interesting idea for you to consider.

A useful technique to practise and use.

A helpful website.

A checklist of practical advice and tips.

An alphabetical list, for easy reference.

You will also find these icons used occasionally. They are explained more fully on pages 83–84:

Your own preferences

Your environment

What you are learning

The 5Rs appear throughout this book. They are a simple way of trying to describe what is involved in lifelong learning. They are shown by the following icons:

Resourcefulness

Remembering

Resilience

Reflectiveness

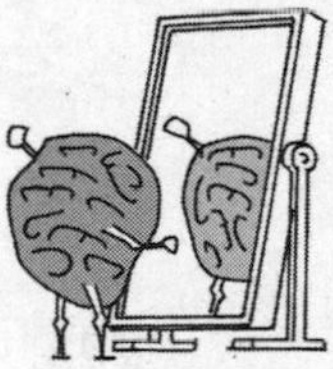

Responsiveness

Health warning Learning is extremely complex and, not surprisingly, there are different views about the validity of some approaches described in this book. I have tried to select ideas and techniques that have some scientific justification and a practical track record of usefulness. Of course I am human and will have made mistakes ...

Part One

You as a learner

one PART

In this part you can find out more about the many ways in which learning can help you throughout your life. You can begin to understand what is going on when you are learning and how you can use the Ready, Go, Steady model to help you. You can also begin to take stock of your life as a learner.

Ready

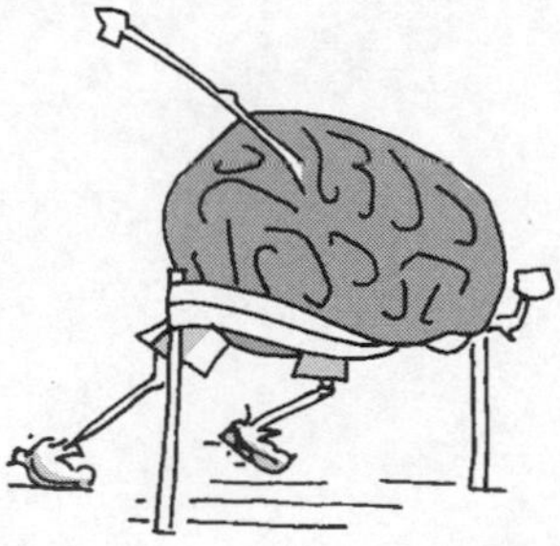

Go

Steady

one PART

Chapter 1

Learning and living

Lifelong learning is the subject of *Discover Your Hidden Talents*. In this book you will find almost everything you could want to know about yourself as a learner living in a time of rapid change and uncertainty.

In the last couple of decades there has been a quiet revolution in many aspects of our lives. You cannot, for example, walk along many high streets for long without bumping into a coffee shop, an internet café or a gym full of people exercising. Yet only a few years ago most people would have scorned the idea of spending their money on such things. Now it is taken for granted that we like to drink decent coffee, want access to the web and our email and need to keep fit.

At the same time there have been radical changes in the way people view learning. Not so long ago learning was another word for education. It was something that you did at school and, if you were one of a lucky few, at university. It was largely thought of as being formal. By your mid-teens, or at the latest by your twenties, you were done with it. Apart from any compulsory training you received in your working life, there was very little concept of the value of continuing learning other than through individual interests and hobbies. This is all changing.

In the 1990s a new phrase entered our language – 'lifelong learning'. First extensively used by Bill Clinton and taken up by European Commission President, Jacques Delors, it suggested that learning was something that you did throughout your life. At the same time as the Blair government has focused on its well-publicised mantra of 'education, education, education', there has been waged a more stealthy campaign for 'learning, learning, learning'.

Learning and living have suddenly become much more closely linked. People learn things in order to live more effectively or more happily rather than just because a teacher tells them to do so or because an examination demands it. Much of this kind of learning happens not in classrooms but in the margins of our lives – valuable know-how that you pick up by reflecting on things that you see or hear. Much of it does not fit under the conventional subject headings you are familiar with from your schooldays, like mathematics or geography. Yet it is precisely the kind of thing that you need to help you get on with your life.

> ‘Significant learning combines the logical and the intuitive, the intellect and the feelings, the concept and the experience, the idea and the meaning.’
>
> Carl Rogers

Learning is what you get when you reflect on the experiences of living. It involves using your entire mind and body, and engaging your thoughts and feelings. Arguably learning is the most important of all human activities and learning to learn more effectively – the theme of this book – is the key skill of the century.

Different kinds of learning

Many different words are used when people talk about learning. The most common of these are 'development', 'training' and 'education'. Each one means different things, as you will find out as you read this book.

> ‘I have never let my schooling interfere with my education.’
>
> Mark Twain

It is important to realize that most of your learning is informal. It takes place on a day to day basis. Effective learners enjoy extracting the meaning from their informal experiences and improving or doing things differently as a consequence.

Informal learning involves watching, listening and copying. It includes: all the things that you do at home, like DIY, gardening or reading; things that you learn from your social life – like noticing how old friends and their family have worked out a very effective way of dealing with teenage requests for sleepovers; and opportunities you acquire during your working day – for example, you may have the chance to see how a colleague from another business handles something of relevance to your own job.

Sometimes you will find yourself plunged 'in at the deep end' with a new experience. A loved one dies, a relationship ends or something unexpected, such as the loss of your job, forces you to rethink the world you live in. At other times you plan to learn, perhaps by taking a course or following the instructions in a new recipe. If you opt to study at a college, for example, this would typically be referred to as 'adult education'. If you are at work, it may be called a 'training programme'.

More often, however, you learn as a result of something that happens to you. This is sometimes called accidental learning. For many people accidental learning, also known in the workplace as 'learning with Nellie', is one of the most powerful and effective kinds of learning at work. Indeed some employers have begun to recognize its importance by encouraging job shadowing and job rotation (see page 233 for more on this).

It is a curious and perplexing fact that you are learning most of the time. I say perplexing because if you are doing it anyway why bother to become more aware of it? You do not, for example, need lessons in breathing (unless you are a professional singer); you just get on and do it. It turns out that with learning, as with most things in life, you can get better at it if you know a bit more about it. Or, put another way, learning is learnable, but only if you are prepared to hold it up to the light and look at it carefully.

In *Discover Your Hidden Talents* I have tried to pull all this together into a kind of guide, with lots of different ways in which it can be used by learners. Incidentally there is a grand word for all of this: 'andragogy'. First coined by American educator Malcolm Knowles in the 1970s, the term describes the science and craft of the way adults learn (like 'pedagogy' does for the way children learn). The essential difference between adult learning and school-age learning is that it is self-directed. Adults choose to do it, while children and young people, by and large, have no option but to take part. Consequently, the process of learning becomes at least as important as the content – adults need to be clear why they need to learn something, tend to prefer to experience learning directly and enjoy solving problems. The process of teaching adults is closer to that of the facilitator than to being a lecturer.

Other relevant factors include the fact that adults:

- have more experience which they tend to like to share
- can be intimidated by formal learning experiences, especially if their memories of school are not happy
- need feedback as well as, or instead of, formal qualifications
- may have different priorities, depending on their age and stage of life
- often see learning as a largely social activity.

In your own life, the more you can create opportunities to learn accidentally the better. And, as you do so, you will get more out of your learning if you have effective ways of reflecting on what you are picking up. After all, learning is one of the key methods by which you extract meaning from your experiences of life. As you process data, you see connections and patterns, and extract meaning. Of course that meaning is subjective; different things mean different things to different people!

How we respond to planned and unplanned learning

Researcher David Megginson has suggested that learners respond to planned and unplanned learning in four different ways:

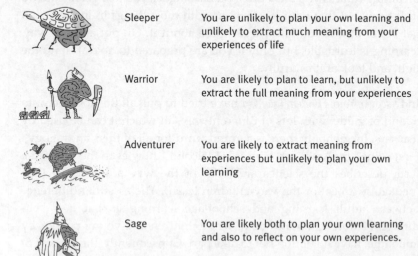

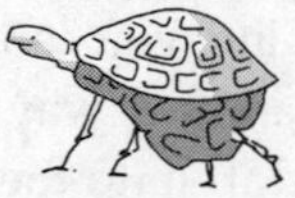	Sleeper	You are unlikely to plan your own learning and unlikely to extract much meaning from your experiences of life
	Warrior	You are likely to plan to learn, but unlikely to extract the full meaning from your experiences
	Adventurer	You are likely to extract meaning from experiences but unlikely to plan your own learning
	Sage	You are likely both to plan your own learning and also to reflect on your own experiences.

He argues that we all need to become 'sages' in our learning lives.

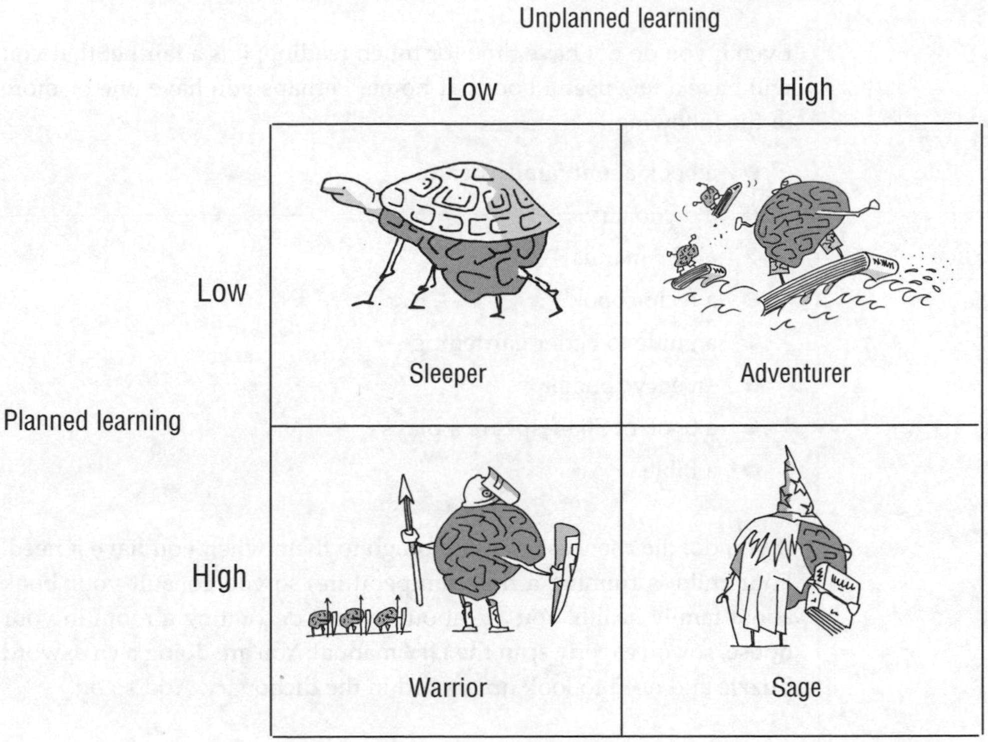

Put crudely, you can choose to sleep your way through life, not pausing to reflect or adapt, or you can be either an adventurer or a warrior, partially learning from what happens to you. Or – and I am not sure that sage is quite the right word – you can be smart and benefit from both your planned and your unplanned experiences.

When you learn you also change and develop. Sometimes it may seem like progress – you take a course and get promotion. Other times it can seem to take you backwards, as when you explore something which you thought at first was very simple and discover that it is actually more complex. By exploring the suggestions in *Discover Your Hidden Talents* you will inevitably be embarking on an exciting journey which may well not always lead you in the direction you thought you were heading!

> Always continue the climb. It is possible for you to do whatever you choose, if you first get to know who you are and are willing to work with a power that is greater than ourselves to do it.
>
> Oprah Winfrey

A new kind of reference book

Even if you do not have time for much reading, it is a fair bet that you will have a few useful books at home. Perhaps you have one or more of the following:

- a book about family health
- a dictionary
- a DIY manual
- a recipe book
- a guide to better gardening
- an encyclopedia
- a book of Shakespeare's plays
- a Bible.

If you do, the chances are that you go to them when you have a need. Your child is running a high temperature, so you consult your book about family health. You are about to start decorating a room in your house, so you eagerly scan the DIY manual. You are doing a crossword puzzle and need to look up a word in the dictionary. And so on.

All of the above books help you to do things. Some are very practical, others are more about your own enjoyment, while some transport you to imaginative worlds far away from where you are when you read them. Such books are full of advice – tips, ideas and experiences – that other people have learned and taken the time to write down.

But look at the list again. There is one important area of your life which is largely missed. It is the thing that matters almost more than your health. The missing subject is you as a learner. Yet the better you learn, the better you will perform and the better you will be able to live your life. For learning is, after all, how you make sense of life. Something happens and you learn from it, perhaps deciding to do it differently next time. You adapt and change. Without learning our species would simply not survive. And nor would you.

Think of *Discover Your Hidden Talents* as a new kind of reference book, one that equips you for a lifetime of learning in the same way as a family health guide helps you to live healthily. Of course there is no direct learning equivalent of being ill. If you are struggling with your learning you do not suddenly break out into a rash! When you are feeling turned off from learning, the malaise is more subtle; *Discover Your Hidden Talents* will help you to spot your own personal symptoms of 'poor learning health'. But, more importantly, it will be there for you with helpful advice, whenever you need it, on a range of useful topics.

Our world has never changed so fast and, unless you are learning faster than it is changing, you may well end up struggling.

Take a moment to start thinking what learning can do for you. Here are just four examples:

1. You do not seem to be able to absorb information, so you find out more about how to get yourself in the right state in order that you are ready to learn.
2. You keep losing your temper when you get stuck, so you practise some techniques to help you become more persistent.
3. You cannot seem to motivate yourself, so choosing different kinds of learning might be the answer.
4. You just cannot remember the things you want to do on a daily basis, so you decide to find out how to improve your memory.

Whatever your concern, you should find the beginnings of an answer in this book.

2

Time for a check-up

Chapter 2

Every year most people take their car to a garage to be serviced. In the UK, at least, cars of more than three years old need to have an MOT or check-up every year. As you get older you have a full medical check-up to ensure that your body is healthy. But what about your mental powers? When was the last time you checked out your own learning health?

The check-up I recommend you take now consists of a series of questions. Unlike an MOT, you do not pass or fail this test and it is free! Instead I hope that the questions help you to see for yourself whether your learning systems are functioning as they should be. At the end of each short section, if you feel uncertain or even concerned, help is at hand in the shape of Part Two, on pages 67–249.

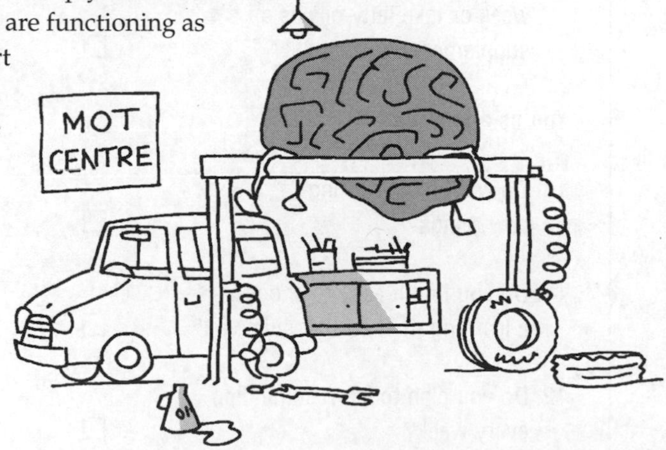

	Never	Sometimes	Very often	Always
State of mind				
1. Do you feel good about yourself?	☐	☐	☐	☐
2. Do you feel curious about life?	☐	☐	☐	☐
3. Do you ever feel too worried to concentrate?	☐	☐	☐	☐
4. Are you relaxed and alert?	☐	☐	☐	☐
Health				
5. Do you take exercise?	☐	☐	☐	☐
6. Do you wake up feeling refreshed?	☐	☐	☐	☐
Diet				
7. Do you drink plenty of water, say a litre, every day?	☐	☐	☐	☐
8. Do you eat at least five fresh fruit or vegetables every day?	☐	☐	☐	☐
9. Do you eat fish at least once a week or take fatty oils as a supplement?	☐	☐	☐	☐
You as a learner				
10. Do you enjoy learning new things?	☐	☐	☐	☐
11. Do you find it easy to choose a learning method that suits you?	☐	☐	☐	☐
12. Do you plan to learn something every week?	☐	☐	☐	☐

	Never	Sometimes	Very often	Always
13. Are you comfortable when you learn with other people?	☐	☐	☐	☐
14. Are you confident about your memory?	☐	☐	☐	☐
15. Do you manage to finish what you start learning rather than giving up?	☐	☐	☐	☐
16. Do you consciously reflect on things that happen to you?	☐	☐	☐	☐
17. Are you able to apply what you have learned to other areas of your life?	☐	☐	☐	☐
18. Do you set yourself clear goals?	☐	☐	☐	☐
19. Are you able to deal with distractions and difficulties?	☐	☐	☐	☐
20. Do you like asking questions?	☐	☐	☐	☐
21. Do you learn from your mistakes?	☐	☐	☐	☐
22. Do you alter your behaviour as a result of what you learn?	☐	☐	☐	☐
23. Do you view the idea of change positively?	☐	☐	☐	☐
24. Do you set aside time for your learning?	☐	☐	☐	☐

How did you do?

The figures below are by no means definitive! Please take them as a very gentle prompt to your thinking and nothing more!

How to score

For each tick in the 'Never' column score one.
For each tick in the 'Sometimes' column score two.
For each tick in the 'Very often' column score three.
For each tick in the 'Always' column score four.

Score

73–96	You already seem to be a really positive, well-balanced, very healthy and very competent lifelong learner. Enjoy using some of the ideas in *Discover Your Hidden Talents* as a further stimulus to your development.
49–72	You seem to be a positive, balanced, healthy and competent learner. Enjoy using this book to find out more.
25–48	You seem to have begun to develop yourself as a learner and may want to focus on some of the other areas outlined in thc book. Read *Discover Your Hidden Talents* to find out how you can become a more effective learner.
0–24	There are lots of areas which you might like to explore about you as a learner.

You might like to compare your results with those of another family member or colleague at work and see what conclusions you draw. What other questions can you think of which might help you check yourself out?

Chapter 3

What's going on when you are learning

Have you ever stopped to think about what is actually happening when you are learning? A child tentatively takes a short, wobbly step forward but in a few days has begun to walk confidently. A teenager learns how to drive a car. An adult discovers how to empathize with someone who is distressed. A grandparent works out how to send an email for the first time, at the age of 80. In each of these examples learning is clearly taking place.

But what is going on? Is learning to drive the same as learning to empathize? Is learning the names of the planets the same as mastering a new program on your computer? Do we all learn in the same way? As you read *Discover Your Hidden Talents* you will discover some of the answers to these questions and develop many more questions of your own.

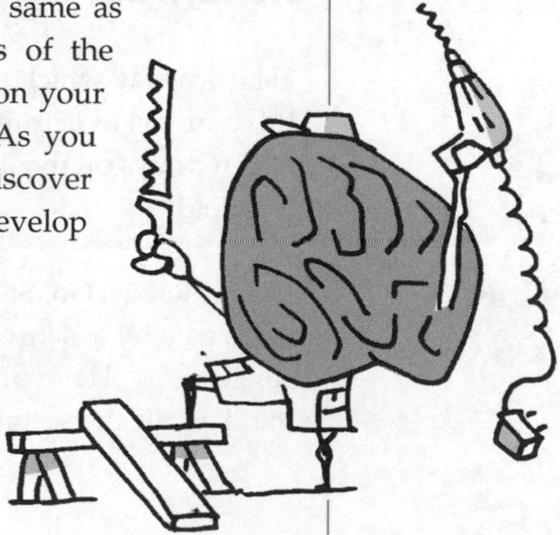

For several thousand years, people have been trying to work out what is going on when you are learning; and in the last hundred years there have been many different theories put forward. You can read more about the most important of these in Part Three, on pages 269–279, and see how some of these can help you as a learner today. In many cases new theories build on older ones. However, sometimes new thinking contradicts what has gone before and needs to be considered with caution.

Hopefully we can all agree that our five senses are very important in learning. We take in data with them which the brain then processes. You have five senses – sight, hearing, touch, taste and smell. Of these, your sense of smell is one of the most powerful. For example, a smell can trigger a whole string of forgotten memories. Olfactory nerves (for smelling) are located within the nasal cavity and respond to particular smells, sending information to the part of the brain that has a role in dealing with memory and emotions. This area connects with the hypothalamus and pituitary gland which in turn cause a number of chemical actions within the body. Aromatherapy exploits this beneficially to help users to be calm and relaxed.

However, exactly what happens in the different parts of the brain is much more complex as are the psychological processes involved. You can read some of the most commonly asked questions by turning to page 257 and find out about some of the things we are discovering about our brains by turning to page 281.

Most recently, with advances in brain scanning technology, it has even become possible to look inside your head as you are actually learning. The more we find out, the more we realize the complexity of it all.

Ready, Go, Steady

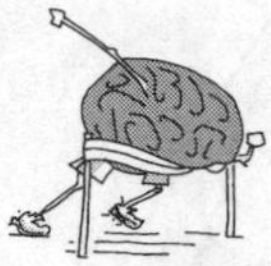

Here is a way which may help you in understanding what is going on. It is a model of learning which I have developed over many years and which draws on the thinking of some of the most respected thinkers in this field.

I call it Ready, Go, Steady. We will be using it throughout this book to help us make sense of a mass of theoretical ideas and practical suggestions. There are three stages. The first is largely about state of mind, while the second and third are more concerned with techniques.

READY	You need to be emotionally ready and motivated to learn
GO	You need to have a range of techniques to harness the full range of your talents and creativity (*Resourcefulness**) You need to be able to recall things (*Remembering**) You need to be able to keep going when learning gets difficult (*Resilience**)
STEADY	You need to be able to make time to take stock (*Reflectiveness**) You need to be able to change, adapt and learn from your mistakes (*Responsiveness**)

* To find out what the 5Rs involve turn to Chapters 6–10.

You could also visualize this as a cycle.

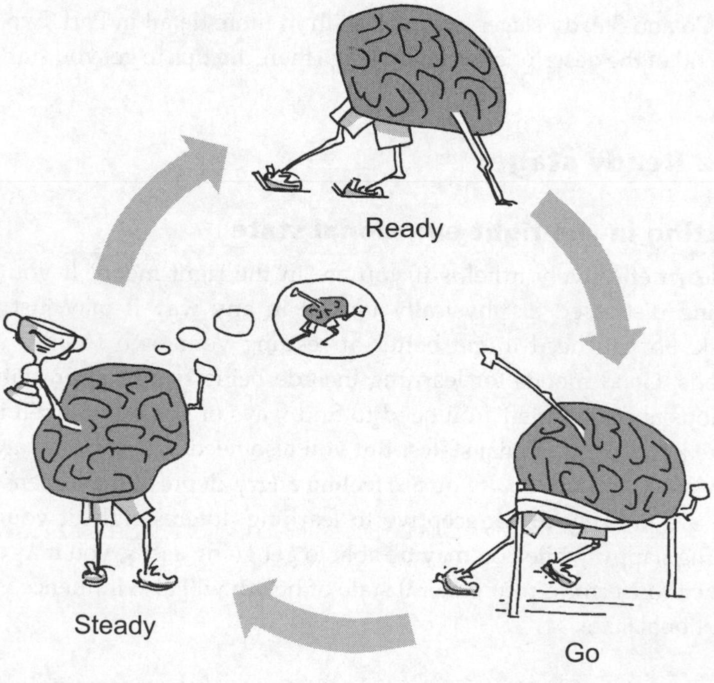

Of course, no one episode of learning is the same, but, put simply, my model of learning recognizes that learning often has three components to it.

You need to be ready to learn before you start learning.

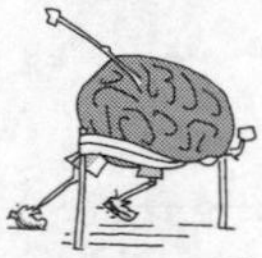

Then you need to choose the best method.

Finally, you need to do things differently as a result of what you have learned.

Sometimes you will not even stop to think about getting ready. You will simply plunge in. Other times you may be so close to the experience that you are not yet ready for the Steady stage and need more time before you can start to process your experiences.

Learning is also unpredictable. Once you are ready, you need a range of techniques to help you at each stage. This is where the 5Rs of the Go and Steady stages come in (see Part Two for a full explanation of this).

In the next few pages you can find out about the main features of each of the stages. The focus of this section is on getting Ready to learn, as the Go and Steady stages are dealt with in more detail in Part Two. At the end of the descriptions of each stage there are tips to get you started.

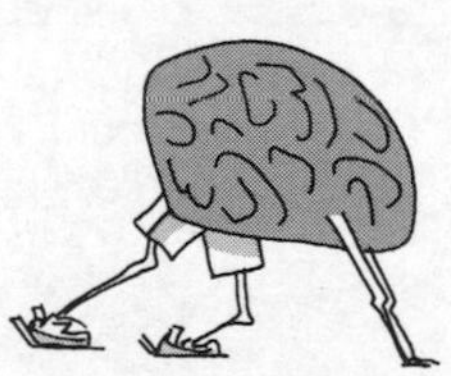

The Ready stage

Getting in the right emotional state

"Learning is not compulsory, but neither is survival."

W.S. Deming

To learn effectively it helps if you are in the right mood. If you are feeling distressed or physically unwell in any way it may just not work. So you need to get better at reading your own feelings and moods. Good moods for learning include being happy, appreciative, curious and interested. You need to find ways of getting yourself into these kinds of emotional states. But you also need to become aware of how moods affect you. If you are feeling angry, depressed or defensive, you are unlikely to be receptive to learning. Interestingly, if you are feeling happy, while you may be able to get going easily, you may also make more errors! Your general state of health will also influence your emotional state.

The best state for most kinds of learning involves a combination of relaxation and alertness. You need to be relaxed enough to be in control of your thoughts but not so laid-back that you are not engaged! For planned learning to be effective, you need to be able to 'pay attention'. While this phrase may bring back unwelcome memories of teachers at school telling you to pay attention, worry not! As adults, this is a different concept involving your own voluntary activity. Attention is the state of mind in which you are focused on your learning. Unless you pay attention it is difficult to learn effectively. Attention is affected by many things, including: mood, emotional state, diet, tiredness and stress. Although we are all different and all learn in different ways, there are some things which may help you to improve your attention:

- Use lively music to energize yourself if you are not alert enough.
- Use calming music if you need to be more relaxed.
- Use unusual colours/shapes/drawings or anything that makes a page of words you are studying more engaging.
- Take regular stretch breaks after 20 minutes or so, unless you do not wish to interrupt your flow.
- Have a change of scenery from time to time.
- Focus on particular things rather than trying to concentrate on everything at the same time.

Music affects us all in different ways. So, not surprisingly, some learners find it helps them to concentrate on certain tasks while others find it positively intrusive. Recently, a number of grand claims have been made for the power of music in learning. You can, apparently, play your baby music and its brain will develop overnight. Or possibly you can play music to improve your performance. If only it were so simple!

However, there is some evidence that playing baroque music (such as Mozart) before certain mathematical tasks can improve performance for some people. Similarly, it appears to be the case that starting to learn a musical instrument early in life helps your brain to develop and possibly enhances memory. It seems that the corpus callosum and certain other areas of the brain are larger in musicians than in others. From which it would seem reasonable to deduce that playing music may alter the structure of the brain (just as doing a number of activities probably does). The truth is that research on this interesting area is still, relatively speaking, in its early days.

What we can be more sure about is that music can be a powerful way of altering mood. So, if you are too stressed it can calm you down. Or, if too calm, a more insistent beat can help to make you more alert. This makes music a very useful aspect of any learner's life.

You can find many more techniques to help you get in the right emotional state on pages 36 and 37.

A hierarchy of needs

Psychologist Abraham Maslow first came up with an idea that helps us to see if we are ready to learn. He said that human beings have a hierarchy of needs starting with basic things like water, food and sleep, moving up to being safe, then to being loved, then to having enough self-esteem and finally to what he called 'self-actualization', in other words a state in which you feel that you have been totally fulfilled. His theory also suggests that we are motivated by unsatisfied needs. We all want to satisfy our needs and we can only do this by moving up the ladder.

Maslow recognized that, although humans are essentially rational beings, they do not act that way, being influenced much more by their emotional response to the world. Maslow's hierarchy of needs looks like this:

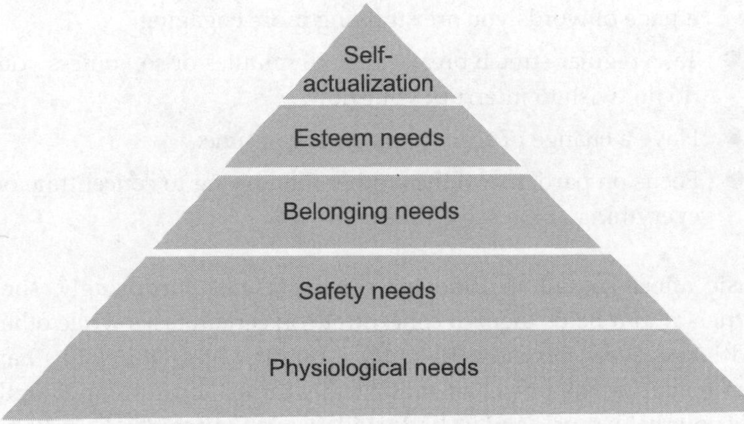

Maslow's views are a radical departure from the beliefs of other influential psychologists like Sigmund Freud and B.F. Skinner. Freud took a fairly pessimistic view of people as animals dominated by their lusts, while Skinner based his views on the power of simple rewards like food or sex.

Maslow's theory helps us to understand why we are unlikely to be ready to learn unless many of our lower-level needs have been satisfied. If we are hungry or miserable, learning may not be on our agenda. Most people find this theory a convincing and helpful one, although it is worth noting that it is possible to do things, even when few of our needs are being satisfied, if we are really desperate.

Getting motivated to learn

> "It is in fact nothing short of a miracle that the modern methods of instruction have not yet entirely strangled the holy curiosity of enquiry."
>
> Albert Einstein

The other aspect of getting ready is motivation. As a learner, your appetite or hunger for learning is a key part of what makes you an effective learner. It is what keeps you going when things get tough. We are all born with an instinctive curiosity – an appetite to learn. This is what drives us to learn how to walk and talk. It is why small children are constantly asking questions. However, many people find their appetite diminishes as they go through formal education. Effective learners know what they have to do to rekindle their appetite. When you explore Resilience, in Part Two, you can find out more about how to boost your own motivation to learn.

Having clear goals and a sense of direction are important. Effective learners regularly think about what they are trying to achieve to be sure that they are spending their energy on the things that they want to do. It is easy to spend an hour copying something out from a book when you know that trying to memorize it would be a better use of your time. If you have clear aims you are more likely to achieve in life and in learning.

> Those who are going nowhere usually get there.
>
> Henry Ford

A key element of motivation will be your own level of self-esteem – how good you are feeling about yourself as a learner. Learning and self-esteem are closely connected: success at learning raises esteem and failure tends to lower it.

Rewarding yourself

External rewards and praise can help, although the best sorts are the ones which come from within you. There are two kinds of rewards: intrinsic and extrinsic. An intrinsic reward is something that comes from within you; you get a feeling of satisfaction on having completed a task, for example. An extrinsic reward comes from outside you. It might be an increase in salary or, for a child, a treat of some kind.

Research shows that intrinsic rewards are better. They last over time, whereas, although extrinsic rewards can help short term ('Do this and I'll give you £10'), unless the learner really wants to learn, the learning will not be as effective.

Another thing about reward is that it can have strange consequences. For example, in an attempt to improve children's reading, some schools introduced a system of rewards for the number of books each pupil read over a period of time. Guess what? Pupils read many more books but they could not recall what they were about. So the outcome was superficial speed rather than proper understanding.

> No use to shout at them to pay attention. If the situations, the materials, the problems before the child do not interest him, his attention will slip off to what does interest him, and no amount of exhortation or threats will bring it back.
>
> John Holt

Effective learners need to be able to use both intrinsic and extrinsic motivation. We all need treats and external feedback, but we also need to be able to cultivate our own internal appetite for learning.

Having a positive attitude

Having a positive attitude to learning will help you. Mind set really matters, as you can see by reading pages 180 and 181. No one can force you to learn. It is a voluntary activity. There are two main components of attitude: the confidence you have in yourself and the interest you have in what it is that you are about to learn. Your own confidence or self-esteem will depend on how successful you have generally been in the past and on various other emotional factors, such as how you are feeling more generally in your life. The interest you have in the learning will be connected to your previous experiences, your view of any teacher involved and your view of the learning method being used. If you have previously failed, your confidence will clearly be lower. If you find computers threatening, for example, then you may have a poor attitude towards using them as part of your learning.

Managing the environment

The environment matters, too. High-challenge, low-threat environments generally help us in our learning. We tend to respond well to challenge, provided it does not push us too far. A challenge is an invitation to 'stretch' yourself. Challenge is essential in your learning. Challenge stimulates you to develop. When this happens your brain literally changes its chemistry. Your neurons are stimulated into growing more dendrites so that they can connect with other neurons.

The impact of stress and challenge on your motivation is something like this:

	High threat	Low threat
High challenge	Feel controlled and compelled	Feel engaged
Low challenge	Feel controlled and de-motivated	Feel bored

We feel engaged when we are asked to do something at the edge of our competence and we rise to the occasion. If it is too easy we get bored. But if we are put under too much pressure we may end up feeling used and controlled.

If you are learning at work, then you may have limited control over your psychological environment, for example the impact of your boss or the culture of your group of friends. But you can still invest some thought into improving it. You can make sure that you are in a comfortable place, with the right level of noise, light and warmth.

Barriers to learning

There are many barriers to learning and it may help to be more aware of these so that you are better equipped to deal with them. These can be divided into cultural, structural and personal issues.

Cultural	Structural	Personal
Suspicion of clever people Lack of previous interest or opportunity in the family For some women, a feeling that it is a man's world For some men, a feeling that learning is not for 'real men' A tradition of leaving school and going straight into a job Alienation because of the accident of location, for example where there is high unemployment Peer pressure	Lack of money Lack of time Lack of childcare Disability Lack of information, advice and guidance	A negative association because of unhappy school memories Language issues Low motivation Low self-esteem Health Age Learning styles not seeming compatible with what is on offer

There are ways of overcoming each of these barriers, many of which are inter-related. It is possible to make huge progress by starting with those barriers over which you have most control: the personal ones. But for you to develop a lifelong interest in learning, you will undoubtedly need to tackle the cultural and structural barriers too.

The following are some of the common barriers with suggestions of how you can overcome them.

	Barrier	Solution
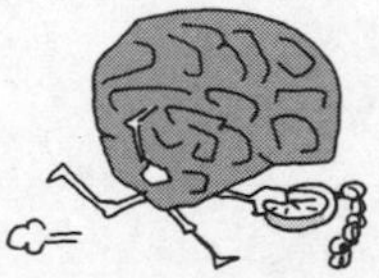	I haven't got enough time.	If it is important then you have to make time for it! Set aside small but regular amounts of time to fit in with your other commitments and think about giving yourself whole days or weekends devoted to something you are keen to learn.
	I can't get the kind of learning I want near where I live or work.	This may be true at first sight. But think more laterally. Can you get it online? Have you really investigated what is available? Try talking about what you want to do to your colleagues and friends and see what creative ideas they come up with. Rather than going on a customer care course, for example, why not go and see how another organization not in your line of work does it?
	What's on offer does not fit with the way I like to learn.	This is an understandable first approach to finding out what you want. But it will be very limiting if you use it as an excuse not to try something different! The point about understanding your preferred learning style is that you may want to learn to use and even enjoy other approaches.
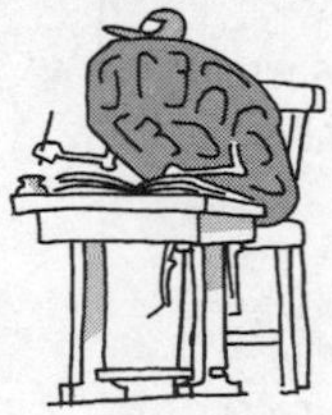	I associate learning with my schooldays: being talked at and sitting at desks in rows.	You are not alone. The good news is that much of the learning you might choose to do today is not like the school experience you remember.
	Learning really turns me off.	Learning does not have a good image for some people because, in their mind, they connect the word with education or training, things they are told to do, sometimes against their will. In fact, most people associate the word learning with 'discovery' or 'searching out their hidden talents'. But it may well be that you do have to overcome a barrier in your head to get started.

Barrier	**Solution**
Where I work learning is frowned upon.	In too many schools, homes and workplaces it is not cool to be smart or to learn. It may be that you have to accept that not all of your friends or colleagues will immediately see why you are choosing to learn something. You can look forward to telling them about how much you have got from your learning at a later stage.
My other responsibilities mean that, much as I'd like to, I couldn't commit myself to a course.	You may well have real issues to work through. Childcare and family or other care responsibilities are good examples of these. The first step is to decide what it is that you want to do and then work through the options for how you can get help to be able to discharge your other duties to your satisfaction. You certainly will not be in a fit emotional state if you are worrying about someone you care for rather then concentrating on your learning.
I didn't realize that DIY was learning.	You learn so much without realizing that you are doing so. In a typical day you may pick up many different tips, learn a new skill, do something in your garden or in the community which without doubt is learning. Often the informal learning that you do is the most valuable and the most real. Congratulate yourself on everything you are already learning!
I am afraid it might change things.	Learning is, most certainly, powerful stuff! You will almost inevitably be changed by what you learn. It is definitely best to be honest about this possibility and try to share your thoughts and feelings openly with others.
I am too old to learn.	This is not true. While you may have heard of the slogan, 'use it or lose it' (see page 201), what we know about our brain does not support this. It is true that your brain cells gradually die off as you get older. But what is more important to remember is that even with half your brain cells intact you have more neural capacity than you actually need. It is true that if you do not seek actively to use your brain you may get a little 'rusty'. It is common-sense that

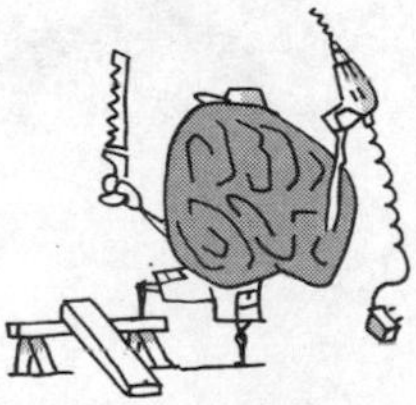

Barrier	Solution
	if you stop using or practising a skill you will be a bit slower. More positively, there is growing evidence that learning makes you healthier in later years.
I couldn't possibly expose myself to ridicule in front of my boss or those who work for me.	A fear of failure or lack of success is the reason why some very senior executives find it difficult to accept the challenge to learn to be different and why coaching and mentoring are such important activities. But the same is equally powerful for those in less senior positions. Nine times out of ten, those around you end up admiring your determination to see something through, even it they do not immediately give you that impression.
I am no good at learning and I'll be humiliated in front of other people.	The same fear is present to some degree in almost all of us. You were born able to learn. You have done it naturally throughout your life. *Discover Your Hidden Talents* tries to help you rekindle your appetite for learning. Mentally rehearsing what you are going to do will help, as will equipping yourself with positive statements to use in the event of comments from others.

Diet matters

If you believed everything that you read about diet you might be forgiven for thinking that, for instance, if you drink enough water and pop enough vitamins you will become a genius. Sadly this is not the case, although drinking a sensible amount of water is undoubtedly a good thing (provided you do not drink so much that you dilute your body's vital minerals!). Also certain vitamins are essential to our health.

Here are three simple suggestions when it comes to diet and learning:

1. stay hydrated
2. balance your intake
3. eat little and often.

Hydration

Your hydration level – the amount of water in your body's system – influences your performance as a learner. It is now generally agreed that you will function better as a learner if you can drink two litres of water a day, more if you are also eating food or consuming drinks that are diuretic (like coffee or alcohol). There is no definitive research on exactly how much you should consume but, for most people, it is more than they currently drink!

Balance

To learn well our brains need to be fed. Glucose – a kind of sugar – is what our brains and bodies run on and is, therefore, essential. It is extracted from carbohydrate. Your brain consumes some 40 per cent of all of the carbohydrate that you eat.

However, not all carbohydrates are the same. Eating a sugary chocolate snack provides you with instant glucose. But to keep you going through an extended piece of learning (or an examination) you need to eat food that does not contain refined sugars and which takes longer to digest. Such food includes grains, beans, potatoes, vegetables, wholegrain bread and nuts.

It helps to eat a balanced diet of protein (egg, yoghurt, fish, chicken and pork) and carbohydrates (vegetables, rice and fruit). Many people eat too much sugary food. Salts are essential to the healthy functioning of all cells; however, most people eat too much sodium salt, typically in crisps and processed foods. Salty food, in its turn, produces the need to drink more water. Caffeine is a stimulant, producing an effect not unlike the release of cortisol when your adrenal gland is working strongly. The brain becomes alert over a short period, but too much coffee, however, causes dizziness, headaches and difficulty in concentrating.

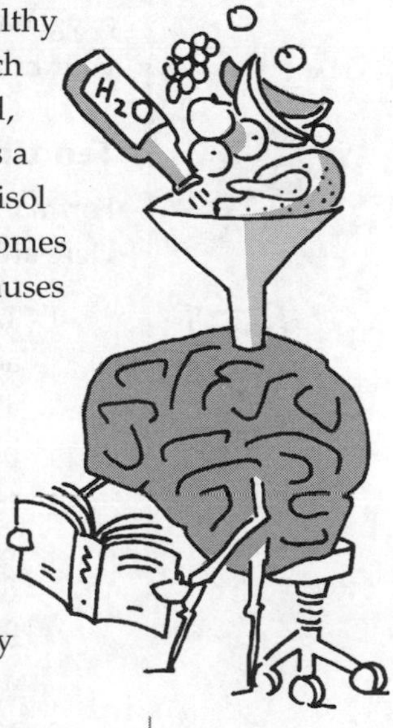

Alcohol causes you to lose inhibition and so, for some, enhances confidence and helps them to be more creative but it is also a depressant. Various additives commonly found in processed food affect the brain adversely, especially when young. Many of us need to consume less fat, less salt, less coffee, less tea, less alcohol and less chocolate. Some of us may want to review the amount of protein we eat.

Vitamins matter, too. The best way to make sure that you have enough of them is by eating the food in which they naturally occur. Recent research suggests that certain nutrients are particularly helpful and enhance performance. The following useful vitamins and minerals are found in fresh fruits and vegetables, except vitamin B12 which is found in meat, fish and dairy products. They can also be obtained as supplements. At the time of writing dietary advice for healthy living is to make sure that you eat at least five helpings of fresh fruit and vegetables a day.

B1 (Thiamine)	Concentration and alertness
B3 (Niacin)	State of mind
B5 (Pantothenic acid)	Memory
B12	General health and memory
Folic acid (and B6/B12)	State of mind
Vitamin C	General health
Vitamin D	Aids absorption of minerals
Calcium	Relaxant
Magnesium	Relaxant

Eat little and often

Regular intake of small amounts of food is sometimes described as a 'grazing' diet and works well for most people. If you eat a big meal, your stomach and digestive system are hungrily consuming oxygenated blood to fuel this process and there is less available for your brain! This is why you tend to feel sleepy after a big lunch.

Ten tips for getting ready to learn

For many people, getting ready is the most difficult part of learning. Here are some activities for you to try to whet your appetite:

1. Take a moment to think about all the things that you have achieved so far. Make a list of all the things you are pleased about. Thinking positively about your achievements is likely to help you to want to go on.
2. If you are feeling in any way not ready to learn, stop and think what you did last time you felt like this. Make a list of all the ways you have dealt with this kind of situation before. The brain loves patterns and by doing this you may help it to make a new connection.
3. You could find something to laugh about. There is evidence that when you laugh your brain releases chemicals called endorphins which act as relaxants and make you feel better.

4. Imagine you have finished your learning. Think about how you would like to feel. What will it look, sound and feel like? Picture yourself having successfully completed it. Visualizing success is a proven way of helping you to be more positive.
5. If any negative thought comes into your head, reword it as a positive one. By doing this you will start to reframe the world in a more positive light.
6. If you are feeling too stressed, take a long hot bath or go for a walk or jog. Getting into a physically relaxed state often helps your mind to relax too.
7. Try setting yourself modest goals for your learning, for example aiming to do half an hour a day. As you start to imagine what you want, your brain will start to connect to it and help you to see things that you did not at first realize.
8. Check that you have really got the big picture. Maybe you cannot see the wood for the trees! Your mind is constantly trying to make connections, so giving it the big picture in advance gives it time to make sense of things and 'gather' all it knows about a particular subject.
9. Organize your learning environment to suit you. Turn heating up or down. Change the light. Turn music off or on as you wish.
10. Feeling that you need some help? Perhaps it would assist you in starting if you were learning with someone else.

The Go stage

Using a range of strategies

So, you are ready to learn. Now what?

Are you interested in concentrating on something in particular, such as learning to give a speech? Or are you trying to make sense of something that has been gnawing away at you in your mind? What kind of a learner are you? What method should you choose? What challenges are you facing which learning could help you with? Would it help to talk to someone? Or do you prefer to mull it over in private? Can you remember what you did last time you felt like this?

> 'In a time of drastic change it is the learners who inherit the future. The learned usually find themselves equipped to live in a world that no longer exists.'
>
> Eric Hoffer

Few would disagree with the statement that 'we are all different', but what about when it comes to learning? Do we all learn in different ways?

We each have an individual learning style

It was Carl Jung who first suggested, more than a hundred years ago, that we have different types of personality, and many people have used his work to help them understand more about themselves (see pages 142–145).

However, when it comes to learning, one of the simplest and most effective ideas was developed by Peter Honey and Alan Mumford. Drawing on the work of David Kolb (see pages 100–101), they suggested that there are four distinct types of learning styles and that we tend to prefer one (or, at most, two) of them.

Importantly they also suggested that:

- No one style is better than another.
- You can change your learning preferences.
- Effective learners need to be comfortable with all of them.

Honey and Mumford's learning styles are:

Activist – Activists tend to immerse themselves in experiences. They will try anything once and are happy to give most things a go. They seem to thrive on the excitement of the here and now and are easily bored. They set great store by getting the job done.

Pragmatist – Pragmatists like learning methods which encourage them to work on real issues and where they are shown techniques with an obvious practical benefit.

Reflector – Reflectors normally enjoy learning methods which give them time to think and ponder, such as keeping a journal. They like to be able to stand back from events and appreciate being given time to think before being plunged straight into a task. They enjoy writing reports. They tend not to like situations where they are forced to give instant responses or asked to act without enough data.

Theorist – Theorists tend to enjoy learning which has a clear underlying concept or model. They like to be able to explore things methodically and enjoy structure. Although the learning may not be immediately relevant, theorists enjoy ideas and concepts. Theorists tend to be less comfortable when they are asked to express emotions or take part in activities which are open-ended or deal with ambiguity.

Not everyone agrees with the idea of learning styles but, if used as one of a number of methods for finding out about yourself as a learner, many people find them very useful.

Individual preference is only one of the things which you might like to consider when deciding which approach to adopt in your learning. For example, if you tend to reflect, you may well enjoy keeping a diary where a more activist approach may be to prefer role play. You will also need to consider the subject matter you are learning. So, if you are trying to learn to counsel others when they are distressed, using a spreadsheet may not be an appropriate approach, whereas if you are learning about how to set up a simple budget it might be the best method. The availability of resources and the location of your learning may also influence you in your choice of approach.

The 5Rs

Opportunities present themselves in many different ways and the majority of them are informal. To be an effective learner you need a range of different approaches to suit different situations. The old 3Rs of your school days are no longer enough. But the 5Rs which I use to structure this book may help you more. They are: Resourcefulness, Remembering, Resilience, Reflectiveness and Responsiveness and you will keep meeting them as you go through *Discover Your Hidden Talents*.

Take a moment to look back at page 25. You will see that three of the Rs are particularly important in the Go stage: Resourcefulness, Remembering and Resilience.

Resourcefulness means having a good range of techniques at your disposal. Think of yourself embarking on some DIY with a full bag of 'tools' suitable for any situation that you may find (see pages 69–112 for a detailed explanation).

Remembering, as its name suggests, involves getting the best out of your memory. But it is more than just remembering facts. Of far greater importance is your ability to recall ways of doing things and to be able to use something you have learned in one place in other situations (see pages 113–131).

Resilience is a special kind of persistence in learning. It involves being able to deal with all the difficult emotions you experience when things get tough so that you can see things through (see pages 133–158).

What you do in the *Go* stage is what most people think of as learning. And they are partially right.

But there is more. What you do afterwards, in the *Steady* stage, will determine whether you have extracted the full value out of your learning, just as what you did in the *Ready* stage, will determine whether you were really able to engage with the challenges you were facing.

Of course *Go* does not just follow *Ready* like night after day. It is much more subtle than this. As so much of your learning is informal, the boundaries between readiness and action are often very blurred. You

will often find yourself in the thick of a situation and hardly have time to realize that you are learning exciting new things.

When it comes to getting going in your learning, you might like to try the ideas in the following section.

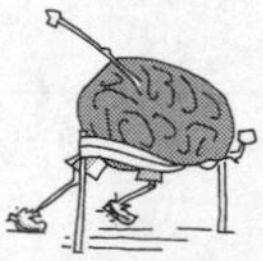

Ten tips for the Go stage

1. Find out more about yourself as a learner. Read about learning styles in the A–Z section in Chapter 16.
2. Before you start a learning activity, cover a blank piece of paper with notes on what you already know about the subject. This is a good way of getting your mind to engage.
3. Make a list of good questions about any learning topic in which you are interested. This helps your mind to begin to explore and find patterns which help it to make sense.
4. Identify the person you most admire in your workplace or family and try to spend time with them. Inevitably your imitating brain will learn from them.
5. Seek out TV programmes that offer opportunities to discover new things about the world.
6. Make up a simple rhyme to help you remember something. Sounds can help you to make connections and remember things.
7. Set a clear objective for any learning session and try not to stop until you have achieved it!
8. When you are trying to concentrate have a list of all the kinds of things that you normally do when you need a break – making a cup of tea, turning on the radio and so on – and ration yourself very carefully by not doing them!
9. If you get stuck come back to the problem at a different time of the day.
10. Try some of the creative techniques described in Part Two, like 'six thinking hats' or 'feed forward'.

The Steady stage

Making your learning work for you

Effective learners view mistakes as their friends and dealing with change as a welcome challenge! But that can be easy to say and hard to put into practice, for we are brought up in educational systems and workplaces where mistakes are seen as the sign of someone who is having difficulties. You fail an exam or you make an error and you are made to feel inadequate or end up being blamed for it.

> Adapt or perish, now as ever, is Nature's inexorable imperative.
>
> H.G. Wells

Yet, as you will discover in *Discover Your Hidden Talents*, real learning takes place when you are on the edge of your comfort zone. And, when you are at the edge of what you feel confident about, of course you are likely to make mistakes. That's how you learn to do it better next time.

Moving from your comfort zone to your grow zone

The zone of proximal development is a concept invented by Russian psychologist, Lev Vygotsky. This simple but powerful idea reminds us that there is always a next step for a learner – the zone of proximal development. Or put another way, we learn well and become 'stronger' learners when our learning muscles are exercised.

For the learner to succeed in the next zone, s/he has to be prepared to come out of his/her comfort zone. The role of those helping the learner is to provide support or 'scaffolding' to help him/her get from where s/he is now to where s/he wants to go to.

Although this theory applies especially to young people helped by a teacher or parent, it also works for adult learners who can be supported to find their zone of proximal development by other adults. We all need the right balance between being pushed and being pulled.

So, you may find yourself needing to take a different attitude to what you used to think of as 'failure'. For your ability to reflect on what has gone wrong will help you to extract the lessons you need to learn throughout your life.

Adaptability is essential for survival. As a result of your reflections you can then respond accordingly, changing as you do so. How you view any such change may depend as much on your emotional response to it as what your head tells you. It may also depend on the degree to which you welcome the change or feel that it has been forced upon you. Typically, people experience anger, denial and a sense of isolation before they become grudgingly aware and are then prepared, albeit reluctantly, to experiment and become engaged in the new way of doing something.

Take a moment to look back at page 25. You will see that the last two of my 5Rs are particularly important in the Steady stage: Reflectiveness and Responsiveness.

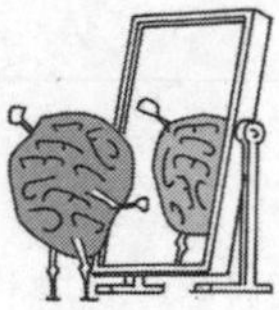

Reflectiveness is the key means by which you extract meaning from an experience. It involves reliving and processing what you have learned and asking yourself questions to help you judge how effectively you performed in any situation. The capacity to reflect is at the heart of what it is to be an effective learner. Indeed, there is a sense in which the difference between living and learning is reflecting. For through reflection you extract meaning from your experiences of life (see pages 159–171).

Responsiveness is about putting into practice what you have learned. You find something out about yourself or about the world about you and, as a consequence, decide to do things differently in the future. Responsiveness often involves you in changing the way you behave which can consequently be very difficult to do as engrained habits are hard to budge (see pages 173–184).

Many learners effectively get stuck in the Go stage. Indeed it is easy to find yourself in this situation, especially when you are busy. Many of us will have heard ourselves saying things like: 'I am too busy to make time to stop and think!'

The Steady stage requires you to be open and exploratory. Ideally you reflect both on an ongoing basis and also after each learning experience. As you learn new things, you need to try and put them into practice.

Some of the most dramatic events are linked with this stage of learning. You take stock of an unfulfilled life with your partner and resolve to get divorced. After years of enduring the unpleasant behaviour of your boss, you finally decide to take matters into your own hands. And so on.

When it comes to reflecting on and responding to your learning experiences, you might like to try some of the ideas in the following section.

Ten tips for the Steady stage

1. Ensure that all meetings you are involved in start with a brief feedback session to learn from what has gone before.
2. Create simple feedback and reflection sheets for every aspect of your life and work.
3. Spend at least five minutes at the end of each day reviewing what went well and what went less well.
4. Ask your friends to give you feedback from time to time.
5. If you are a parent, ask your child to give you feedback from time to time.
6. Find out more about the feelings of change and how you can best deal with them.
7. When you are changing something, so as not to throw out the baby with the bath water, build on the past.
8. Try not to go it alone when you are changing things; use those around you as a support network.
9. Don't be afraid to ask for help.
10. Don't forget to keep your sense of humour intact!

4

Troubleshooting

Chapter 4

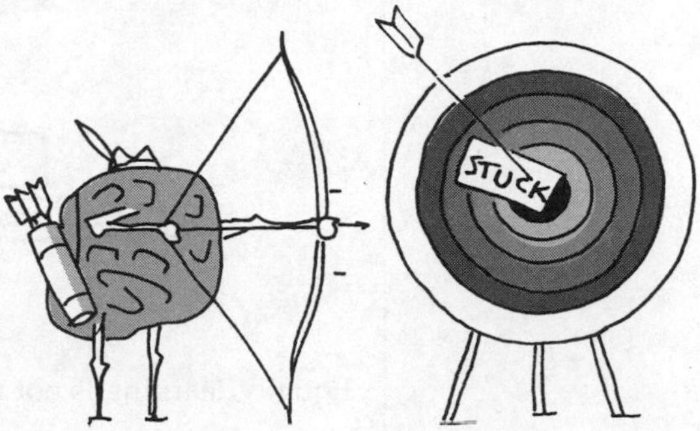

Of course, even very confident and experienced learners experience challenges. Unexpected events happen. Things go wrong. That's the nature of learning.

Being able to be your own troubleshooter is really helpful. If you can work out what it is that is bugging you, you may be able to fix it. Indeed, realizing that being temporarily 'stuck' is a smart place to be is an important part of becoming an effective learner. For being stuck is an indication that you may be moving from your comfort zone to your grow zone. And if you want to develop, then this is the zone you want to spend time in.

You might like to look through this section now to see if it stimulates some of your own questions.

Maybe you should consider the next few pages as if they were the section of a computer manual which tries to deal with commonly experienced difficulties or a home health guide which assists in helping you to diagnose the cause of your symptoms.

The following are a few of the solutions to some common problems you may encounter while learning.

Obviously your mind is not a computer and many of the issues you encounter as a learner will, therefore, be much more complex.

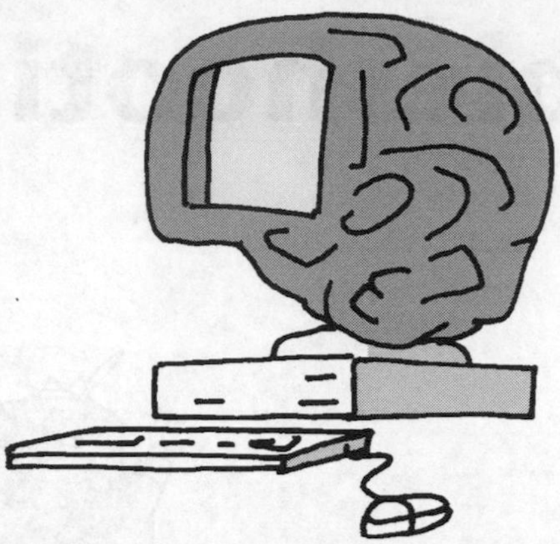

Equally, learning is not the same as health for two reasons:

1. you do not have to be 'unwell' as a learner to want to get better, and
2. if the equivalent to being unwell is being in a state where you are not learning effectively, the symptoms of this are much more subtle and difficult to recognize.

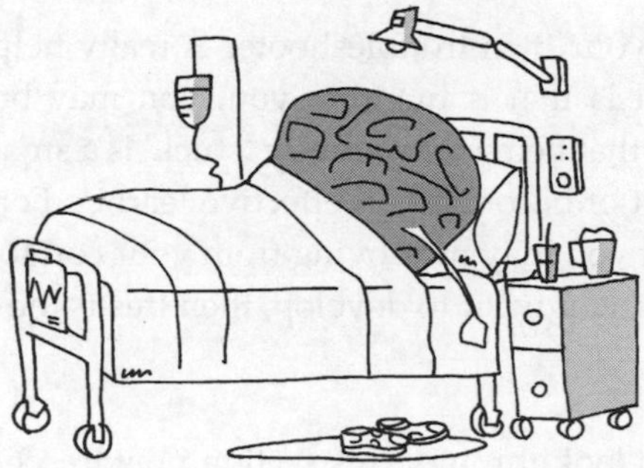

Incidentally, a common source of trouble for learners is careless treatment of the mind or the body! So, there is a sense in which troubleshooting can alert you to things you really do need to take care of. If the answer to your problem involves formal learning, then, in the UK, you may be able to find out what you need by calling learndirect (tel. 0800 100900) or going online and searching at www.learndirect.co.uk

You and your attitudes

I do not know what kind of learner I am

Possible cause	What to do
Nobody has ever said that people have natural preferences about the way in which they learn.	Work out whether you are an activist, reflector, theorist or pragmatist by looking at page 38 and then using this as a way of broadening your repertoire.

I have been a failure all my life

Possible cause	What to do
Your schooldays were miserable.	Recognize that this was indeed the case and take a conscious decision to move on. You could start by thinking of all the things you have achieved since leaving school and then read the sections on learning from mistakes and mind set on pages 170 and 180–181.
You have had a bad experience.	Put it behind you. Think about it in the past tense: 'Yesterday I did x, but I am aiming to do y tomorrow.' Look at the section on setting goals on page 151.
Your mind set has got stuck on 'pessimistic'.	Find out more about the 3Ps on page 180 and look at the section on putting optimism back into your life on page 180.

I am scared of computers

Possible cause	What to do
You are an older person who has never had the chance to learn.	You might like to ask one of your children or grandchildren to show you how to do some simple things on a computer. Or try your local college, which will probably run taster or bite-size courses for you to have a go with someone who understands that you are nervous about it.

Possible cause	What to do
You have had bad experiences of being asked to use them without support.	Get yourself on a computer skills course or try sitting by someone at work or at home who can help you to learn about computers without putting any pressure on you.

I feel very nervous if someone asks me to speak in public

Possible cause	What to do
It is totally natural to feel nervous.	There are some tried and tested ways of calming yourself down, from deep breathing to relaxation exercises. Look at pages 76 and 200–201 for more advice.
You have never done it before.	Make a point of watching a variety of speakers at work, at home and on television. Note how they start and finish, and watch where they look. See what kinds of notes they use. After you have read the section on public speaking, on pages 110–111, do some practice in a safe place, like with your family.
Everyone around you seems so good at it.	Recognize that when you feel unable to do something there are others who can seem so much better than you. That's life! Use them as a secret learning resource by watching how they do it!

I do not feel motivated to learn

Possible cause	What to do
You had awful experiences of learning at school.	So did many other people! But learning need not be like it was at school. Use what you know about learning styles to select something that really suits your preferences.

You cannot see the value or impact on your life.	Flick through the why bother sections of Part Two and see if you can find ways in which learning can really connect in to your life.
You have chosen a topic that neither interests you nor seems currently relevant to your life!	Read the section on motivation, check out your goals, and then use the PLAN on pages 61–66 to help you be clearer about what you want to learn.
You are trying to be too ambitious.	Break up what you are trying to learn into manageable chunks.

I am afraid of failing

Possible cause	What to do
It is only human to be afraid of failure.	You need to try to think about failure in a different way. Read the sections on failure, feedback and Neuro-Linguistic Programming (NLP). Start to appreciate that there is no such thing as failure, only feedback. See failure as a great way of learning how not to do things!

I keep getting stuck

Possible cause	What to do
You do not have enough strategies for coping when the going gets tough.	Read the section on Resilience on pages 133–158 and try some of the ideas suggested.

My memory keeps letting me down

Possible cause	What to do
You are trying to remember too much.	Break it up into smaller chunks. You tend to remember the beginnings and endings of what you learn!

You have not made the connections.	Try to find the patterns or connections between the things you have learned by classifying them in ways that work for you.
You need to take a different kind of notes.	Try Mind Maps™; see page 97.
You are tired.	Sleep on it! This is not as silly as it sounds as sleep seems to help you to process information unconsciously.
You are not fixing it in your brain enough.	Review things regularly: after an hour, a month, a day.
Your learning is too passive.	Make it more active!

I do not think I could ever be creative

Possible cause	What to do
Everyone has the potential to be creative and to develop their multiple intelligences; you just have not yet learned how!	Stop believing the myth that only some people are creative. Read the section on multiple intelligences on pages 136–140, or try relaxing for a while. Creativity is as much about state of mind as about techniques. Keep a diary for a day of all the ideas that you have, however trivial they seem. Try out some of the techniques on pages 93–97.

I am terrified of change

Possible cause	What to do
You are human! If we are truthful, most of us find change challenging but you do not need to be terrified.	Read the section on dealing with change on pages 173–174. Start to recognize that the best way to getting less terrified is to identify the feelings involved in change and deal with them by talking them through and coming up with positive suggestions for the way ahead.

You and your skills

I cannot spell properly

Possible cause	What to do
You were never taught or perhaps you have always found it difficult.	Use a computer's spell-checker when you can. Make a list of the words you often spell incorrectly and have a go at learning them, using things like rhymes, rules, mnemonics, jokes or anything else that can help you to remember them. Make short lists to begin with of just a few words and do a little bit each day.

I find it difficult to say what I mean

Possible cause	What to do
You do not know what you think!	Spend some time working out what it is you really want to say. Write down no more than three keywords on a piece of paper and then start to think through what you think about each of them. Read about chunking down.
You find it difficult to express what you think.	Read the sections on public speaking, telling stories, persuading others and developing an argument, in Chapter 6.

I cannot get started

Possible cause	What to do
You do not really want to get started.	Think more carefully about why you want to undertake the learning, and about the new opportunities that it is going to give you.
You have temporarily lost your sense of curiosity.	Stop watching so much uninspiring television! Plan an evening to do something that you have never done before!

You are under too much stress.	Your mind is elsewhere, worrying about something else. Try and work out what that something else is and what you could do to improve things. Ask for help from someone you trust.
Your environment is wrong.	Prepare a special place to learn at home or at work where you feel really good and where you have all the equipment you need at your fingertips. Turn all mobile phones off and put other phones on voicemail.
You are simply not ready.	Read the section on getting ready to learn on pages 26–31.

I always seem to lose arguments

Possible cause	What to do
You lack confidence.	Read the sections on creative visualization and boosting self-esteem.
You have not thought through your own argument clearly enough.	Read the sections on developing an argument, getting the big picture and persuading others, and then do some practice with a friend.

I cannot seem to absorb information

Possible cause	What to do
You are tired.	Try to get at least seven and a half hours of sleep each night.
You are being talked at.	Seek a more interactive approach to your learning.
You have not really connected.	Make sure that you ask for and get the big picture. Do not be afraid to ask someone to explain their overall aim for a session several times.

I am a slow reader

Possible cause	What to do
You had bad experiences at school and are now too embarrassed to do anything about it.	Feeling embarrassed or even ashamed are very common feelings. It may help to talk about it with a family member, friend or work colleage. Then you may want to get some help. Most colleges run sessions to assist you in ways that will identify your feelings and there are various campaigns in the UK that may help. Try learndirect on 0800 100900 for more information. You could also look at the section on speed reading, on pages 91–92.

I do not seem to be able to concentrate

Possible cause	What to do
You are tired.	Take a break. Get up and have a drink and a quick stretch.
You need to take a break.	Take one and, as you do so, work out a plan for the rest of what you have to learn. Split it up into manageable sessions.
You keep getting interrupted.	Read the sections on dealing with distractions and saying no on pages 156 and 157.
You need to set yourself some realistic goals.	Perhaps you are aiming to do too much. Look at the section on setting goals, on page 151.

I find listening really difficult

Possible cause	What to do
You have never learned how to listen.	Read the section on active listening, on page 106, and try it out.

I do not know how to reflect

Possible cause	What to do
You are very busy.	Try and make time. Use the PLAN on pages 62–66 to help you.
You do not see the value of it.	Think about it. Learning = Life + Reflection. If you never stop to reflect, how can you know what you might want to do differently?
You are active by nature.	Activists can find reflection difficult. See if you can find a way of doing it that suits you. Read the sections on the benefits of having a Learning Practitioner or LP (like a GP but for the learner), on page 200, keeping a learning log, giving and receiving feedback, asking good questions and reviewing experiences to give you some ideas.

I do not know how to change

Possible cause	What to do
You have always been a passive recipient of change.	Take control! Learn to predict some of the feelings that commonly go along with change (see page 174). Read the sections on learned optimism, altering behaviour, dealing with change, unlearning and life planning.

You and your life style

I work for too many hours

Possible cause	What to do
Your life is out of balance.	Be realistic about the tough situation you are in at the moment. Use the quiz on pages 20–21 and the PLAN on pages 62–66 to help you. Within a definite timescale, no more than a month from now, adopt some of the suggestions you have read about.

I constantly have low energy

Possible cause	What to do
You are stressed.	Put yourself through the simple quiz on pages 20–21 and do something about it! Listen to music. Try some of the relaxation techniques on page 76.
Your diet is poor.	Try to eat a more balanced diet, as suggested on pages 34–36. Drink more water and less alcohol and coffee.
You are not taking enough exercise.	Remedy this either on your own, for example by walking, or as part of a planned social activity, like a dance class.

I never have time to learn

Possible cause	What to do
You have not stopped to work out how important your planned learning is to you.	Complete a PLAN, see pages 62–66.

I get very stressed

Possible cause	What to do
Life! Plus some recurring ways of dealing with it which you have that could be different.	You might like to tackle this on a number of fronts. First of all, start taking regular exercise. Next, identify situations which seem to cause you most stress. Focus on one of them. Work on your mind set and on altering your behaviour so that you gradually start to deal with it in different ways; see pages 77–78 for more on this. Review the many things that are crowding in on you to do. Take some hard decisions about putting off all but the non-essential items for the next month and seeing if this brings you some respite.

My relationships always go wrong

Possible cause	What to do
There are many things that learning alone cannot fix. But it may be that there are some basic relationship skills that you are lacking.	Read the sections on showing empathy, understanding points of view, managing feelings, giving and receiving feedback, and dealing with conflict. Choose a few of the practical ideas here to work on. But, most importantly, focus on your mind set. Talk about past failures as if they no longer exist: 'Relationships used to go wrong for me, but now I am taking steps to fix that.'

You and your family

My child hates school

Possible cause	What to do
S/he is being bullied.	Talk to him/her and ask directly about it. Be sympathetic and show that you are taking it very seriously. Find out all the facts that you can. Reassure him/her that talking to you is the right thing to do. Calmly talk to your child's teacher and insist that the bullying must stop.
S/he has a poor relationship with a teacher.	Encourage your child to talk about it. The likelihood is that there are factors on both sides of the relationship which can be worked upon. If the problem continues ask to see the headteacher.
S/he has special educational needs.	Read the section in Part Three on common conditions, for example special educational needs, attention deficit hyperactivity disorder (ADHD), dyscalculia, dyspraxia and dyslexia, and share your concerns with your child's teacher or tutor. If necessary, make an appointment to see an educational psychologist.

My child cannot read properly

Possible cause	What to do
S/he is dyslexic.	Read the section on dyslexia on page 302 and then seek specialist help.
S/he is a slow reader.	Many children develop the reading habit later than their peers. Try not to make a thing about it. Gently keep encouraging your child to read everything, from road signs to the backs of cereal packets. Make it fun and wait for a breakthrough to happen.

My child cannot concentrate

Possible cause	What to do
Oh yes s/he can!	Sit down with your child and help him or her to set some realistic goals and then set aside short periods of study. Help him or her to break down the bigger tasks into manageable chunks. If s/he is successful then give a reward.
S/he is eating too many sugary foods and drinking too many additive-full drinks.	Try cutting these out and see if there are any improvements.
S/he has ADHD.	Read the section on ADHD (page 300) and seek help from the school or an educational psychologist.

You and your workplace

I cannot be creative at work

Possible cause	What to do
The environment is seriously uncreative.	Leave! Or find some like-minded people who can work with you to change it from within.

Your full range of intelligences is not being realized.	Read pages 136–140 for ideas as to how you might do this.

I do not get on with my boss

Possible cause	What to do
Your boss is a difficult person.	Recognize that this is the case and stop blaming yourself. Focus on minimizing the situations in which your boss is awful and maximizing those areas that you can work on.
You are not handling it well.	Read the sections on explaining problem solving, building relationships, working with other people, saying no, managing feelings, and giving and receiving feedback, and try out some of the ideas.

My boss will not support my learning

Possible cause	What to do
S/he does not see why it is important.	Pick a good moment to explain some of the ways in which your learning will help the organization, for example greater efficiency, improved performance, dealing with change better, understanding customers more and motivating you and others.
S/he is too busy and stressed.	Seek a brief meeting. Start by acknowledging the pressures on your boss and explain that you have some solutions (all involving learning) which will help. Present learning as the answer to business issues rather than as something that the training department has organized to take you away from your job!
S/he has had bad experiences of learning.	If you think this is the case, suggest s/he tries something that is really enjoyable. Make sure you have something to suggest!

I never get offered any training

Possible cause	What to do
You are working for a small organization.	There are two possible approaches. You could stop worrying about formal training and concentrate on creating informal learning opportunities for yourself, like job swaps and job shadows. Or you could tackle it head on by showing the benefits (for example greater efficiency, improved performance, dealing with change better, understanding customers more and motivating you and others) and start insisting that it happens!
You are working for an unsatisfactory organization.	Leave and go to one that is seeking to be a 'learning organization'!

5

Chapter 5

Your PLAN (Personal Learning Action plaN)

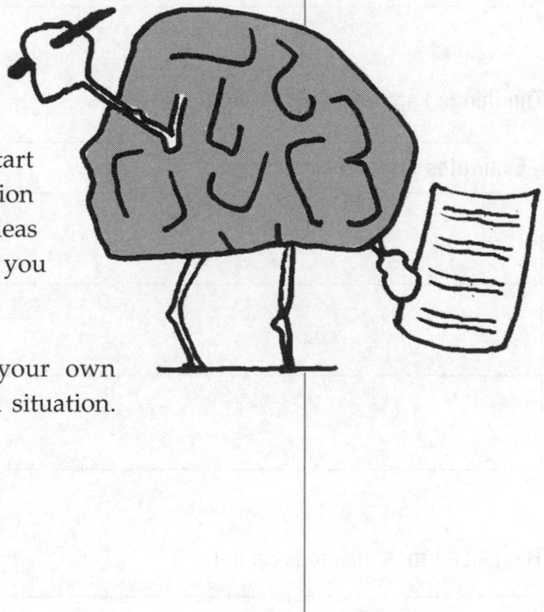

Before you start to explore Part Two, you might like to start your own personal learning plan. Or you may not feel ready to start on your own PLAN (Personal Learning Action plaN) until you have explored some of the ideas in *Discover Your Hidden Talents*, in which case you can return to it later.

Use these ideas as a starting point for your own thinking. Customize them to suit your own situation. And feel free to do lots of versions.

Looking back

1. My most enjoyable learning in my life so far has been:

Example	When?	Where?	How?	Why?

2. The things I am best at are:

Examples

3. The place I most like to learn in is:

4. The times I like to learn best are:

Time	Reason

5. The people I most like to learn with are:

6. The ways I prefer to learn are:

Method	Reason
1.	
2.	
3.	
4.	

My wish list

7. The things I want to achieve in the next three years are:

Home	Work	Social	Personal	Other

8. The things that are changing most in my life are:

1.	
2.	
3.	

To survive and thrive during these changes, I need to learn how to:

1.	
2.	
3.	

9. The things I most need to help me realize my goals are:

Home	Work

Social	Personal

Other	

10. The things I plan to learn in the next 12 months are:

What?	Why?	How?	When?	Where?

11. The people who might help me most over the next few months are:

12. Other helpful things to consider are:

To stimulate your thinking about learning you might like to visit:

www.campaign-for-learning.org.uk
www.infed.org
www.bbc.co.uk
www.bbc.co.uk/webguide
www.niace.org.uk
www.dfes.gov.uk

Part Two

Becoming a better learner

In this part you can find out more about the 5Rs and the main ways in which you can become a more effective learner.

Clear entries help you to:

- understand what you need to learn
- find out about new techniques
- practise the techniques which are most relevant to you
- focus on the particular learning environments of home and work.

Resourcefulness

Remembering

Resilience

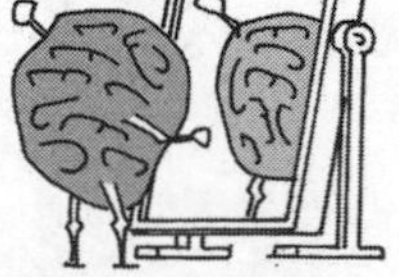

Reflectiveness

Responsiveness

two PART

Resourcefulness

Chapter 6

Learning to be a better learner

It's a curious fact that while most people think they can learn how to cook, to speak another language or to become a better parent they do not naturally assume that they can learn how to become a better learner.

But you can. The good news is that learning is learnable.

There are three elements to learning how to learn, all of which are covered in this book.

First you need to have a clear enough idea of what is going on when you are learning. (That's the Ready, Go, Steady that you met earlier and which appears on the next page.)

Second you need to be able to use some practical techniques to help you become a better learner. (These are the 5Rs which you are about to explore in this section of the book.)

And third, you need to have a simple but effective language to be able to talk about what is going on when you learn. That's what every page of *Discover Your Hidden Talents* is trying to help you with.

Of course you may not have picked anything like this up from your schooldays! For, while you will probably have learned the facts and processes associated with subjects, you may not necessarily have picked up the helpful approaches you need to become a more effective learner. (Schools, today, often find themselves helping children to pass tests and examinations when they might be better off helping them to become better learners.)

Take a moment to look at the following chart, which you first met on page 25.

READY	You need to be emotionally ready and motivated to learn
GO	You need to have a range of techniques to harness the full range of your talents and creativity (*Resourcefulness*) You need to be able to recall things (*Remembering*) You need to be able to keep going when learning gets difficult (*Resilience*)
STEADY	You need to be able to make time to take stock (*Reflectiveness*) You need to be able to change, adapt and learn from your mistakes (*Responsiveness*)

Most of you will have heard of the 3Rs – Reading, wRiting and aRithmetic. But what you need to get to grips with today is not the 3Rs, although of course you definitely do need to be able to cope with English and maths, but the 5Rs:

Resourcefulness 

Remembering 

Resilience 

Reflectiveness 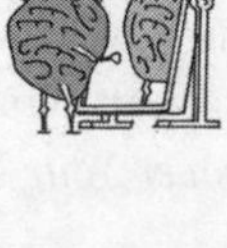

and Responsiveness. 

Unlike the 3Rs, the 5Rs focus on know-how rather than know-what. Taken together they provide a curriculum for lifelong learning.

You could think of the 5Rs as a way of describing the kinds of habits which will help you to learn better. Habits are typical or customary ways of behaving. If you are trying to become a more effective learner and realize your hidden talents, then some habits are more helpful than others. The table below gives you a flavour of the kinds of things we will be looking at as we explore the 5Rs.

Three of the 5Rs	Helpful	Less helpful
Resourceful	Giving ideas time to germinate	Being too quick to judge
Resilient	Being patient	Always rushing
	Being persistent	Getting angry when things get difficult
Reflective	Keeping a diary	Being too busy to take stock
	Asking questions	Only being interested in answers

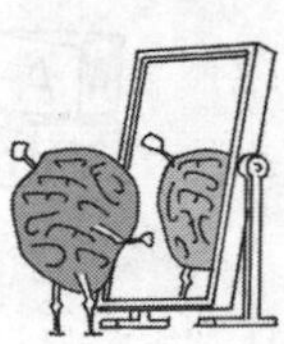

I first developed the idea of the 5Rs in *Power Up Your Mind: Learn Faster Work Smarter* while I ran the UK's Campaign for Learning (a charity that helps people to learn). But I am not alone in thinking like this. Guy Claxton and Louise Stoll, both Professors of Education, are just two other examples of well-regarded authors and thinkers who have reached very similar conclusions.

In the next five chapters you will be finding out more about each of these ideas and seeing the many ways in which you can apply them in your life. The last two chapters in this part explore some issues particularly associated with two key environments in most people's lives – home and work.

A word of caution

Some of the techniques you will find in each of the next chapters under a particular 'R' heading could just as easily appear under another of the Rs or, indeed, under 'at home' or 'at work'. That's the messy nature of learning! It's often difficult to tie things down! So do not worry if you read something under 'Reflectiveness' and find yourself thinking 'Shouldn't that be under 'Resourcefulness''? It is very likely that it could have been put under both headings. A good example of this is 'asking and answering questions'. This appears under 'Reflectiveness' because without this skill it is impossible to be reflective. Equally you could argue that questioning is an essential tool of any effective learner and, therefore, should be part of 'Resourcefulness'.

'Learnacy'

'Learnacy' is a word that was first coined by Guy Claxton in the 1990s to describe the over-arching idea of learning to learn. It was adopted and further defined by many people, including the Campaign for Learning.

Learnacy is to learning as literacy is to writing and reading. It describes the overall concept. Learnacy is close in meaning to another word sometimes used – meta-learning.

If you are using *Discover Your Hidden Talents* to find a particular technique there is an A–Z list of all of the techniques in Chapter 13 on pages 253–256 to make this search process easy.

There is also a very comprehensive index (starting on page 309) at the end of the whole book with lots of cross-referencing to help you if you are not sure quite what you want to find out about.

Being resourceful

Effective learners are resourceful; they have a full toolkit of techniques. When approaching any challenge that life throws them, they know how to deploy the most appropriate learning 'tool'. They know when to use the learning equivalent of a screwdriver or a saw, rather than persisting with a hammer.

> People who are only good with hammers see every problem as a nail.
>
> Abraham Maslow

In this chapter you will see that the idea of resourcefulness has been broken down and explored under a number of different headings. Under each of these headings you will find useful techniques and methods for you to try. Before each technique or method is described you can see a clear explanation as to why you might want to bother with it. Then the technique is explained and, finally, there is a simple 'how-to' guide to help you to learn how to do it.

There are three headings under 'Resourcefulness': 'Managing your learning', 'Developing and organizing ideas' and 'Working with people'.

Resourceful learners know how to manage their learning. This involves being able to see both the big picture *and* the detail, cultivating a receptive and open state of mind and being confident with a range of techniques.

They also know how to develop and organize their ideas. This requires both the ability to imagine new thoughts and to shape these so that their meaning is clear.

And finally, resourceful learners need to know how to work with people, understanding their points of view, explaining their own views and building networks of helpful relationships. Sometimes, of course, they will know that it is smarter to be solitary rather than sociable.

Managing your learning

There are very many different kinds of 'tools' or techniques that you need to have mastered to be a resourceful learner.

Fundamental approach, for example getting the big picture ↔ Particular method, for example using a book

The entries which follow start at the fundamental end of the spectrum and end with specific methods. Both types of techniques are useful, depending on the situation you find yourself in.

Getting the big picture

Why bother with the big picture?

It will help you to understand what is going on.
You will be able to plan which order to do things in more effectively.
So that you see the 'wood' and do not get lost in the 'trees'.

If you are not able to get the big picture you will often end up not seeing the wood for the trees, as the saying has it. For most situations, our brains work most efficiently if they have the big picture first. Data comes into our brain through our senses and our brain processes it, looking for patterns, connections and generally seeking to make sense of what it finds. Give yourself a big picture and this process generally becomes much easier. Think of the way you solve a jigsaw puzzle. With the picture on the lid in front of you, it is immediately possible to see that the mass of blue pieces go to form the sky while the various green pieces are for the landscape. The red is for the flag and the grey belongs to the road. Suddenly, it is clear how the whole fits together. You can make the connections which are necessary for you to solve the puzzle quickly.

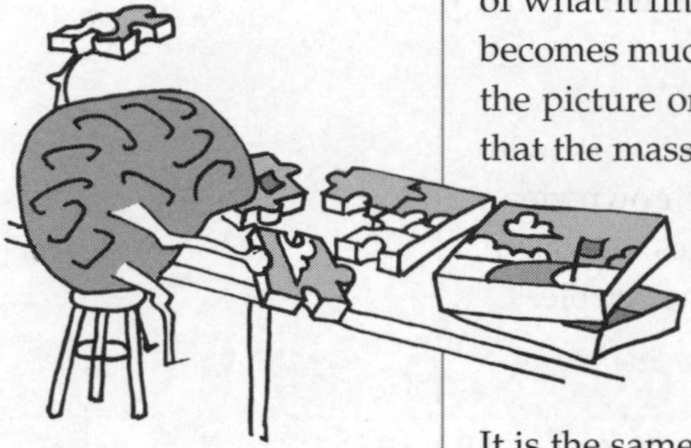

It is the same with your learning. It normally helps to be given the big picture first. You can then break it up into manageable pieces. Different contexts and different situations call for different responses. If you do not have the big picture you may misread the situation.

How to get the big picture

1. Always ask yourself why you are doing something.
2. See if you can create headings or keywords to describe what the main purpose of your learning is. Write them down on paper. Use techniques like lists or mind maps to help you clarify the relationship between things that are very important and part of the big picture and those which are less significant.
3. Be prepared to stop what you are doing from time to time and check that you have not lost sight of the bigger picture.
4. If you are not clear about something you have been told to do, ask for clarification. Seek more information on what the overall picture is, on what other people are doing and how your task fits in with this.
5. Take time to work out what the most important thing in your month, week and day is. That way you are more likely to think in big picture terms and less likely to get dragged into details which do not fit.
6. In meetings, develop a range of non-threatening ways of asking for clarity about what is going on, for example:

   'I am really sorry, but I do not know what this is about. Could you explain?' 'Could you just go back over what it was you were planning to do in this session?' 'Could you help me to see how this fits into the bigger picture?'

Gestalt theory

Gestalt is German for 'pattern' or 'shape' and gestalt theory was developed by psychologists to explore the ability of people to see the whole picture rather than just the constituent elements.

Modern thinkers about learning increasingly see the importance of taking a holistic view of learning; one that takes account of the whole person. This is sometimes also referred to as taking a holistic view.

Chunking down

While it is important to be able to see the whole picture it is equally useful to be able to break it down into smaller, more digestible pieces.

Why bother to learn chunking?

You need to see the trees and the wood.

It helps you to focus on manageable goals.

Chunking or 'chunking down' material is a way of breaking down larger issues or activities into smaller, more manageable elements. Effective learners are able to break down any piece of learning they are undertaking into its constituent parts, or chunk it down.

How to chunk your learning down

You might like to try one of these approaches:

1. Write the word that describes what you are trying to chunk down at the top of a piece of paper and then make a long list of all its 'ingredients'. When you have finished see if any patterns and connections emerge.
2. Put the word in the centre of a piece of paper and make a Mind Map™ of the issue you are exploring.
3. Imagine you have a magnifying glass in your hand. Keep on asking yourself what is beneath each 'layer' of the issue you are learning and, as you do so, make notes of what you 'see'.
4. Think of what you are trying to chunk down as a machine and to label each part of it. Use a pad of yellow sticky Post-it notes to write down your labels as you think of them. Say you were wrestling with a big family issue, such as ensuring that your child does his or her homework. You might write things like the following on your labels: need to make time; need to plan the whole week; need to talk about amount of TV watched; and so on.
5. Think of your learning as a recipe and write out all the instructions you will need, in the order that they occur, to help you see it through successfully.

Often it helps to start with the big picture and break it down into smaller chunks. But, sometimes, you may find that you simply need to get started and then stop and take stock. Many authors find this to be particularly the case when they are beginning a story. Sometimes it is possible to plan out exactly what the big picture looks like. At other times it is better simply to plunge in and get started. The same is true for many learning experiences.

Resourceful learners need to be able to see both the distant horizon and what is close up to them.

In Part One you found out about the importance of being ready to learn – whether in respect of things that you are specifically planning to learn or regarding the many haphazard opportunities that life throws at you. Resourceful learners need to manage their state of readiness. You need to cultivate a state of relaxed alertness in which you are receptive and open to new experiences.

> Man is so made that he can only find relaxation from one kind of labour by taking up another.
>
> Anatole France

Different ways of getting ready

To learn effectively or to come up with good ideas, you need to be in a state of relaxed alertness. While it is comparatively easy to make yourself alert (a good night's sleep, a cup of coffee or some adrenalin, for example) it is often more difficult to relax. Indeed an increasing number of people say that they are too stressed to sleep when they go to bed at night.

You can learn to relax by using a number of techniques. Some involve your body and some your mind. You might like to try one or more of the following:

How to relax

1. Have a long soak in a hot bath or go for a jog and then have a bath.
2. Arrange an evening with a friend who can normally help you to pick up emotionally.
3. Soothe your mind with some calming music.
4. Arrange to go somewhere or do something that will lift your spirits, for example a walk in the country or a visit to a favourite restaurant.
5. Try listening to a relaxation tape (there are many on the market).
6. Learn yoga.

As well as being able to relax when you need to, you may also find certain other techniques helpful in getting you into the right frame of mind. It is, for example, particularly helpful if you are able to motivate yourself by developing a positive attitude. Positive affirmations are a technique that you may find useful.

Making an affirmation

An affirmation is a positive statement of your belief in yourself. Affirmations feed your subconscious mind and there is evidence to show that this can help you in a variety of situations. Affirmations are 'can do' statements, such as 'I can do this', 'I am good at maths', 'I will do well in my test' and 'I will stand up to my boss'.

Athletes have long known the power of affirmations, but they can be equally useful for all learners who simply want to build their self-belief and change their mind set.

You might like to try:

Helping your child to develop affirmations to deal with their schoolwork or a sporting challenge.

Or:

Thinking of all the situations at work in which you currently feel least confident – with your boss, with colleagues, on the phone, in meetings, whatever – and developing affirmations which you can practise saying to yourself each day as you journey to work.

As well as preparing for specific events, resourceful learners also know the value of positive thinking more generally. They have discovered that it actually helps them to be more effective as learners.

Sometimes it helps to shut out the world around you and look inside yourself, using all your senses to help you engage with your chosen 'subject'.

Creative visualization

Creative visualization is a relaxation and motivation technique. The simplest way of achieving it is to close your eyes and try to summon up whatever you want into your mind. It helps to focus on each of your senses.

So, for example, if you were trying to imagine a strawberry, then imagine biting into it, imagine the texture of it, the look of it, the smell of it, and so on. It can also be used to help you imagine what it might be like to do something, especially something that you are not yet confident in, for example speaking on a public platform or winning a race.

You might want to have a practice run at something. This is particularly important when you are learning to do things which have an element of performance involved, for example giving a presentation, being interviewed or chairing a difficult meeting.

Or you may find it helpful to do a 'dry-run' in the privacy of your own mind by rehearsing whatever you are planning to do.

Mental rehearsal

Rehearsing in your mind involves imagining you are undertaking an activity and running through a 'film' of it in your head.

Originally used widely in sports psychology to help athletes get in the winning frame of mind, it is also a very valuable more general learning tool for any situation in which you want to improve your performance, from giving a presentation to dealing with your children's bedtimes!

Here are the kind of steps you might go through if you were going through a mental rehearsal. At every stage of this rehearsal, think of all your senses and imagine what each one would be sensing.

1. Think of the situation you want to rehearse and the result you want.
2. Ask yourself what state of mind you want to be in for it. How do you want to feel? Imagine you have completed the activity successfully. What sort of words come to mind?
3. Now imagine you are creating a film of yourself in action! Run it through from start to finish. Then do it again in fast forward mode!
4. Focus on the ending. Do you want to win? Do you want to reach a new understanding with someone? Do you want to overcome a personal fear? Think carefully and spend a few moments imagining the ending. What will it feel like?

Mind set matters hugely. Whether you are getting in the right frame of mind to start learning or are dealing with things that happen to you as you learn, if you are resourceful then you will have a number of techniques which you can use depending on the situation in which you find yourself.

NLP

Neuro-linguistic programming, or NLP as it is popularly known, was the idea of linguist John Grinder and mathematician Richard Bandler. It draws ideas from a number of disciplines and combines them together. It is not a specific philosophy grounded in science, rather a mixture of ideas.

The NLP approach involves increasing awareness of the way your mind processes experiences – the 'neuro' – being aware of how the way you use language affects the way you see things – the 'linguistic' – and creating new models or ways of doing things – the 'programming'.

A key concept in NLP is the idea that having a positive mind set is essential in life and learning. Consequently there is no such thing as failure, only feedback. NLP involves 'reprogramming' your feelings so that you do not see a setback as a failure.

NLP is always looking for the positive slant on behaviour. Two techniques already covered in this chapter are helpful: positive affirmations and creative visualization.

Managing your emotions

Emotions are an inevitable part of almost all learning. Indeed, if you are not emotionally involved, you may not be engaged in your learning. There are exceptions to this, of course. Learning a new computer program or a specific technical skill may not obviously involve an emotional response. But even with an apparently 'dry' activity, there can be a real thrill and strong emotional response if you succeed (or fail) at it.

When you are appropriately 'aroused' and your emotions are engaged, you often remember things better. (So people can often recall their first day at school, their first kiss or where they were when J.F. Kennedy and John Lennon were assassinated or, more recently, what they were doing on 9.11.01).

However, if negative emotions are engaged – fear, anger, disgust and sadness, for example – then you are less likely to be an effective learner.

Managing your emotions is one of the key skills of being an effective learner. Many people mistakenly assume that to be smart you only need to use your brain. In fact most learning involves feelings too. And to be an effective learner you need to begin to understand more about your own!

> 'Ability is not a fixed property; there is a huge variability in how you perform. People who have a sense of self-efficacy bounce back from failure.'
>
> Albert Bandura

In the past various people have tried to make an artificial distinction between feeling and thinking. René Descartes' saying 'I think therefore I am' is perhaps the most famous statement of this point of view. More recently people have suggested that our brains are divided into two or three distinct parts, with the feeling 'bit' in one part only. This is simply not the case.

Emotional intelligence

Emotional intelligence, sometimes also known as EQ (like IQ), is the ability to deal with emotions effectively. Unlike IQ, it is not a fixed concept, in other words you can get better at it! The term was first used by a student, Wayne Payne, in a dissertation in 1985 and has been made famous by Daniel Goleman. Goleman drew on work by Howard Gardner on multiple intelligences (see pages 136–140). At the same time as Gardner, two other American researchers – Peter Salovey and John Mayer – were coming to similar conclusions.

Key aspects according to Goleman include: knowing your own emotions, managing your own emotions, motivating yourself, recognizing other people's emotions and handling relationships.

There is increasing evidence that having a well-developed emotional intelligence is a much better indicator of success than having a high IQ. Certainly common sense suggests that, when dealing with people, recognizing and managing emotions is at least as important as processing thoughts. By the same token, it is clear that emotions can account for considerable fluctuations in individual performance.

It is worth noting that Howard Gardner does not see emotional intelligence as a single intelligence, rather a combination of at least two intelligences – interpersonal and intrapersonal.

Think of Spock in the popular sci-fi series *Star Trek*. As a citizen of Vulcan, he has no feelings and consequently is always depending on others to invest knowledge with meaning and decide which possible course of action demands attention. Our feelings help us to set our priorities and goals. One moment studying for an exam may seem to be your life's goal. Then your mother has to go into hospital and your feelings help you to set a new goal – finding time to be with a sick parent.

A list of feelings includes the following: interest, enjoyment, surprise, fear, distress, anger, shame, disgust, excitement, joy, terror, anguish, rage and humiliation. Each feeling can be experienced at different levels, with anger and humiliation being particularly powerful feelings for learners.

Why bother to explore new feelings?

It is essential to getting on in life.

It will help you to establish and keep relationships.

You will be able to interpret experiences better.

How to explore your feelings

There is a paradox when dealing with feelings. People and situations can make you feel things, but only you can decide what you feel. In other words, you are responsible for your own feelings. You can let feelings control your actions or you can learn how to control your feelings and act differently.

1. Get to know what gets you going! Notice when you feel certain things.
2. Name your feelings. When your feelings are running high, pause and give your feeling a name. Say to yourself 'I am feeling angry', 'I am feeling sad' and so on.
3. Talk (and/or write) about what you are feeling.
4. Find ways of dealing with your feelings. These could include:

- find something to laugh about
- think of a time when you dealt well with the feeling before

- think about something else
- relax by running, listening to music, having a bath and so on
- face up to the feeling – you might like to imagine what it looks like from a different viewpoint and see if this helps.

Do not be surprised if strong feelings take lots of time and much work to deal with.

Sometimes calling on your feelings involves being alive to your intuition. Intuition, sometimes called 'having a hunch about something', is a kind of sixth sense which everyone can learn to use more. It is a way of knowing that is derived partly from experience and partly from feelings which lie deep within you. Intuitions can be right or wrong, and effective learners know when to back theirs by balancing insights acquired using it with those from other senses.

When feelings become too intense they can get in the way of life and learning. The better you get at reading your own tell-tale signs of an impending difficulty the better for you it is

> 'A fact is like a sack – it won't stand up if it's empty. To make it stand up, first you have to put in it all the reasons and feelings that caused it in the first place.'
>
> Luigi Pirandello

> 'Intuition will tell the thinking mind where to look next.'
>
> Jonas Salk

Using your pause button

American management expert Stephen Covey has suggested that we all have a 'pause button' which we can press if we choose to when our feelings run away with us. This button is like the switch on a video or DVD recorder that freezes the frame. Covey has shown how we can learn to 'freeze' a situation when it begins to get out of control.

For example, if you were heading for a family argument and you decided to 'press the pause button' you might stop in mid flow and gain some breathing space to see if there were smarter ways of continuing. Often there are, and like the 'quiet corner' used by schools with young children, the breathing spaces are enough for individuals to re-think a course of action which otherwise could end in tears.

The pause button idea also works in your learning. When the going gets really tough, and you are concentrating so hard that you feel as if you are about to explode, you can release new energy by taking time out and 'walking around the block'.

If you were interested in putting this into practice in your life, for example, you might like to:

1. Explain the idea to a member of your family or a colleague.
2. Recall some moments when, in the past, emotions have run high and pressing the pause button might have been a good idea. (Do not bother to relive the details or you may start arguing again!)

3. Agree to start practising the pause button idea.
4. Give people positive feedback when they try! Tell them what worked and what worked less well! Gradually you should find a useful way of slowing things down when they are heading out of control!

Choosing the best method

1. If you wanted to learn how to drive a car, would it be enough to read books about it?
2. If you had a terrible temper and wished to learn how to manage your anger more effectively, would you prefer to listen to a lecture about current thinking or practise some different approaches using role play?
3. Or, if you simply want to learn a new recipe for cooking curry, would you like to have someone give a PowerPoint presentation to help you?

While the answers to the above questions may be relatively easy (1. no; 2. role play plus some kind of advice or feedback; 3. no!), it is often more complicated if you consider that these are just examples of planned learning when so much of what you actually do is accidental.

With many skills the best method may well be simply to practise it with someone alongside you able to comment and advise on your progress.

The cycle of competence

The idea for this cycle is sometimes credited to W.C. Howell, although it is not absolutely clear who first thought of it.

Many learning activities have a reasonably predictable. When you are acquiring a new skill, you tend to go through the following progression:

Unconscious incompetence	You do not know that you want to learn it
Conscious incompetence	You become aware of something you want to learn
Conscious competence	You become able to do something, albeit a bit mechanically
Unconscious competence	You have learned it so well that you do it without even thinking about it

Of course learning rarely proceeds in straight lines or even a regular cycle or circles. The concept of a cycle, therefore, though useful is not to be taken literally but to help learners understand more about what might be going on at any one moment.

You can find out about other versions of the learning cycle on pages 38 and 92.

When it comes to choosing the best method or approach, there are three key areas that you may wish to consider:

Your own preferences	Your environment	What you are learning

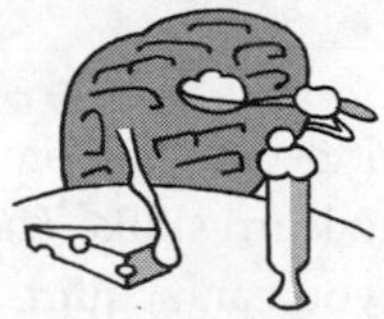

Your own preferences

You have already begun to explore this on page 38, and you can find out more on pages 142–146. As a general rule, the less confident you are about the learning you are about to undertake, the more you may want to choose methods which suit your preferences.

Of course, you will want to remember that truly resourceful learners are confident with lots of different approaches.

Your environment

You may be at home or at work (see Chapters 11 and 12), alone or in a group, with or without someone whose job it is to help you. The kind of environment that you find yourself in may well influence your choice of method. If you were embarking on a really new technique, for example, you might want a bit of support! Or you may be in an online environment.

Categories of learning

Benjamin Bloom, an American, suggested that there are three categories or domains of educational activities. The three categories are cognitive, affective and psychomotor. Each, it is argued, is a fundamental aspect of mental ability. Often these three areas get reduced to knowledge, attitudes and skills.

> Cognitive literally means relating to the faculty of cognition. It involves investigating, thinking and knowing. A 'shorthand' for cognitive is knowledge.
>
> The affective domain is concerned with feelings, beliefs and attitudes. Some of the most significant aspects of lifelong learning fall into this domain. A shorthand for affective is attitudes.
>
> The psychomotor domain is concerned with physical skills, like holding a pencil to write, learning to walk and learning to make eye contact. Psychomotor skills can mostly be learned through practice.

What you are learning

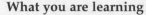

The content of your learning will inevitably vary considerably. One day you might be thinking about how to plan a party, the next you may find yourself needing to remember the key points of a talk you have to give, and on another you might be curled up with a good novel, enjoying letting your imagination run wild. *What* you are learning will affect how you choose to learn.

My view of content goes beyond the ideas developed by Bloom to include 'insights' and, most importantly, learning to learn skills. These are, in many ways, the most important skills that you can acquire for life. For with them you have the know-how to thrive in any situation where your previous knowledge is not enough. I use the word 'learnacy' to describe these skills. I am particularly grateful to Dr Peter Honey whose thinking about different kinds of learning has stimulated my own.

So, in my view of the world, there are five different types of 'content' that you are likely to experience when you are learning. These are:

Developing knowledge

- Information (for example, the number 11 bus leaves at 33 minutes past the hour)
- Facts (for example, my house was built in 1856)
- Theories (for example, eating five portions of fresh fruits and vegetables every day is good for your health)

Developing skills

- Interpersonal skills (for example, how to give feedback to a colleague)
- Motor skills (for example, how to drive a car)
- Techniques (for example, how to prime wood so it is ready to be painted)

Developing insights

- Making connections (for example, by seeing the way another business does something and realizing how you could use it in your work)
- Understanding complex issues (for example, why the USA and the UK went to war in Iraq in 2003)
- Self-awareness (for example, a realization about your preferred ways of learning)

Developing standards

- Values (for example, the importance of treating each member of your family fairly)
- Attitudes (for example, your colleagues need to have the total picture of what is going on before they can make an informed decision about an issue)
- Beliefs (for example, if you treat other people with respect they will respect you)

Learnacy skills

- Learning to learn skills, for example, the 5Rs – Resourcefulness, Remembering, Resilience, Reflectiveness and Responsiveness – that you are reading about in this part

You may find it helpful to think about, consciously or unconsciously, the different methods, approaches and techniques that you have at your disposal. The following is a prompt list to start you off. See how many you feel confident to use. If you are not sure about a particular item then use the index at the end of this book. Do not worry about the fact that it is a very long list!

Accidental learning	Action learning sets	Audio-tape
Audio-visual	Case studies	Classroom-based
Coaching	Conferences	Courses
Critical incidents	Dialogue/debate	Discussion
Diaries	Drama	Email groups
Exhibitions	Family learning	Formal study
Formative assessment	Games	Imitation
Informal learning	Instruction	Interactive learning
Job swaps	Job shadowing	Job rotation
Knowledge management	Knowledge sharing	Learning by doing
Learning through libraries	Online learning	Open learning
Opportunistic learning	Trial and error	Leading a team
Learning from mistakes	Learning from role models	Lectures
Mass media	Meetings	Mentoring
Networking	Observation	Outdoor pursuits
Peer review	Performance review	Personal dev't plans
Placements	Presenting	Problem solving
Projects	Questioning	Reading
Receiving feedback	Reflecting	Residentials
Reviewing papers	Role play	Sabbaticals
Scenario planning	Searching	Secondments
Simulations	Slide show	Spreadsheets
Study guides	Teaching	Team-based learning
Telephone conferences	Toolkits	Video conferencing
Videos	Visits	Writing

Choosing a method

Using the three boxed headings on page 83, you might like to apply them to something you are currently learning and begin to experience the kinds of choices you can make for your planned learning.

Start with what you know about **your own preferences**. Look back to page 38. If you have a strong activist preference, then the kinds of techniques which may appeal to you from this list would include:

Action learning sets

Drama

Job swaps

Trial and error

and many more. Of course, the goal is to become a more effective all-round learner. Then you will not just want to choose those methods which come most easily to you.

If you are more pragmatic, then you may like:

Critical incidents (where you explore the effects of important moments in your life)

Informal learning

Networking

Visits

and many more.

If you tend to be reflective by nature, then you may enjoy:

Coaching

Diaries

Peer review

Questioning

and many more.

And finally, if you tend to the theoretical, then your preferences may be for:

Instruction

Knowledge sharing

Learning through libraries

Study guides

and many more.

Now think about the **environment** in which you will be learning.

Will you be able to move around as you learn?
Will there be anyone to help you?
Will you be learning on your own or with others?
Will you have access to computers? (See below for more on this.)

You can probably influence your environment considerably if you are at home or less so if at work (see Chapters 11 and 12 for more information about learning in these two particular environments).

If you are able to move around then methods such as role play, games and simulations may work well.

If there are skilled people available to help you then coaching, mentoring and peer review (where a colleague gives you feedback on your work or learning) may be helpful.

If you are with others then the more sociable kinds of learning, like dialogue, discussion, observation, scenario planning and team-based activities, are likely to be effective.

And if you have access to computers then email groups, knowledge management, searching and simulations become possibilities.

Perhaps the most significant of the three influencing factors is the content of your learning. Take a moment to look back at the headings on pages 84 and 85 which describe most of the different kinds of **content** you are likely to encounter.

If you are developing your knowledge, then learning through case studies, conferences, exhibitions, lectures, libraries, reading, reviewing papers and visits are just a few potential methods.

If you are developing skills then the following may work for you:

Coaching
Imitation
Trial and error
Instruction
Learning by doing
Observation
Placements
Problem solving
Receiving feedback.

If you are developing insights then action learning sets, formative assessment, job swaps, job shadowing, learning from role models, peer review, sabbaticals and visits may be helpful.

If you are developing values then case studies, family learning, role play, informal learning, mentoring, questioning and residentials are useful.

And if you are developing your skills as a learner, then you might like to go no further than Chapters 6–10 which are full of ideas to help you. Of course, these are only my suggestions and are in no way to be seen as a prescriptive set of ideas.

A checklist of questions to ask yourself when selecting a method

You have already covered three key areas:

Does it suit my style as a learner?
Will it work in the environment I will be in?
Is it likely to work for the content I have chosen?

But there are others you might like to consider:

Do I have time for it?
Can I afford it?
Am I ready for it?
Do I like the way it is assessed (if it is)?
Has it worked before in situations like this?
Can I adapt it to suit me?
Will it support me?
Will it stretch me?
Will it help me understand?

As you become a more resourceful learner, you may well think of other good questions.

Using computers

In recent years one method in particular has grown in importance – the use of computers. Ownership of a home computer has risen steadily and, in the UK, the majority of people in work either have a computer on their desk or make use of one during a typical working day. The computer is as important to us now in our learning as the book once was (and still is to a large extent). While computers can never replace people – the social interaction of learning together – they have opened up enormous possibilities for learners.

> The computer is a moron.
>
> Peter Drucker

Using computers is such a big subject that it is difficult to know what to include in a reference work like *Discover Your Hidden Talents*, so all this brief section seeks to do is to touch on some of the different views about their use.

Internet access and the advent of broadband technology have meant that, from your desk at home or at work, you can access books, pictures, films, music, chat rooms and much more beyond. At the same time email has led to a revival of letter writing and, as we tend to write at speed, the development of a whole new language (just as texting on mobile phones has done). Meanwhile computers themselves enable us to word-process, use spreadsheets, create slide presentations, design spaces, look up train and air timetables, book hotels, print out maps and process digital photographs. The computer is not itself that smart or reliable, as Peter Drucker points out, but in the hands of a smart learner it can be an extraordinarily powerful and effective tool.

> I do not fear computers. I fear the lack of them.
>
> Isaac Asimov

Why bother with computers?

They are everywhere and, whatever your age, you may want to find out more.
They are excellent for seeking out information and opinions of all kinds.
They are useful for communicating with friends and colleagues.
They can be a good means of supporting your learning.

There are some obvious benefits of using computers. You can undertake it when you want to, simply by flicking a switch. You can do it where you want to. You can also, potentially, choose different methods of learning (although all of them necessarily involve the computer). And you can go at a pace that suits you.

Useful as computers are, they have become so pervasive that, like the television, they have come to dominate some homes and some workplaces. The dangers of this include:

- Computers take up far more of our time than is necessary and leave us less time to focus on becoming a more effective learner.

- We depend too much on the reliability of the information to which they give us access.
- When they are not available we can find that we have become less resourceful ourselves.
- We waste time on computer 'processes' – which fonts and colours to use, for example – rather than spending it on real thinking about any issues we are exploring.
- We let a program dominate our mind set. PowerPoint is a good current example of this phenomenon. As a consequence we end up sitting though slide shows at work with an endless series of bullet points of dubious intellectual merit, where the presentation method has become more important than the content.

There are some issues with regard to children's use of the computer that are worth mentioning. The most important of these is a decision about the location of your child's computer or the home computer which has internet access. It is strongly suggested that you do not put a computer with internet access in your child's bedroom as it will be far more difficult to monitor the use of it. It is much better to put it in a central place where it is easy for you to be aware of its use, without having to consciously intrude. As with television, it is worth establishing clear rules for the use of a computer, especially the overall amount of time spent on it.

How to get the best out of computers

1. Be clear in your own mind about the kinds of learning activities that the computer can help you with.
2. Specifically seek out the kinds of e-learning (learning with computers) that work best for you.
3. Always try and have a back-up method which does not involve a computer.
4. If you are a parent, limit the amount of time your child uses a computer.
5. In the workplace, ensure that you continue to have regular face-to-face time with your colleagues.
6. Be discriminating in your use of emails.

At the same time as individual computer technology has been developing, so have global communication networks. The internet, which is part of the world wide web (from which the 'www' bit comes from), is a network of millions of computers linked together by telephone lines and other means. It exploded onto the scene in the 1990s, although over the previous 30 years various aspects of it had in fact been invented. Websites and email are now a major component of the web, along with all kinds of clever ways of searching for information. The name of one of the search engines, Google (like the name Hoover), has become so popular that a new verb has emerged, 'to google', meaning to search.

The internet has opened up huge possibilities for learners, with almost limitless virtual libraries available to them. When NASA put a probe onto Mars, for example, it was possible to watch film of Mars live on the internet.

Conversely, the internet has led to whole new, malicious types of antisocial behaviour – computer viruses and spamming (sending junk emails), for example. It is also difficult for a learner to tell whether the site they are exploring is accurate or not.

> Getting information off the internet is like taking a drink from a fire hydrant.
>
> Mitch Kapor

The dramatic developments in information technology have also been accompanied by a more general information explosion. More and more data are being created. Websites pop up overnight. A new book is published somewhere in the world approximately every 30 seconds. With so much information to absorb, you may find it helpful to find out about speed reading.

Speed reading is something that you can learn. The average reader can take in 240 words per minute and it is possible to double or triple this with practice.

Why bother with speed reading?

It will help you to acquire information more rapidly.
It will give you more time to spend on other things if you can be a super-efficient reader.

How to speed read

1. Skim the contents page and index first.
2. Read whole sentences and paragraphs for their key ideas rather than looking at individual words.
3. Use a guide – a pencil or ruler, for example – to drag you eyes speedily down each page.
4. Miss out examples.
5. Skip things you already know.
6. Read inside your head not out loud.
7. Do not go back.
8. If speed reading on the internet, cross-reference what you are reading with your own common sense!

Remember not to speed read your favourite novels!

There are many speed-reading courses on the market which might help you.

If you can read faster can you also learn faster? Many people think that you can.

Accelerated learning

The idea of accelerated learning developed in the 1970s from the work of Georgi Lozanov, a Bulgarian professor of psychiatry and psychotherapy, who developed a teaching method known as 'suggestology'. It is an approach that attempts to engage all the senses and capture the naturally positive feelings towards learning with which we are born (and which we tend to lose as we grow older). The underlying assumption is that if you use certain techniques you will learn faster and more effectively.

These days, the term accelerated learning covers a whole spectrum of techniques including those previously listed. The accelerated learning ideas of writers and trainers like Colin Rose and Alistair Smith, for example, have become influential in many schools. They include learning styles, memory techniques, music and the creation of positive emotions. Enthusiastic followers of this approach tend to overemphasize the value of individual aspects of the approach, for example, by suggesting that playing Mozart to a child will make him or her more intelligent! Sadly this is not true.

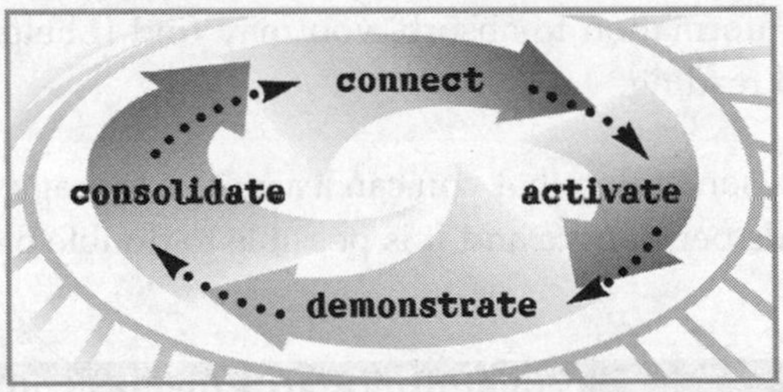

Source: Alistair Smith, Mark Lovatt and Derek Wise (2003) *Accelerated Learning* (Network Educational Press)

If you were going to put the principles of accelerated learning into practice, you might try making up rhymes to help you to remember the things you want to do. You could use music to create a mood of relaxed alertness at the start of a meeting. Or you might choose to use pictures where you would normally use words.

It seems logical to assume that anyone can learn faster.

However, the key to being an effective lifelong learner is probably something to do with whether you can learn better.

> Creativity is the ability to introduce order into the randomness of nature.
>
> Eric Hoffer

Developing and organizing ideas

The second area of resourcefulness to explore is the ability to develop and organize ideas. It is through this that you can begin to release your own creativity and make sense of the world around you. There are hundreds of different definitions of creativity. Some stress the ability to generate good new ideas and others focus on the desirability of ideas being practically useful. Most definitions involve the ability to see new relationships between things. Creativity is a very important part of learning and learning to be more creative is, consequently, a key skill for an effective lifelong learner. When we are at our most creative we tend to feel most fulfilled.

The state of flow

The state of flow was first identified and described by American psychologist Mihali Csikszentmihalyi (pronounced 'Chick-sent-me-high-ee') in the 1990s through detailed analysis of the way creative people performed and lived. Flow is when you are totally absorbed and oblivious to external pressures (time, noise and so on). This state involves both relaxation and alertness and is increasingly being seen to be a state in which you are likely to have more creative thoughts.

The state of flow appears to be ideal for both creativity and learning. Self-consciousness disappears. There is no fear of failure. The activity you are engaged in becomes an end in itself.

You may be able to think of situations when you have been in a state of flow. Perhaps you were imaginatively absorbed in a good book and could not put it down. Or, as a child, you were totally absorbed in making a complicated model out of old cardboard boxes. Maybe, as a student, you forgot time as you wrote an essay.

Being creative is a subtle and complex process. It involves getting in the right frame of mind, generating ideas or new thinking, absorbing and sensing what is already there, feeding your ideas so that they grow, testing them out and reflecting. Very rarely is there an 'ah-ha' moment, despite what Archimedes and his famous cry of 'eureka' would lead you to believe.

A specific aspect of resourcefulness, in a fast moving world, is the ability to come up with new thoughts and ideas. Indeed, in a real sense, being creative is just this: being able to come up with a good idea when you need one.

Why bother learning how to generate ideas?

It will help you to solve problems at home and at work.
It will help you to develop your own creative self.
You might create something new that will make you rich and famous!

How to generate ideas

Traditionally, the emphasis has been on the ideas themselves and one technique – brainstorming – has become widely used. In fact research suggests that having good ideas is as much about mind set as about any specific techniques. Standard techniques include brainstorming, synectics, feed forward, plus, minus and interesting, action learning, double-loop thinking, thinking of outrageous opposites and many more. (Use the index at the end of the book to find out more about each of these.)

You may also find it helpful to allow more time for sleeping, walking and thinking, and to consciously expose yourself to new ideas.

However, the right frame of mind for generating ideas is a state of relaxed alertness. Often you need to:

1. Slow down, using a relaxation technique of some kind (including taking a bath, going for a walk or jogging).
2. Look inwards rather than outwards by finding some quiet time for yourself.
3. Learn how to think softly rather than straining at the leash to come up with great ideas. When you feel yourself straining to look at something and almost end up trying too hard, go into soft focus mode with your eyes – almost as if you let them go out of focus – and, at the same time, tell your mind to wait and see what it sees.
4. When faced with most issues it is helpful to get into the habit of:
   - asking good questions
   - delaying judgement so that you do not squash other people's ideas
   - approaching things from different perspectives
   - empathizing with other points of view, and
   - becoming more comfortable with the often conflicting and ambiguous feelings that these kinds of habits may create in you.

Good luck! There is no one way! Develop your own blend!

Metaphors make connections between one thing and another. Ice cold is an example of a simple metaphor. The cold is like ice in its coldness!

> "There are few things as toxic as a bad metaphor. You can't think without metaphors."
>
> Mary Catherine Bateson

Your mind likes metaphors because making connections is one of the key principles of the way it works. When you create a metaphor your mind is holding two ideas in the same space and looking at them from different angles. This is a key element of creativity.

Lateral thinking

Invented by Edward de Bono in the 1960s, lateral thinking is sideways thinking. It attempts to see all problems as opportunities and create more original and effective ideas. It assumes that, as De Bono puts it: 'You cannot dig a hole in a different place by digging the same hole deeper.' Or, put another way, it is easy to get stuck digging an ideas hole in one place when you would be better off starting again somewhere else.

Many of the methods associated with lateral thinking are now widely used throughout the world.

When you are looking closely at a problem there is a great tendency to view it in black and white terms, and so reduce it to opposites. This can lead to closed thinking. One of the techniques De Bono invented to avoid this limiting kind of thinking is called 'plus, minus, interesting'.

Plus, minus, interesting

Plus, minus, interesting allows you to categorize ideas, thoughts and propositions in ways that allow you to appreciate both sides of an argument while, at the same time, suspending your judgement and seeing things from a different point of view. It encourages breadth of thought and open-mindedness. It also encourages creative conversations.

1. Take an idea or proposition.
2. In pairs explore what is positive, what is negative and what is interesting about it.
3. See how many ideas you can generate under each of the above labels.
4. Then review your lists. Often you will find that the germs of some really good ideas are in the 'Interesting' column, for the tendency of our mind is to classify things in black or white terms.

You might like to try this technique on something that you are grappling with yourself at the moment.

So, if you were considering the proposition that we should abolish all schools, your columns might look a bit like this:

Plus	Minus	Interesting
It would cost less in taxes You could learn what you like You could learn when you like	Many teachers would lose their jobs Children from poorer families might suffer	You could use the buildings for other things Parents might get more involved

Already you can see that there are some fascinating ideas shaping up under the 'Interesting' heading.

Making connections

As we generate ideas, we are often stimulated by something else from another part of our life. Indeed the ability to make connections is a key element of learning. We experience something and immediately try to find some connection with it. 'Where was it I saw her before?' 'That reminds me of …' 'That's just like …' This ability to make connections rapidly was, and is, an essential survival skill. 'That animal looks like a lion. I'm going to run for it.'

> 'An idea is a feat of association.'
>
> Robert Frost

We take in data with our senses and millions of brain cells miraculously process it all by seeking to connect themselves in different parts of our brain.

Today, making connections is at the heart of what we need to do to be a more creative learner and have good ideas. Who would have thought the connection between glue that does not stick and small bits of paper would have led to Post-it notes? Or that the invention of the internet combined with the idea of a supermarket and the humble book would have produced a bookstore like amazon.com? Creative learners see novel ways of combining things. They draw experiences from one part of their lives and use them in another. Above all, they know how to ensure that they are connected to their learning.

Why bother making connections?

It will help you to engage in any type of learning by connecting with it.

It will help you to have good ideas.

Your memory will improve.

How to make connections

1. Deliberately expose yourself to new situations by visiting other organizations and places.
2. Try shadowing a colleague from time to time or even doing a job swap for a day.
3. Try this standard test of creativity – see how many uses you can think of for a paper clip. (Each time you do so you are forcing your mind to make improbable connections!)
4. Learn how to Mind Map™; see the next page.
5. Always look at problems from at least three different points of view and see what connections this stimulates.

Seeing connections is important not only as a means of generating ideas but also as a way of making sense of your ideas. It helps to organize your thoughts, as 'plus, minus, interesting' demonstrated. Some people find lists or charts work well for this purpose. Others prefer to arrange things more visually.

Mind mapping

Invented by Tony Buzan in the late 1960s, a Mind Map™ is a colourful way of organizing and visualizing what is in your mind onto a piece of paper. Many people find the interconnectedness and networked features of a Mind Map™ more helpful than a traditional list running from the top to bottom of a page. If you are working with an A4 page then you may find it easier to have it horizontal, like this

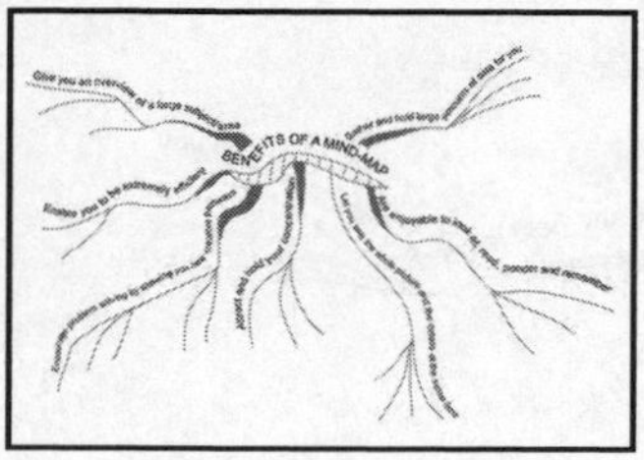

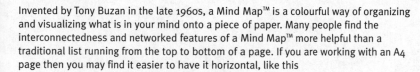

rather than vertical, like this

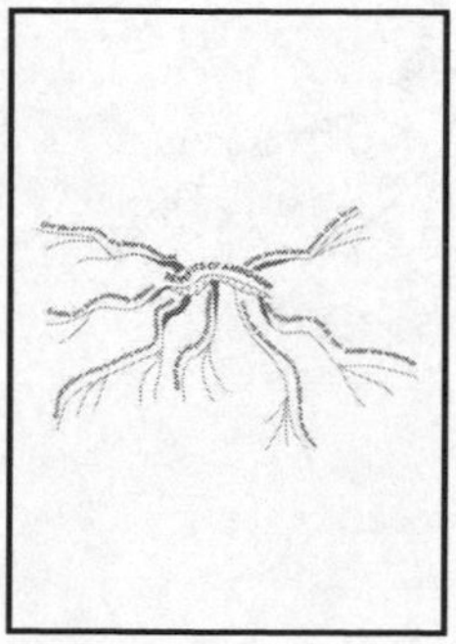

1. Start by putting a key word or picture in the centre of a piece of paper and work outwards from this.
2. Draw lines out from the centre, like a spider web, and put your thoughts or ideas down as words or images on these lines.
3. Use branches off these for related ideas.
4. Use colour.
5. Use arrows or any other visual aids to show links between different parts.
6. Do not get stuck in one branch. If you dry up in one area go to another.
7. Put ideas down as they occur, wherever they fit. Do not judge or hold back.
8. Enjoy the process.

Mind Maps™ work really well for many people and not for others, just as lists do. This is what a Mind Map™ of the benefits of using Mind Maps™ might look like!

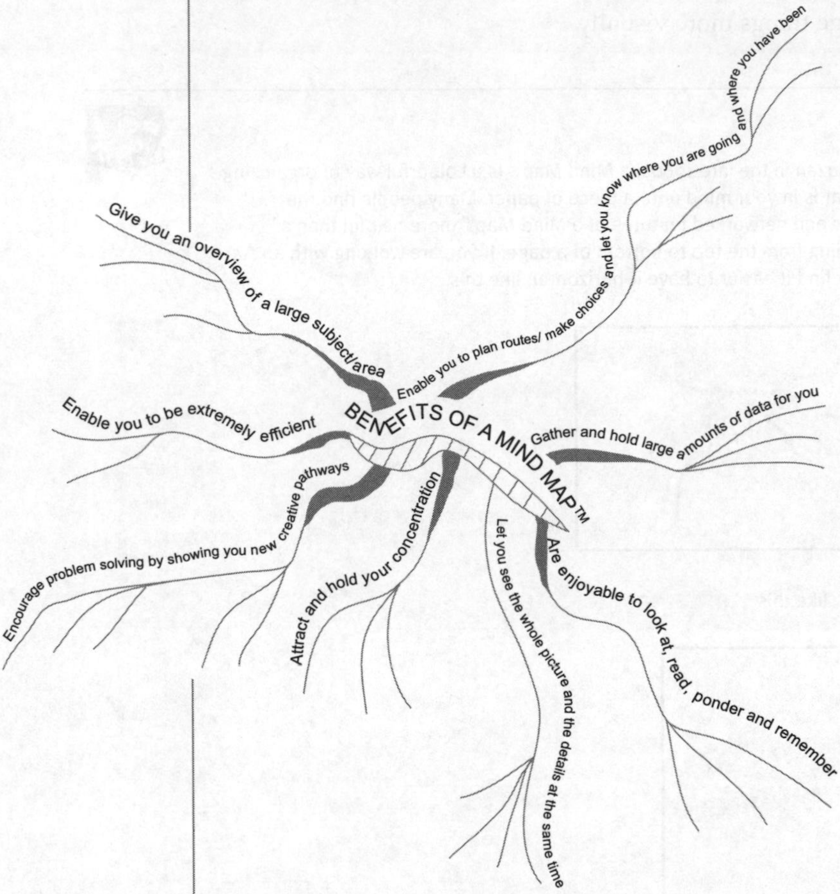

> A day without an argument is like an egg without salt.
>
> Angela Carter

Arguing a case

Being able to generate ideas is important. But there are many times when you need to be able argue your case in life and learning. Developing an argument involves persuading other people to agree with your view of the world and is a key element of your resourcefulness.

Why bother learning to argue?

As a parent you will need to explain your views to your child.

At work you may need to persuade your boss to back you.

If you want to be able to stick up for yourself you need to be able to argue your case.

How to develop an argument	

1. Work out your position
What's your point? Be clear about what you are trying to say.

2. Find the best way to put your argument across
Have a number of different approaches. These might include:

Describing the benefit	for example,'The reason you ought to do this is ...'
Examples	for example, 'Here are some examples of other people who have found this to work ...'
Anecdotes	for example, 'Other people who think this said that ...'
Facts	for example, 'Eighty per cent of people who tried my approach found that ...'
Emotions	for example, 'You know it feels right ...'
Empathy	for example, 'Put yourself in my shoes and you might see how I ...'

3. Make sure you have thought of the other points of view
Work out what you would say if you were arguing against your position and then think of good counter arguments. Often it helps to anticipate what your 'opponent' might say.

Working with people

Sometimes you learn on your own: you are reading something or keeping a diary, thinking or designing. But much learning is sociable and involves working with people; often this may be in teams. Consequently, being able to work well with others is an important aspect of what it takes to be an effective learner. Of course everyone is different and this inevitably leads to tensions when people are working together. Effective learners anticipate this and have ways of dealing with the tensions that it creates.

Why bother learning how to work with people?

It's an essential life skill.
You will make and keep more friends.
You will get on better at home and at work.

How to work with people

Here are some general guidelines for you to adapt:

1. Make sure that you have an agreed, common goal.
2. Try to ensure that each person's role is clear. Some people prefer thinking, some doing. Some are better at the ideas stage, others at seeing things through. Some like to research before testing, others prefer trial and error. Some are opinionated and hard to shift, others are more flexible in their approaches. A successful team needs different approaches.
3. Most projects have a fixed time limit, so make sure that someone has the role of checking on progress against time.
4. In most teams there are moments of tension. Ensure that there is at least one person who is good at conciliating and facilitating.
5. Watch out for emotions – they are much more likely to disrupt, both positively and negatively, the smooth running of a group of people who are working together.
6. Keep communicating – listening, speaking and picking up non-verbal cues.
7. Take a break if things get difficult.
8. Remember the importance of praising others for their contributions.
9. Gently seek to involve quieter members of any group.
10. Do not be afraid to abandon one course of action in favour of another!

“Tell me, and I will forget. Show me, and I may remember. Involve me, and I will understand.”

Confucius

Unless you are a hermit, you will inevitably spend time with other people and need to learn how to get the best out of these situations. But there is another good reason why the social dimension is important to understand – much learning is rooted in experience and experiences often happen with other people around. While it is perfectly possible for you to wander the moors alone and learn about the natural world, for much of the time other people will be involved in the experiences you have.

Experiential learning

Do we actually need to experience things to learn them? Or can we just read about them in books?

The idea of experiential learning was invented by David Kolb in the 1970s. Kolb argued that, in any learning cycle, experience is a key element. He argued that there are four processes which together go to make up most learning, as per the diagram on the next page. Most people find that experience is essential to their learning.

Crucially, Kolb showed that many people need to experience their learning for it to be meaningful and effective. Peter Honey and Alan Mumford's learning styles on page 38 draw from Kolb's thinking.

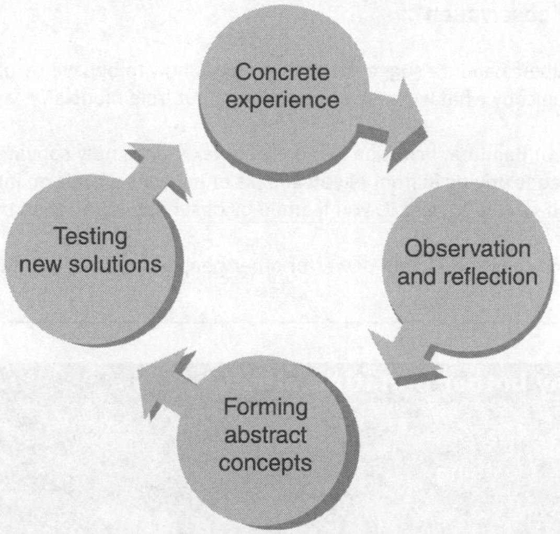

There are two kinds of experiential learning. The first is the learning that happens simply by living: something happens to you and you reflect on it. The second occurs when you have a direct experience of whatever you are studying rather than being told about it second hand. Part of learning to be a teacher or a doctor, for example, involves experiencing being a teacher or doctor.

Kolb also recognized that you can enter the learning cycle at any one of the four points in the diagram. You might like to think of something you are learning at the moment and see how this compares with your own experiences.

> Imitation is the sincerest form of flattery.
>
> Anon

Learning from others

Of course one of the most fundamental ways in which we learn is by watching and imitating others. It is one of the five principles of mind for which we, as human beings, are 'hard-wired'; see pages 281–285. So, we learn to walk and talk largely though imitation. Of course, not everyone likes imitators! At school it is called cheating, at work it is intellectual property theft and, at national level, it can be espionage!

Effective learners are always on the look-out for people from whom they can learn by imitation. It follows that, if you want to become more effective then you need to choose your close friends carefully! For you are likely to pick up the habits of those around you. This is why parents are right to be concerned about their children's peer groups.

The power of observation

Psychologist Albert Bandura suggested that we learn how to behave by observing people. We then copy what we have observed from our 'role models'.

But, according to Bandura, imitation is more complex than simply copying. For example, if you see someone driving in front of you and his or her car's wheels go into a hole in the ground and you swerve to miss it, you learned by observing rather than by imitating!

There is disagreement about the power of other people's actions to influence our own behaviour.

Why bother imitating others?

It is a great way of getting new ideas.
It is a quick and practical way of learning.
You cannot stop doing it any way!

There are some straightforward things that you can do to ensure you have more opportunities to observe from others and learn from them.

How to imitate others

1. Consciously put yourself in as many situations as possible where you can learn from others.
2. At work, see if you can take part in a job swap and learn from this.
3. Spend time with people you admire and notice what they do well.
4. Identify those things in your life that you want to improve and find people who are good at these things to learn from.
5. Read the biographies of those you admire.
6. Cultivate friends from different walks of life.
7. When you see a tough situation being handled well make a note of it.
8. Avoid spending unnecessary time with people who are negative or pessimistic.

Working with people does not mean that you have to do everything with them all the time. Indeed if you try and do this you are likely to end up with no time for yourself. An aspect of resourcefulness is your ability to delegate things to other people. Delegation means giving responsibility to someone else to do something that you would otherwise have done yourself, as leaders the world over have found out how to do.

It is important to remember that you cannot delegate someone else to do your learning for you! But you can delegate things which will help others learn more effectively and also help you. Many people find it difficult to let go, but there are some simple steps which may help you to do this.

> Surround yourself with the best people you can find, delegate authority, and don't interfere.
>
> Ronald Reagan

Why bother delegating?

So that you concentrate on the things that only you can do.

So you can help others by giving them a chance to take on new things.

How to delegate

Start by thinking why you are delegating.

1. Is it because you want to give someone else the chance to develop and to motivate them? If so, check that s/he has the ability/confidence to do it and, if not, ensure that you provide support.
2. Is it because you do not want to do the task yourself? If so, check that it is something that is appropriate to delegate. (You would not want to delegate a sensitive meeting with someone, for example, whereas routine matters may be just right to pass on as activities in which you have little interest.) Assuming that it is appropriate, ensure that:
   - the task is clear
   - it is clear how the person to whom you are delegating can get support
   - the deadline, when the task needs to be completed, including any interim deadlines, is known.

If you want someone to learn from doing this, tell them what needs to be done, but avoid telling them how to do it. Make sure you give both praise and, more helpfully, critical feedback.

Once you start working closely with people in any activity it rapidly becomes clear that some are better than others at learning together. One of the most helpful skills to acquire is the ability to show empathy with those around you.

Empathy involves understanding and identifying another person's situation, seeing the world from their perspective.

> I hope to leave my children a sense of empathy and pity and a will to right social wrongs.
>
> Anita Roddick

Why bother with empathy?

It is essential for maintaining friendships.
It helps when dealing with difficult situations.
It is useful when bringing up children.

Some helpful suggestions for becoming more empathetic include the following.

How to show empathy with someone

1. Make regular eye contact.
2. When someone tells you that they are feeling something, acknowledge what they say and always avoid telling them what they feel! (If someone tells you that they are feeling something, who are you to contradict them?)
3. Consciously try and see the world from someone else's perspective.
4. If they seem to find it difficult to express their feelings, gently suggest possible views, for example, 'I guess you must be ...' 'Perhaps you are feeling that ...'
5. Acknowledge other points of view, especially when you do not agree with them. (This is often the case when parents are dealing with their children!)

A well-known technique to help you see things from other people's perspectives is role play.

Role play

Role play involves two or more people taking on the character of someone else and exploring what might happen in certain situations. For example, you might decide to make up a short scene in which a confident learner tries to persuade a less confident one to enrol on a course at their local college.

Role play was first introduced as a concept by Jacob Moreno in the 1920s as a part of psycho drama. It gives lots of scope for creative exploration of different points of view and a chance for people to practise their reactions in a number of new situations.

Extroverts love it. Introverts may take time to become involved and may prefer to explore ideas in the privacy of their own mind.

You might like to practise role play by playing role-play games (like 'charades' and 'guess the famous person') in the safety of your own home. Or if you have a difficult situation at work, get your partner to do a role-play rehearsal with you of how you might handle it. (You could also do similarly with your child if s/he is worried about dealing with something at school.) Or you could think about the opportunities for role play at work and gently suggest that you and your colleagues give it a try.

Once you have tried something out one way round, you could try some role reversal, a kind of role play where participants swap roles.

Another useful technique comes from NLP (see page 78 for more about this).

Reframing

Reframing is a term used in NLP to describe the important skill of being able to see information and situations from different perspectives or frames.

Imagine that you overslept, your car had a puncture, you missed an important meeting and have lost the keys to your house. On the face of it this is a disastrous situation and you could choose to spend the rest of the day raging around like an angry bull. Or you might like to start by thinking how much worse it could have been. You could have had a serious road accident. Your house might have been on fire rather than just locked up until your partner arrived with the spare set of keys.

Reframing a situation gives you the chance to see three different perspectives:

1. your own
2. the other person's, and
3. that of a bystander who is not involved.

By beginning to reframe any situation you start to give your mind some options. Something that seemed like the end of the world is reframed as an unlucky but not life-threatening experience. And you can move into a mode of operating where you start to look for solutions.

> The real magic of discovery lies not in seeking new landscapes, but in having new eyes.
>
> Marcel Proust

Effective communication

For people to be able to learn together effectively good communication is essential. While empathy is essential for effective communication, so are talking and listening skills.

Resourceful learners are good at explaining things. For without this there will be confusion, irritation and time-wasting.

Why bother learning to explain clearly?

It helps to break down a complex task into smaller chunks.

If you cannot explain clearly you will end up wasting your (and other people's) time!

How to explain clearly

1. Choose your language carefully so that you are using words which are understood by the person to whom you are explaining.
2. Break up what you are trying to explain into small chunks and work out what you want to say about each. Think whether any of your explanation would be helped by a diagram, picture or action.
3. Start your explanation with the big picture 'I am going to say how to …'
4. Then go through the smaller chunks.
5. Then sum up and check that your listener has understood you!

> ‘I like to listen. I have learned a great deal from listening carefully. Most people never listen.’
>
> Ernest Hemingway

Equally important is listening. Indeed some would argue that this is a much undervalued skill today.

Why bother to listen attentively?

People will like you.

You are more likely to learn from others.

You will be a better parent, lover, friend, manager, citizen.

How to listen attentively

1. Maintain eye contact.
2. Focus on what someone is saying not how they are saying it.
3. From time to time, make sure that you show your interest.
4. Be patient and check your understanding of what is being said now and then.
5. Avoid jumping in with too many questions.
6. Try to empathize, imagining what it is like to be in the other person's shoes. Draw him/her out.
7. Pick up non-verbal cues that suggest a response from you would be helpful.
8. Try not to let your mind wander.
9. Treat listening as a challenging mental task and feel good because you are managing to achieve it.
10. Stay active by asking questions about what you are listening to.

Sometimes you will need to combine your explaining and listening powers to persuade those around you to adopt your suggestions. For it is worth remembering that the most persuasive people often get their way in life. Being able to know how to argue your case persuasively is, consequently, an important skill.

Why bother learning to persuade people?

Getting your way helps you to get on in life.

Working out an argument is a great way to keep your brain active.

How to persuade others

1. The most important thing is to be clear about what you want.
2. Then there are a number of possible approaches which you might take:
   - Work out what is in it for them. Bargaining works. Give and take.
   - Make an appeal to the emotions.
   - Give a clear explanation. Saying 'because' rather than just demanding is known to improve your power of persuasion.
   - Ask for a difficult thing first, possibly one that you do not actually expect to get. Then introduce the request you really want to be heeded.
   - Get their commitment to helping you to get a good result before you seek to persuade them. Commitment is a positive force.
   - Have some evidence ready in a language that you know will be understood.
   - Make yourself liked. Smile, listen and empathize. It may seem corny, but it is much more difficult to refuse a request from someone with whom you have established a good relationship.

Building networks

These days, networks are incredibly important. And 'networking' is a key element of resourcefulness. All of us have networks – the people we send cards to at Christmas, the people we work with, those who live near us, for example. Networking is the word used to describe getting to know people so that you can count them among your circle of contacts.

But networking is a more active process. It involves continuously meeting new people and staying in touch with those you already know. Contacts can be especially useful when you need advice or a recommendation for a job. Successful people tend to be well networked.

It is worth remembering that extroverts (see page 143) tend to find networking comes to them more naturally than introverts.

Why bother to network?

Friends and contacts really matter in today's world.

It is a great way to share and learn.

How to network effectively

Networking is a two-way process, so it is important to give as well as to receive. If your life is heading in a new direction you may be particularly interested in refreshing your contact network.

1. How many people do you know well enough to be able to describe their current professional or personal interests, including members of your own family?
2. Set time aside on a regular basis to call or email or write to each of them and exchange news.
3. Given where your life is currently heading, do you have the right kind of network to help you? If not, think how you might find new people. This could involve consciously seeking to get to know new people at work or in your local community or through family members. Ask existing members of your network to suggest people.

As you work and learn with different people you will probably begin to notice how some are better than others at maintaining their relationships. Effective learners recognize this and are likely to want to invest time and thought in cultivating important relationships.

Why bother to learn how to make and keep relationships?

It is essential unless you plan to be a hermit!

Everyone needs to work at relationship building.

It will give you more confidence.

There are no absolutely hard and fast pieces of advice that will work in all situations, but the chart on the opposite page may be helpful in getting you to think more about this area.

How to make and keep relationships

Making

1. Some people find it easy to make relationships. They just naturally start talking and getting to know people. Others find it much harder. The important thing is to be yourself and not put on an act.
2. Stop and think about your own current friends. Where did you meet them and how? Are there any clues here about which situations work best for you?
3. If you find it difficult to talk to strangers, set yourself very modest goals like trying to talk to one new person at a party or a meeting.

Keeping

4. Always respect another person's feelings. Saying something like 'That sounds like it was really upsetting for you ...' does not cost you anything and can help to make the other person feel better.
5. Sometimes just listen.
6. Take time to find out what is on other people's minds/agendas and set aside time to deal with any issues that arise.
7. Keep lines of communication open with friendly emails and notes and calls that are just about saying 'hello' and make no particular demands.

Sometimes it may help you to develop a relationship if you can see yourself as others see you. The following technique can help with this.

The Johari window

The Johari window is a way of helping people understand the ways in which they interact with others. Johari is a made-up word from bits of the names of the two people who invented it: Joe Luft and Harry Ingram. You can use the window (shown on the right) and its four panes to help you understand more about yourself. Imagine you are exploring your relationship between you and your manager:

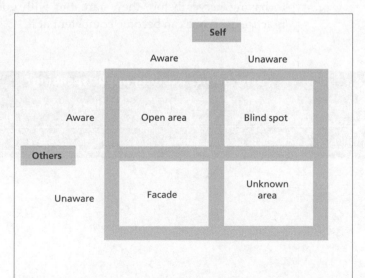

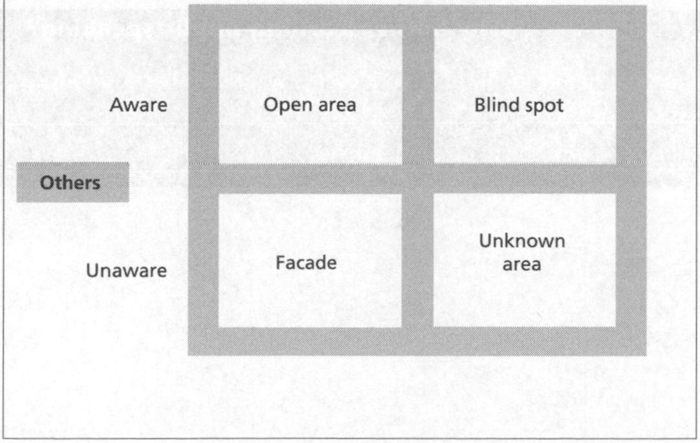

The open area is the information that you and s/he both share.

The facade contains other things you are aware of but have not disclosed to others.

The blind spot consists of things others have noticed about you, of which you are unaware.

The unknown area contains unconscious factors influencing your behaviour which are not known to you or your manager.

You can expand the open panel by telling people things. And you can find out more about the blind spot by asking questions. Effective relationships occur when there is a fair and reasonable balance between self-disclosure and feedback.

Although this may first appear rather complicated, the four-paned 'window' is a very useful tool in analysing all sorts of issues in life.

You might like to try this approach on a relationship which you are developing at present and about which you have some concerns. You could then use what you learn in a conversation with the person concerned.

So far most of the focus in this section on exploring working with people has been on small group situations. But, at some time in your life, you will probably have to give a speech to a larger group. If you are extrovert by nature this may not worry you. If you are an introvert it probably will. Most people, even those who are confident at speaking, get anxious beforehand. Indeed, many great speakers admit to having nerves before they start. But with good preparation and practice everyone can become competent at it.

Why bother learning public speaking?

Giving speeches at family and work events will be embarrassing for you, and others if you do not!

It will help you to speak up at meetings.

How to get better at public speaking

Before you speak

1. Preparation is essential. Find out who your audience will be and how long you are due to speak. The way you speak at the 80th birthday of your father will be very different from what you might say if you were speaking at a conference!
2. Decide clearly on your content. Almost always the temptation is to have too much to say. So, focus on a few key messages.
3. Concentrate on the beginning and the end, but mostly the beginning. Most listeners decide on whether they rate the speaker within a few minutes of him or her starting. Good ways of starting include:
   - Simply giving your listeners the big picture of what you are going to say (not forgetting to introduce yourself if they do not know you).
   - Telling a short funny and relevant story that leads you into what you are going to talk about.
   - Making a connection with the place where you are speaking or the people who are listening.
4. Decide whether you are going to use any visual aids. These days PowerPoint dominates the market for public speaking and it can be extremely tedious to sit through lots of identical slides, each with a heading and then some bullet points. So, think carefully before you opt for this unless you can create a small number of really visual slides.
5. Make sure the main bulk of your speech has some variety in it. This could include: mini-stories to make a point, images, quotations, statistics, video clips and so on.
6. Work out how you are going to end. A one sentence summary is a pretty good way, possibly with a light-hearted comment to round it all off.
7. Practise it in front of a mirror or a friend or both. Make yourself some prompt cards with key headings on them. If you get very nervous, write out your first two sentences so that you can be sure about the start. But, except in very formal situations, reading a speech that you have written out can be very stilted.

As you speak

8. Take deep breaths and have some water to hand. Try to make eye contact with your audience. But if this really throws you, concentrate on looking at the back row where you cannot make out facial expressions. Try to enjoy yourself!

Sometimes it also helps to be able to use narrative. Being able to tell stories is a skill that some people find easier than others.

As stories are such a powerful method of communication, it is a skill worth trying to acquire. An anecdote is the story of an interesting incident. Examples can be very powerful in real learning, showing that 'people like you' have had similar experiences and helping to boost confidence more generally. Using anecdotes is a really helpful way of bringing your learning alive or remembering things.

> Stories have the magic that make you run into the backyard at night and stare up into infinity to see what's there.
>
> Mark Twain in *Huckleberry Finn*

Why bother learning to tell stories?

It is a great way to share your experiences.
It makes experiences real and memorable.

How to tell good stories

1. Decide what the key moments of your story are and hold onto these in your head.
2. How will you start?
3. How will you end? Does it have a punchline? If so, how will you remember it?
4. Where will you start your story? In the middle and then go back to explain how you got there? At the beginning? At the end and then work back?
5. Will you tell the story with any prompts or would you prefer to have key 'headings' or scenes written out on cards?

When you think you have worked out the answers to these questions, have a practice on your own and then try it out in front of a friend or family member.

Remembering

Chapter 7

> An education isn't how much you have committed to memory, or even how much you know. It's being able to differentiate between what you do know and what you don't.
>
> Anatole France

It is hard to be an effective learner or do well in any education system if your memory constantly lets you down. Life becomes like shifting sand, with your never being quite sure what you are certain about and what you have forgotten.

Without memory the human race would rapidly die out. It would not be able to recall which animals were dangerous and which friendly; which food was safe to eat; how to get back to the home, and so on. There would be no learning either, because as soon as you had learned something you would forget it!

As more and more data floods our daily lives, knowing how to remember becomes increasingly important. You might think that memory is less important these days, with the growing power of the computer and the world wide web. And you would be partially right. Certainly it is no longer a problem if you cannot remember the capital city of Denmark or the chemical formula for something because it is much easier to look it up. But, paradoxically, more and more aspects of life require you to remember a password or memorable phrase or four-digit PIN (personal identification number) as the role of technology requires protective codes.

This is memory of a 'know-what' kind. However, these days it is much more likely that you need 'know-how' memory (for example for many of the techniques you have just been reading about in Chapter 6).

A particular challenge our society will be dealing with in the coming decades is the product of our increasingly healthy society – longevity. This is a wonderful opportunity for us all, but it means that we need to focus even more on learning how to remember. For the many people who will have active lives beyond the age of 70 – when it is generally agreed that changes in the brain tend to lead to changes in the operation of memory – a good grasp of techniques for enhancing memory will be very helpful. Luckily we are discovering more and more about this subject as we penetrate the mysteries of the human mind.

Memory is a hugely complex subject and, like an iceberg, huge parts of it exist at an unconscious level and therefore cannot be processed in any straightforward way. Nevertheless, there are many useful things that you can learn about your memory which may help you become a more effective learner. The following are three elements to consider:

1. It may help if you can understand the basics of how memory works.
2. It may be helpful if you can see the patterns between things and group them accordingly. Seeing the bigger patterns which knit your experiences together can bring self-knowledge. Being able to apply things that you have learned in one part of your life to another part helps to increase your learning power.
3. It may help if you can gain confidence in a number of specific memory techniques which are drawn from an understanding about the way memory operates.

In this chapter you may explore some of the ways in which you can become a more effective learner by getting more out of your memory. It is organized around three headings: 'How your memory works', 'Seeing patterns' and 'Specific techniques'.

How your memory works

There are three aspects to memory: creating (or fixing it) in the first place, storing it, and recalling it when you need to. Each of these stages is affected by your emotional state, your general health and your degree of engagement, as well as by a number of other factors that we do not yet fully understand.

Every time you sense anything at all, an electro-chemical connection is made in your brain. It leaves a trace, or pathway, of synaptic connections between the neurons in your brain. Each one of these is, potentially, the beginnings of a memory. The more that a particular pattern of connections is activated, the more likely it is that a memory will be created. For the memory to stick it has to mean something; your brain has to find some meaning in it. Relevance to something you are already interested in may help. Emotions also play an important part.

Chemicals are produced which act as effective transmitters and mean that you are likely to lay down effective memories. It seems possible that two neurotransmitters, epinephrine and norepinephrine, act as fixers, helping to ensure that a memory becomes long term. (Remember where you were and who you were with when you had your first kiss, for example.)

However, if the emotion is so intense that your survival is threatened, then your adrenal glands start to produce adrenalin, a neurotransmitter, in case you need to fight it out or run away. If the stress continues, you may start to produce another chemical called cortisol which can decrease your effectiveness to learn or remember.

No one single part of your brain is involved. The amygdala seems to be involved with emotional content, the hippocampus appears to have a sorting and disseminating role and the front cortex has a part in overall planning and determination. (See more on parts of the brain in Chapter 17.) We are constantly learning about which parts of the brain play certain roles. This information comes directly from experiments on human volunteers, which are possible now that brain scanning equipment is so much more sophisticated, and also from experiments on other animals such as rats.

For example, researchers in America have recently identified two different areas of the brain that share the function of storing and remembering events for short-term memory, the subiculum and the hippocampus, where before it was thought that this role was played only by the hippocampus. They found that the shortest memories were controlled almost exclusively by the subiculum, which is exactly opposite from what was previously believed. For the first 10–15 seconds of a task carried out by rats the memory function of the hippocampus actually shuts off. Of course, human beings are not the same as rats, but over the decades it has become clear that it is often possible to successfully deduce human brain functions from those discovered in rats!

Most useful research into memory falls into two types of studies: those that seek to explore the different parts of the brain involved in memory (like the example above); and those that relate aspects of learning to the effectiveness of recall later on.

Creating a memory

Much of what we do or learn never becomes fixed. Our brains simply do not register it except in the most fleeting sort of way. So much of the trivia we are involved in on a daily basis never gets stored. If it did, it is easy to imagine the whole memory system becoming clogged up.

The primacy–recency effect

In the first half of the twentieth century psychologists started to explore the different effects information created in people depending on the way it was ordered.

Successive experiments showed that, when presented with a list of items, people tend to be most influenced by the first and the last item that they hear. It seems that this primacy–recency effect also works for the way we remember things. In other words beginnings and endings assume great importance in our learning.

Good teachers and good learners have, therefore, deduced that it helps if you break up topics into small chunks, thereby producing lots of beginnings and endings and improving the likelihood of things being remembered.

In a typical day there are many items which are only ever going to last for a few seconds, for example what a passer-by is wearing or the number plate of the car in front of you. Although, as the primacy–recency effect suggests, you may be more likely to remember what you did at the beginning and end of your day.

Then there are short-term memories – what you need to take to work, who is picking up your children, where you are going and so on. Interestingly, research has shown that we remember pictures better than we remember words. And this is true even when words and pictures appear together during learning.

Storing memories

If information is important it will be transferred into your long-term memory. You learn and remember how to cross a road safely, for example, by noticing and recalling the noise and sights that indicate the presence of cars. You store memories of what a particular gesture or tone of voice conveys, for example those that indicate happiness and those that suggest anger. Many of your stored memories exist at an unconscious level, waiting to be used at some time in the future.

> Memory is the diary that we all carry around with us.
>
> Oscar Wilde

The Zeigarnik effect

Named after its creator, Russian scientist Bluma Zeigarnik, this is the psychological tendency to remember an uncompleted task rather than a completed one.

Break off from telling someone an interesting story and they will be hungry to find out what happens and remember what you told them more than if you had finished it off for them.

We can see this in action on a weekly basis with the storylines in soap operas which inevitably leave viewers on a cliff-hanger ending and guarantee their attentive memory until the next episode!

There are all kinds of ways in which you can influence the likelihood of memories being stored, of which the Zeigarnik effect is one. You may also have fixed and stored something in your mind, but, unless you use it in some way or unless it was a very powerful experience, it is unlikely that you will retain it for long.

The following are just a few suggestions of ways in which you can improve your ability to store memories.

Things that help you to store memories

These include the following:

1. Use more than one sense whenever possible.
   For example, as well as writing something down, you could try saying it aloud.
2. Turn random information into some kind of order.
   For example, using mnemonics like acronyms and acrostics (see the facing page).
3. Exploit deviations from the norm – the opposite of the order above.
   For example, using odd-one-out rules like the ones for 'i before e'.
4. Concentrate hard during the learning you are trying to remember.
   For example, shutting the door so that you can really concentrate on preparing for a speech without competing noises.
5. Use regular repetition to embed the memory.
   For example, reading through a list of key points every day for a week or learning your times tables by rote.
6. Review what you have learned over a long period of time.
   For example, going back to something important once a week for several months to check that you have remembered it.
7. Reorganize things so that you see the way that they fit together.
   For example, summarizing the key points of a lecture you have enjoyed using your own headings.
8. Train your memory by practising.
   For example, trying to remember everything when shopping without looking at your list.
9. 'Tag' things you really want to remember by associating them with something else.
   For example, tying a knot in your handkerchief or using keywords that act as cues to trigger memories when public speaking.
10. Use multiple methods.
    For example, by not assuming that one method alone will work and using several to ensure that you remember something important.

Mnemonics

A mnemonic is an ancient technique for using sounds to help you remember things. A mnemonic can help you to remember all sorts of information from spelling, 'i before e except after c', to the number of days in a month '30 days hath September, April, June, and November. All the rest have 31, excepting February which has 28.'

There are two special kinds of mnemonics that may be helpful – acronyms and acrostics.

An acronym is a real or made-up word that has been created by using the first letters of other words. For example, NATO is the word, now widely used, to stand for the North Atlantic Treaty Organization. Whereas ASAP – as soon as possible – is a made-up one. Acronyms are helpful as a means of remembering other words or ideas.

Like an acronym, an acrostic is a way of remembering a word or idea. Originally it was a poem which had first letters of each line that spelled out a word, for example:

> Hot sun
> And I need one of
> These
> Soon.

An acrostic is a sentence or phrase that uses the first letters of the words you are trying to remember, for example, 'Richard of York gave battle in vain' for the colours of the spectrum (red, orange, yellow, green, blue, indigo, violet). Children find acrostics particularly helpful when they are trying to remember concepts. So, a child learning to play the piano and struggling to remember the names of the notes which sit on the lines of the treble clef may be taught 'Every good boy deserves favour' to help them remember E, G, B, D, F.

Acrostics have another benefit. Because it does not matter if the sentence makes sense or not, you can deliberately make up funny and personal ones to ensure that the words you are trying to recall stick in your memory.

You might like to think of all the acronyms you know. You could start by seeing which of the following you recognize:

SMART RADAR DINKY

(Answers are at the end of this chapter.)

See if you can make up an acronym for something you are currently trying to remember, like a short shopping list (for example, PHONE: potatoes, haddock, oranges, nuts, eggs).

Or you might like to try out an acrostic. Make up a really silly sentence to help you remember something you are currently struggling with at work. If you have children, see if you can think of an acrostic to help them remember something in every subject that they are studying.

A number of people have made claims that music, especially baroque music, can help you to store memories. Some people feel that it helps them, others that it distracts their attention, but in both cases the data is not conclusive so far.

Recalling memories

Of course, you constantly need to retrieve memories that have been stored. You are asked a question about something you have learned for a test or examination. You meet an old friend and remember their name. You revisit a place you knew many years earlier and memories come flooding back. These are all recalled memories of which there are essentially three kinds:

Straight recall	When you bring information out of a memory 'store' and reproduce it, for example in a test or when you recite a favourite song off by heart.
Recognition	When you realize that you have encountered something before because, when you see, hear or read it again, you recognize it.
Reconstruction	When you re-create a memory as you go along, for example when the police get volunteers to act out a crime in the hope that it will jog the memories of witnesses and help them to reconstruct their memory of the crime.

We know that the mind does not just record events passively. So, for example, when a series of things that have happened are presented in random order the brain, when trying to recall them, reorders them into patterns that make sense.

We also know that your ability to recall memories can often be adversely affected by high levels of stress: a phenomenon to which many people will attest when they look back over examinations they have taken.

As you get older your long-term memory tends to get clearer and your short-term memory may become less reliable.

> A strong experience in the present awakens in the creative writer a memory of an earlier experience (usually belonging to his childhood) from which there now proceeds a wish which finds its fulfilment in the creative work.
>
> Sigmund Freud

Things that help you to recall memories

These include the following:

1. Retrace your steps.
   For example, retracing your steps if you have walked into a room and forgotten what you entered it for.
2. Use a process of elimination.
   For example, thinking of the last five things you did before you noticed that you had lost an item.
3. Search for cues that you associate with the original memory.
   For example, using photographs or music as triggers or prompts.
4. Use posters as visual reminders.
   For example, showing a simple list of things to do when you get stuck.
5. Use relaxation exercises.
   For example, using a tape that you know calms you down and frees up your mind to try again to remember what it was trying to recall in a less fretful way.
6. Sleep on it.
   For example, going to bed telling yourself you want to recall something and seeing if it will come to you during the night or the next morning (it often does!).
7. Try and visualize it.
   For example, closing your eyes and trying to conjure it up in your mind's eye.

There are other ways of considering the way you remember things which may be helpful.

Is it implicit or explicit?

Implicit: you remember how to walk, talk, kick a football, drive a car or ride a bicycle implicitly. In other words, you do not have to consciously remember what to do.

Explicit: you have to be explicit about remembering how to use the keys to someone else's front door if you have only been shown once.

Is it procedural or declarative?

Procedural: this kind of memory concerns processes and skills – learning to type or learning to ride a bike, for example.

Declarative: deals with facts and figures.

Your memory clearly has to deal with individual items, the image of your own house, a particular face, a word or a symbol. But it also has to store memories of important procedures.

Declarative memory is itself made up of two elements – semantic and episodic:

> Semantic memory is about information that does not connect to you personally – the distance from the Earth to the Moon, for example.
>
> Episodic memory is part of your experience, such as a memory of your last birthday party.

These categories are offered to you as some of the conventional ways in which we can view such a big topic as remembering. But it is important to realize that, as we learn more about the way the mind works, it becomes clear that many such categories are interrelated.

For example, just stop to consider episodic and semantic memory for a moment. It is possible to imagine a situation in which you are recalling a story that is partly about things that have happened to you and partly about information of which you have no direct knowledge but which you are including as part of the detail of your tale.

What about other categories?

Another set of categories you might like to apply are:

> Sensory memory: you recall the smell of the polish or the floor of your infant school and this triggers other memories.
>
> Motor memory: you remember how to drive a car or ride a bike (largely implicit) or recall how to start your gas boiler after it has being turned off for nine months (largely explicit).
>
> Visual–spatial memory: you manage to grope your way to the bathroom in the middle of the night without waking up your partner.

Linguistic memory: you use a really appropriate and interesting word, drawn from one of some 20,000 or so basic word families in a typical adult memory. You constantly manage to select the best word to use in any given situation!

The tip of the tongue phenomenon

This is that moment when something slips out of your mind and is temporarily forgotten. You feel that you know the answer; that it is fixed in your memory. But you just cannot seem to recall it when it is needed. You walk into a room and forget what you were coming in for. Or it can happen halfway through a conversation without warning when suddenly words desert you.

Sometimes retracing your steps to the room that you have just left seems to help. Or deliberately trying not to think about it may work. For often it will magically pop into your mind!

When the novelist G.K. Chesterton wrote 'The chief object of education is not to learn things but to unlearn things', he unwittingly put his finger on a truth about memory. There is a real sense in which we need to be able to forget. For memory is a dynamic thing and if our minds simply filled up with memories that could never be erased, or if your memory was perfect, then life would be a terrible experience. There would be no such thing as uncertainty. You would never want to go back and revisit something to work it out again.

'Memory is the centripetal force which pulls together learning, understanding and consciousness.'

John Ratey

Seeing patterns

Patterns are key to our survival and an important principle of the way the mind works (see page 284). Through patterns we create languages, lists, alphabets, filing systems, maps – all the ways in which we organize information.

Patterns help us to predict what will happen next and explain what has just happened. We have developed as a civilized race largely because of patterns that we have noticed and acted upon. If you want to become more creative there will be lots of times when you need to break out from your current pattern of seeing the world or doing things.

You have already seen on page 114 how the brain tends to organize data into patterns as it is storing it. And this is an important and helpful tendency when it comes to remembering things.

Try to remember a page of text and you may well struggle. But add four or five keywords or headings and you are likely to find it much easier. Clustering things together in small digestible chunks helps.

There is a game called 'Categories' which provides excellent practice for your memory. It is best played in a small group of between three and six persons. It is played as follows: on a piece of paper write out the letters of the alphabet in the margin, one letter per line. One person acts as the categorizer. He or she calls out 26 different categories and the players choose one of their letters to come up with a word that fits the category. So if the category is fruit, you might write orange under 'O'. But you do not need to limit your imagination to simple categories like fruit. You could go for 'things that would fit in your pocket' or 'fears', for example.

Why bother trying to see patterns?

It will help you to organize information and experiences to best effect.
You will see new connections.
You will remember things better.
It will help you to transfer learning to new situations.

How to see patterns

You might like to try some of the following ideas:

1. Practise seeing patterns in:
   numbers, words, shapes, colours, music.
2. Use simple tools to help you make connections:
   - a two-column page headed 'Similar' and 'Different' to help you classify objects;
   - a three-column page headed 'Plus' 'Minus' 'Interesting' (see page 95 for how to do this);
   - a quadrant (window with four panes like the Johari window on page 109) to help you compare items to two different ideas.
3. Try making up similes: 'x is just like y ...'.
4. Keep a good-ideas file of thoughts that you have during the day which seem to make unusual connections.
5. Try a relaxation exercise to get your mind in the mood for gentler searching.
6. Stand up. Fold your arms the way you normally do. Now try and fold them the other way. Keep this metaphor in your head as you notice the many habits you have unconsciously adopted.
7. Try an alternative route to work or school or do something different today.

Being able to see patterns is essential for our survival. But the danger of patterns is that you can get set in them. Think of the folding arms activity from the list above. How many people do you know who can only fold their arms one way (metaphorically speaking)? In other words, they are set in their ways and challenge any new way of working or being.

Patterns, while essential to survival, can be a curb on creativity. But effective learners recognize this and are constantly seeking to try out new ways of doing things.

> Creativity involves breaking out of established patterns in order to look at things in a different way.
>
> Edward de Bono

Transferring learning

Effective learners constantly seek to transfer the knowledge and skills that they have learned to different parts of their lives. For instance, you learn how to work more effectively with other people on a training course and want to be able to apply it to your family life.

Consider the following example from American psychologists Mary Gick and Keith Holyoak. They gave college students the following problem:

> Imagine you were a doctor faced with a patient who has an inoperable stomach tumour. You have at your disposal rays that can destroy human tissue when directed with sufficient intensity. At lower intensity the rays are harmless to healthy tissue, but they do not affect the tumour either. How can you use these rays to destroy the tumour without destroying the surrounding healthy tissue?

Few of the students found it easy to solve this problem. But 90 per cent of them were able to do so when they were also given the next passage and told to use the information in it to help them:

> A general wishes to capture a fortress located in the centre of a country. There are many roads radiating outwards from the fortress. All have been mined so that while groups of men can pass over the roads safely, a large force will detonate the mines. A full-scale direct attack is therefore impossible. The general's solution is to divide his army into small groups, send each group to the head of a different road and have the groups converge simultaneously on the fortress.

> All perception of truth is the detection of an analogy.
>
> Henry David Thoreau

The students were able to see the analogy between dividing the troops up into small groups and using a number of small doses of radiation which converged on the same bit of the tumour. But they did much better when the explicit connection between the two bits of information had been pointed out.

Transferring knowledge is a complex matter. You may be able to use your arguing and persuasion skills very easily with someone you know and love, for example with your partner, but go to pieces when you try to use the same knowledge in front of your over-bearing boss. Context and environment do matter.

Transfer certainly requires memory, but it also seems to depend on other things.

Why bother transferring what you have learned?

The more you can transfer skills, the more your learning will affect all of your life and the more you will save time.

Successful transfer seems to depend on a number of factors (see below).

Things which seem to help the transfer of learning

1. Achieving a threshold of knowledge before you try using it elsewhere.
   For example, making sure that you are really confident about your presentation skills in front of your family before you try them at a conference.
2. Spending a significant time actively practising before you try it elsewhere.
   For example, you may find it a lot easier to read detailed spreadsheets outlining an organization's accounts if you have really spent time familiarizing yourself with them and developed your own set of home accounts.
3. When the tasks share some common elements.
   For example, learning Spanish after learning Latin, when you have already grasped some key principles of the way languages work.

4. Organizing information into some kind of pattern or conceptual framework.
For example, having a clear model of how you learn, so that whenever you are faced with learning new things you are sure where you are in the process.
5. Learning similar content in different situations.
For example, a child learning the same way of making notes in all the different subjects at school.

Specific techniques

In this chapter you have already found out about some useful techniques to help you remember things more effectively. The following are a few more.

Summarizing

An obvious but sometimes overlooked aspect of remembering is the ability to reduce the content of what you are trying to remember by summarizing it.

Summaries are shortened versions of something. You can summarize in writing or verbally. Both are useful skills.

Why bother to learn how to summarize?

We all need to be able to have a sense of what really matters.
It is very helpful whenever you are working with other people.
It will help you to remember key points.

How to summarize

1. Focus on keywords and concepts. You may find it helpful to underline or circle things if you are reading.
2. Ignore all extra details, especially when you are presented with a list of things. Come up with a word to describe all the items in a list if they all seem to matter.
3. Ignore unimportant information.
4. Reduce whole paragraphs to a single word or sentence.
5. Make your own headings.

If you are making a verbal summary, you may want simply to have a small number of key points.

If you are summarizing in writing, it is helpful to have the number of words you want to end up with in mind, as well as the number in the original. If they are different by a factor of, say, five, then that will give you a sense of how much you need to reduce it by.

> A man would do well to carry a pencil in his pocket, and write down the thoughts of the moment. Those that come unsought for are commonly the most valuable and should be secured, because they seldom return.
>
> Francis Bacon

Related to summarizing is the ability to make notes. This can be as simple as items on a shopping list, a few helpful headings for a speech or the detailed notes that you might be required to take for some examinations.

How to make notes

Whether you like the idea of taking a pocket notebook around with you or not, you may still like to be aware of the following:

How to make notes

1. Before you start, think about how you want to use your notes. If they are for a speech you may need a few headings only. If you want to recall something in detail your notes may need to be more substantial.
2. Give each page a clear title and date.
3. Be selective (see 'How to summarize' on page 127).
4. Leave plenty of space to add things later.
5. Experiment with different styles (see Mind Maps™, for example, on pages 97–98).
6. Use colours, pictures, arrows, underlining and so on.
7. Develop your own shorthand/abbreviations for common words, for example &. (Mobile phone text messaging has produced many good examples for this.)
8. If you are making notes while someone is speaking, listen out for signal words and phrases, for example 'There are four reasons why ...', 'for instance', which act as useful indicators of important things to remember, or suggest that a summary is to follow: 'to conclude ...' or 'the important points you need to know ...'. Also, listen out for 'change of direction words' – 'however', 'on the other hand'.
9. Review your notes on a daily basis to start with and then on a weekly basis if you are keen to remember them.

Obviously organization skills are important to all aspects of learning, including remembering. But one special set are those associated with revision. Revision is something we all have to do at different stages throughout our lives: for examinations, for important meetings and for many other occasions.

Effective revision should not be a last-minute panic attack in the week before a test. It is much better when it involves regular, planned sessions.

Why bother learning how to revise?

Life is full of tests and examinations and revision is a key skill.

Regularly revising what you have learned is the best way of remembering it.

How to revise

There are many different ways to revise. The following are only a selection to choose from. If you are a parent, you might like to pass on some of the ideas to your child well before his or her examinations happen:

1. Find a comfortable place without distractions (telephone, television, radio, noise, passers-by and so on).
2. Plan a schedule for your revision.
3. Use a highlighter pen to go through your notes, picking out all of the key points, and then reread them concentrating only on these points.
4. Turn over whatever you are revising and fill a blank piece of paper with all you can remember from it.
5. As you read, think of the questions you might be asked and rehearse the answers.
6. If you find yourself getting too stressed, take a break and go and do something else for a while.
7. (Some learners) Play music – not too fast, not too slow, not too interesting and no words – from time to time.
8. Use cards or Post-it notes to help you summarize the key points.
9. Ask a friend to test you.
10. Keep eating food and drinking water. A grazing diet of fruit, like bananas, and bars made from grains, dried fruit and nuts should help to keep you going.

The key issue for any learner remains, apart from learning some of the specific techniques in this chapter, how to put the principles of effective remembering into their learning lives.

Overleaf are a few suggestions.

"Though I do not deny that memory can be helped by places and images, yet the best memory is based on three important things: namely study, order, and care."

Erasmus

"The illiterate of the future are not those who can't read or write but those who cannot learn, unlearn, and re-learn."

Alvin Toffler

Practical tips for organizing your learning to improve memory

Amazingly, Erasmus was right in suggesting three general principles for remembering (see the margin quote) at the start of the sixteenth century!

1. *Rehearse (study) what you would like to remember.* Reviewing things on a regular basis will help you fix your memories. Re-read things that are of importance to you. Your degree of understanding depends on what you already know!
2. *Organize (order) things in your own way.* Organize things you want to remember in ways you find helpful: from acronyms to pictures. Creating a framework into which you can put more detailed elements helps, for example moving from the general to the specific. Try to make connections between apparently unconnected items.
3. *Pay attention (care).* You are, in general, more likely to remember things which you care about and have invested your energies in.

You might also like to try these:

4. *Use the primacy–recency effect.* Break your learning up into chunks, wherever possible, to create lots of mini-beginnings and endings. The same applies to meetings! Take regular short 'stretch' breaks too.
5. *Visualize yourself explaining it.* Share what you know with an imaginary audience. You will have to organize your material, think about what they might ask you and generally engage on many levels.
6. *Talk it out loud.* It can help to speak your ideas or thoughts as you go through them.
7. *Consciously decide to remember things.* Deliberately engage your memory. Learn how to 'tell' yourself that you wish to remember something, especially before going to sleep at night.
8. *Relate things to you.* Always try to think of examples that engage you personally.
9. *Use pictures and colours.* Learn in Technicolor wherever possible, using images as well as words.
10. *Keep a memory file and review it weekly.* It is important to consolidate what you have learned and a good way of doing this is to review it regularly.

The acronyms on page 119 stand for:

SMART:	specific, measurable, achievable, realistic, on time
RADAR:	radio detection and ranging
DINKY:	dual income, no kids yet

8

Chapter 8

Resilience

> Courage is going from failure to failure without losing enthusiasm.
>
> Winston Churchill

There are three elements to this chapter on resilience, 'Understanding yourself as a learner', 'Staying motivated' and 'Being persistent'.

Effective learners know how to be resilient. They understand themselves well enough to know how to choose the methods that suit them best. They are able to keep motivated. And they are able to enjoy the complex and sometimes unsettling feelings which tend to accompany any worthwhile learning.

In Chapter 6 you explored some of the many tools and techniques that a resourceful learner needs and how you might go about selecting the most appropriate method for the task in hand.

In this chapter you will also explore the idea that some kinds of learning are more difficult than others. You may also begin to adjust your sense of what it is to be intelligent; beginning to appreciate that, through the application of resilience in your learning, most things are learnable and intelligence is expandable.

Nature v. nurture

In the early twentieth century two celebrated anthropologists, Margaret Mead and Derek Freeman, first debated an issue which has since become known as the nature v. nurture issue.

Are you born the way you are, or do you become so through your experiences in the world? Are your genes more important or does culture matter more?

Mead argued that it was all down to nurture; drawing on fieldwork studying teenagers in Samoa, Freeman disagreed with her (as Steven Pinker has done more recently).

The truth probably lies somewhere in the middle. But in this book I argue that nurture is probably more important than nature. Of course not everyone is going to be a genius, but most of us can do much better than we are led to believe.

What it is to be smart these days

> 'Intelligence is what you use when you don't know what to do!'
>
> Jean Piaget

Intelligence is a highly contested subject. The word 'intelligence' entered the English language in Europe during the early Middle Ages. In recent years it has become closely associated with IQ or intelligence quotient.

For most of the time that it has existed as a concept, intelligence has been linked to the brain. The Ancient Egyptians believed that a person's ability to think resided in their heart, while their judgement came from either the brain or the kidneys! Not surprisingly, scientists have, for some time, tried to link particular intelligences or attributes with particular parts of the brain. The most famous of these is the idea of phrenology, which grew up in the nineteenth century, originally developed by Franz Gall in Germany (see below).

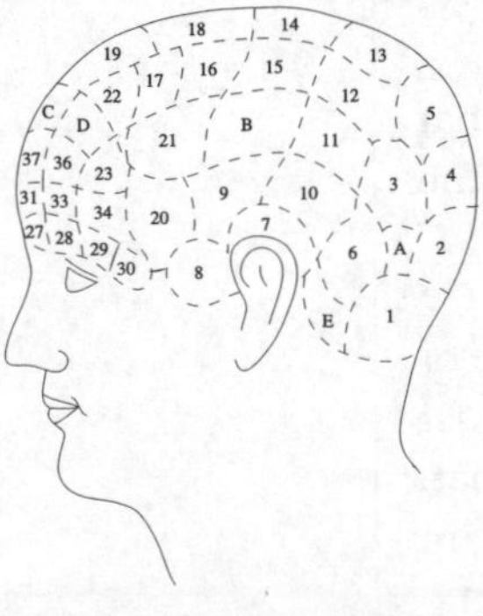

1 Amativeness
A Conjugal love
2 Parental love
3 Friendship
4 Inhabitiveness
5 Continuity
E Vitativeness
6 Commativeness
7 Destructiveness
8 Alimentiveness
9 Acquisitiveness
10 Secretiveness
11 Cautiousness
12 Approbativeness
13 Self-esteem
14 Firmness
15 Conscientiousness
16 Hope
17 Spirituality
18 Benevolence
19 Benelovance
20 Constructiveness
21 Ideality
B Sublimity
22 Imitation
23 Mirth
24 Individuality*
25 Form*
26 Size*
27 Weight
28 Colour
29 Order
30 Calculation
31 Locality
32 Eventuality*
33 Time
34 Tune
35 Language*
36 Causality
37 Comparison
C Human nature
D Suavity

* Not shown on the illustraion.

Phrenologists believed that each separate part of the brain had a distinct purpose and could be 'mapped'.

Yet we now know that intelligence involves a combination of 'know-how' and 'know what' across a multitude of contexts. If you are intelligent you are good at using your mind in many different ways. If your mind is working well you are able to learn to do many things that you did not think you could do. Nurture not nature is in the ascendancy.

In the early part of the twentieth century, Alfred Binet invented the first intelligence test to identify students in Paris who might benefit from extra help at school. Binet's formula was altered by William Stern and another version was published at Stanford University in the USA. This became known as the Stanford–Binet Scale, the direct precursor of what we now know as the IQ test. IQ is an abbreviation for 'intelligence quotient'. This is a score from standardized tests which seeks to measure a person's cognitive abilities in relation to their age group. An IQ score is expressed as a number where the norm is 100. So 115 is above average and 90 is below. Scores have tended to rise across time throughout the history of IQ testing.

It is only comparatively recently that we have really begun to grapple with what we mean by intelligence, largely as a result of the emergence of psychology as an accepted science in the second half of the nineteenth century and, more recently, as advances in neuroscience have offered tantalizing glimpses of the mind at work.

In the last two decades we have found out an enormous amount about intelligence. Many books have been published on the subject, some of them becoming best sellers. They have shown us that there are many different intelligences and in doing so they have released us all to begin to recognize our potential across all our talents.

According to many people, IQ's influence has been pernicious, artificially inflating the importance of language and figures and taking no account of creativity, common sense or the ability to manage emotions. The most powerful challenge to thinking about intelligence has come from Harvard professor, Howard Gardner.

Multiple intelligences

The idea of multiple intelligences was developed by Harvard professor, Howard Gardner. Instead of the narrow numerical measure of IQ, it suggests that we have eight different intelligences: linguistic, logical–mathematical, musical, naturalist, spatial, bodily–kinesthetic, interpersonal and intrapersonal.

Subsequently, Daniel Goleman has proposed a concept called emotional intelligence (largely a combination of Gardner's interpersonal and intrapersonal intelligences).

Recently, Danah Zohar has suggested the idea of spiritual intelligence and both Charles Sternberg and Charles Handy have argued for some kind of practical intelligence.

With multiple intelligences the emphasis shifts away from what seems like a fixed examination score to an empowering description. IQ tests give you a measure of a certain kind of cleverness, telling you how 'smart' you are. Multiple intelligence approaches give you a sense of where your talents lie, helping you to realize how or in what areas you are smart and opening up potential avenues for lifelong learning and further development.

You might like to take a moment to look at the following descriptions of intelligences, starting with Gardner's (whose original titles are in brackets) and then going on to include others. The titles have been simplified for ease of understanding.

Linguistic (Linguistic)

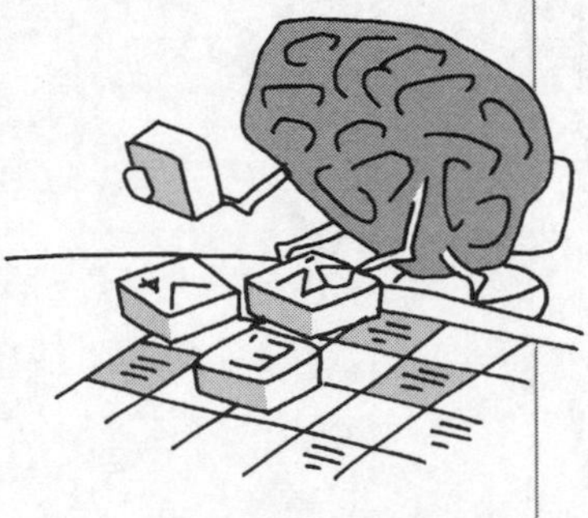

You probably like words and stories. Word-play intrigues you. You may be the kind of person who enjoys proofreading and has a distinct view of what is correct or a sloppy use of language. You are likely to be an avid reader. You express yourself with clarity and have a good vocabulary. You probably enjoyed learning languages and literature at school and may have gone on to study it at a higher level. You enjoy writing and may well be able to speak and write more than one language. Possibly you will be able to remember lists of words and be able to remember and tell good stories.

Mathematical (Logical–mathematical)

You probably like figures and abstract problems. You like to understand the relationships between different things and are likely the sort of person who enjoys knowing how things work and fix them when they go wrong. You may well be the sort of person who enjoys doing brain-teasers and playing chess or Trivial Pursuit. You probably enjoyed learning mathematics at school. You like argument and evidence. You enjoy patterns, categories and systems. You probably make lists at home and at work and tick off the things that you manage to achieve. You like logical order. You may well enjoy reading financial figures, although this is not always the case.

Visual (Spatial)

You probably like pictures and shapes. You tend to notice colour, form and texture. You quite likely make use of diagrams, maps and doodles when you are in meetings, listening to others or simply thinking on your own. You might use pictures to help you remember things. You may well be able to draw, paint or sculpt. You possibly spent time in the art department at school. You probably enjoy visiting galleries and noticing architecture or landscape. You like maps and cartoons and prefer to be supported by material which is illustrated rather than relying on the written word.

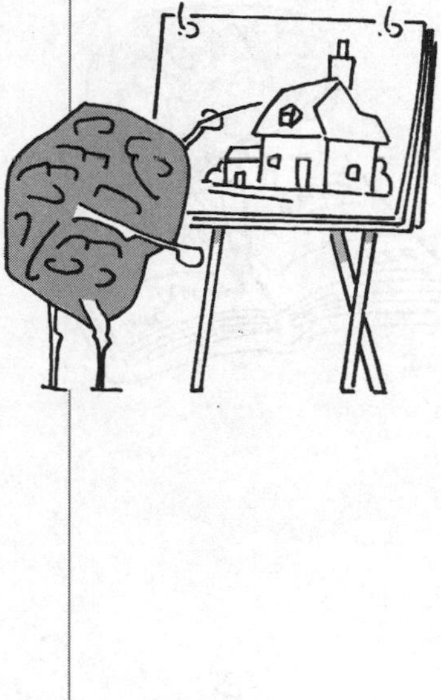

Physical (Bodily–kinesthetic)

You probably like to work with your body and use your hands. You enjoy physical exercise and probably take part in sporting or dance activity of some kind either now or in the past. You may well be the kind of person who gets up on your feet at the first opportunity when in a group meeting at work or on a dance floor at a party. You like to handle things directly and enjoy the sensation of new experiences. You may well use your body to aid communication, waving your hands, gesturing with your shoulders and using facial expressions. You possibly enjoy mime and games like charades. You like to learn by doing and the first to roll up your sleeves and get on with things.

Musical (Musical)

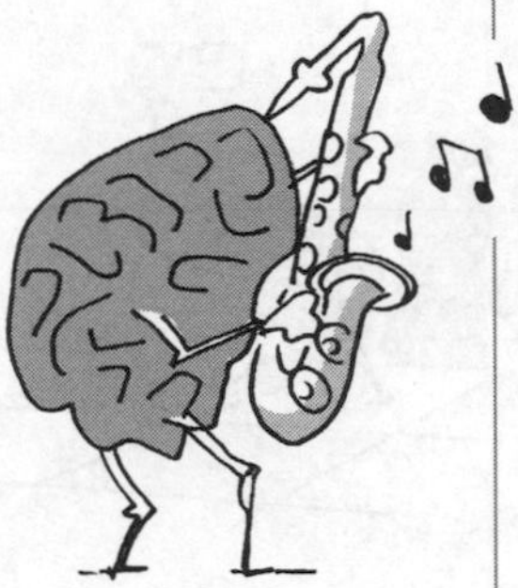

You probably like sounds and rhythms. You may also be interested in the tonal qualities of different sounds and can probably pick out different instruments when you listen to music. You probably enjoyed singing and listening to music from an early age. You may well be actively involved in making music and will almost certainly enjoy going to concerts and listening to music at home and on journeys. You have a good sense of rhythm and can remember songs and melodies well. You remember advertisements mainly for their music. You often hum to yourself and can easily be emotionally transported by a piece of music. Music acts powerfully on your moods.

Emotional (Intrapersonal)

You probably like to look within yourself, an instinct which has you constantly questing for self-knowledge. You are continually analysing your strengths and weaknesses and setting goals to do something to improve yourself. You may well keep notes, a diary or personal log of your experiences, moods and thoughts. You explore those situations which give you pleasure and those which cause pain and seek to act accordingly. You understand and manage your own emotions well. You enjoy having time to think and reflect. You may well have pursued some kind of counselling or self-improvement activity.

Social (Interpersonal)

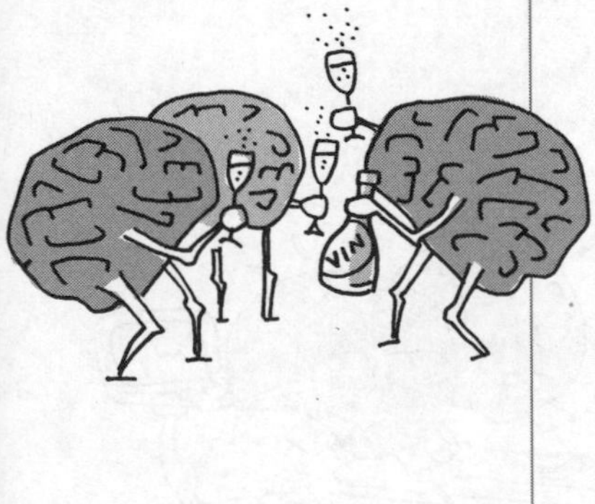

You probably like to be with and understand other people. Not surprisingly you enjoy parties, meetings, team games and any gregarious activities. You have the ability to understand and relate to other people. You can read the moods and plans of others, so that people tend to seek you out when they need advice. You are often the person who is called on to sort out difficult situations and resolve differences of opinion. You have a number of close friends with whom you share much. You show high levels of empathy with others. You like talking over people's problems and people turn to you to be their coach, buddy, mentor or critical friend.

Environmental (Naturalist)

You probably like the natural world. You see meaning and patterns in nature which pass others by. You have a good knowledge of plants, animals and landscape, knowing not just names but the characteristics of the elements of the world about you. You probably have or have had pets. At school, you probably enjoyed botany, zoology and biology. You like being outside and when walking are a fountain of knowledge about what is going on in nature. You take a keen interest in your own home environment, inside and outside. You notice the weather and the seasons and may be deeply affected by them. You know a fair amount about the workings of your own body. You enjoy classifying species.

Spiritual (proposed by Danah Zohar)

You probably like to deal with the fundamental questions of existence. You are the kind of person who, when faced with difficult issues, will tend to act according to your principles, possibly questioning the normal ways of behaving in the situation you find yourself in. You seek constantly to explore your whole self and to heal those bits which seem not to be well. You are interested in values. You will probably hold particularly well-developed beliefs but may or may not practise any particular religious faith. You think about issues of duty. You tend to see some value in different sides of an argument. You could be involved in some kind of community service. You would be ready to stand up and be counted for what you believe in.

Practical (proposed by Robert Sternberg and Charles Handy)

You probably like making things happen. You have the capacity to sort things out and are often called on to fix, mend or assemble things. Where others talk about what needs to be done, you prefer to get on and do it. You probably enjoy difficult or stressful situations because of your ability to come up with workable solutions. When things go wrong you are constantly thinking of useful ideas to help others. You like to explain by doing. You constantly want to put theory into practice. You may well enjoy gardening and DIY. At school you enjoyed practical subjects. In domestic life, you are the person who is happy to spend hours assembling flat-packed goods of all kinds. As a child you were always taking things apart to see how they worked. You enjoy seeing the inner workings of many items.

How did you find these descriptions? Did any of them fit you? Or did they begin to describe others close to you? If linguistic and mathematical were the key intelligences for the twentieth century, then there is a strong case to suggest that emotional, social and spiritual intelligences will be critically important in the twenty-first century. This is because in a world that was largely static and where everyone knew their place, IQ worked fine. However, in a constantly changing world, where we are all encouraged to learn, what we think about things and believe in is constantly under scrutiny.

To someone intent on becoming an effective lifelong learner, Gardner's work begins to lay out a kind of informal agenda of areas where you might choose to develop yourself.

Not everyone agrees with Howard Gardner. Professor John White, for example, considers that they are only one way of describing the full array of talents that we may develop.

The difficulty of learning

Is some learning more difficult than others? If some of your intelligences are more developed than others (as they probably will be) does this mean that you may find it harder to learn certain things?

These questions also have a bearing on what it is to be a resilient learner. For, if the answer is 'yes' to either of them (which it probably is) then this will impact on the likelihood of your being able to stick with it.

At school, learning difficulty is often signposted by terms like Key Stage 3 or GCSE or A levels. But, when it comes to describing the largely informal learning which you encounter in life, it is more difficult. There have been various attempts to classify different kinds of learning.

Levels of learning

Benjamin Bloom and Gregory Bateson have both tried to describe the different levels of learning that you may experience.

Bloom's six levels of learning (also known as Bloom's taxonomy) are:

1. Knowledge
   This level deals with facts, information and simple theories. It involves learners describing, listing, defining and so on.
2. Comprehension
   This level deals with understanding meaning. It involves learners comparing, contrasting, discussing, estimating and so on.
3. Application
   This level deals with applying knowledge. It involves learners applying, demonstrating, calculating, solving, classifying and so on.
4. Analysis
   This level deals with breaking learning down into smaller parts and seeing the relationship between them. It involves learners analysing, ordering, connecting and so on.
5. Synthesis
   This level deals with reassembling the constituent elements of more complex subjects to make a new whole. It involves learners in synthesizing, composing, integrating, reconnecting and so on.
6. Evaluation
   This level deals with the assessment of learning material using criteria. It involves learners assessing, evaluating, ranking, measuring and concluding.

Bloom was quite clear that there was often overlap between the categories. The higher up the scale you go, in other words above level 3, the more likely it is that you will be using skills from across the three areas or domains – mental, physical and emotional.

Bateson's levels are:

1. Direct experience	Simple change
2. Generalized experiences	Change from which a principle can be learned
3. Contextualized learning	Transferring from one situation to another
4. Profound learning	Level 2 with a change of life as a result.

However you define difficulty, it would be logical to assume that the higher you go the more helpful it will be to have some of the attributes of a resilient learner!

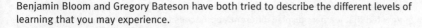

Deep or surface learning

In parallel with the ideas of Benjamin Bloom and Gregory Bateson, Noel Entwhistle has suggested that learners display different approaches to learning – deep or surface – depending on their attitude to the task, and that those intentions are closely related to how they go about learning and the quality of the learning they achieve. Some learners focus on facts and on the surface level of what they are reading. Other students look more deeply at the underlying meaning and seek to integrate the ideas they are presented with. Those who adopt a deep approach are consistently more successful as learners.

Deep learning

Learners:

intend to understand material for themselves;
interact vigorously and critically with content;
relate ideas to previous knowledge/experience;
use organizing principles to integrate ideas;
relate evidence to conclusions;
examine the logic of arguments.

Surface learning

Learners:

intend simply to reproduce parts of the content;
accept ideas and information passively;
concentrate only on assessment requirements;
do not to reflect on purpose or strategies in learning;
memorize facts and procedures routinely;
do not recognize guiding principles or patterns.

Part of becoming a resilient learner is about learning to feel comfortable with deep learning strategies, as defined by Entwhistle.

Understanding yourself as a learner

Why bother with learning styles?

You will understand more about yourself as a learner.
It will help you choose learning methods that suit you.
It will help you to keep going when the learning is difficult.

The more you understand yourself as a learner, the more resilient you are likely to become.

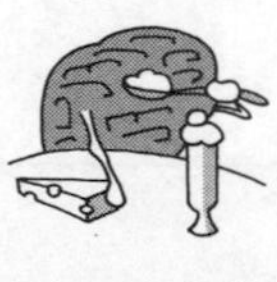

There are hundreds of organizations purporting to offer ways in which you can describe learning styles, not all of which have any basis in science.

In this book are four examples of different approaches. One you have already met on page 38; three more are listed below.

Of course learning styles are not like blood groups which you are born with and which remain with you for your lifetime.

1. You *can* change and develop your current preferred style.
2. An effective learner will be able to operate across the range of learning styles.
3. Most learning 'personalities' do not begin to 'settle' until their late teens.
4. Understanding your learning style is only one helpful way of becoming more confident as a learner.

One of the most profound views of personality, and also one of the most heavily validated, is the Myers–Briggs Type Indicator® (MBTI®) which draws on Carl Jung's theory of personality. The MBTI® is a personality profiling system, developed by Katherine Briggs and Isabel Briggs Myers. It is one of the most respected personality indicators in the world.

MBTI® has four scales, each with two alternative perspectives denoted by a different letter in bold type. Consequently there are 16 different combinations, each one of which can be described in ways which most MBTI® users find useful and accurate. No one combination is any better than another; they are just different. While the MBTI® is a widely used method of finding out about your personality and learning styles, not everyone accepts its validity.

Source of energy	Extrovert	v.	Introvert
Focus of attention	Sensor	v.	iNtuitive
Way decisions are made	Thinker	v.	Feeler
Attitude to world	Judger	v.	Perceiver

Extrovert If you are an extrovert, then you derive your energy from outside. You tend to be sociable, enjoy interaction and often find yourself working things out as you go along.

> How do I know what I think until I have heard what I said.
>
> W.H. Auden

Introvert If you are an introvert, then you derive your energy from inside. You tend to have a small number of deep relationships, reflect much and think carefully before you speak.

Sensing If you are a sensor, then you gather your information in an exact and sequential manner. You tend to be realistic, down-to-earth and specific about this.

iNtuitive If you are an intuitive, then you gather your information in an imprecise, big picture sort of a way. You tend to rely on hunches, on your sense and on generalizations which may not always be realistic.

Thinker If you are a thinker, then you take decisions in an impartial, fair-minded way. You tend to be detached, logical and firm.

Feeler If you are a feeler, then you take decisions in a collaborative, interpersonal and subjective way. People's feelings matter to you and you are unwilling to upset people if you can avoid it.

Judger If you are a judger, then your orientation towards life is likely to be fixed, controlled, planned and with tight deadlines.

Perceiver If you are a perceiver, then your orientation towards life is likely to be 'wait and see', adaptable, flexible and open-ended.

The 16 permutations are:

ISTJ	ISFJ	INFJ	INTJ
ISTP	ISFP	INFP	INTP
ESTP	ESFP	ENFP	ENTP
ESTJ	ESFJ	ENFJ	ENTJ

Depending on which of the 16 profiles is most like you, it is possible to see likely dispositions to be aware of. For example, ISTJs tend to be perfectionists who like to think things through and prefer to be in charge. ISTJs will often benefit from learning how to see the big picture, be more comfortable with ambiguity and stress the positive more when giving opinions. By contrast, ENFPs tend to be full of enthusiasm, always starting new projects and exhausting to be with. They may become more effective in life and in learning if they learn to be more disciplined and more prepared to do the detailed work which gets things done.

Another well-used alternative has been developed by Ned Hermann. Again there are four categories:

Analyser	Applies logic to facts. Likes formal learning.
Organizer	Likes seeing patterns, and testing and using theories. Likes planned learning.
Sensor	Listens and shares ideas. Enjoys group discussions and movement.
Explorer	Likes taking the initiative and tends to be intuitive. Likes to experiment.

Rita and Kenneth Dunn (known as Dunn and Dunn) describe learning styles in terms of a range of preferences:

Environmental: sound, light, temperature and design;

Emotional: motivation, persistence, responsibility and structure;

Sociological: such as private, pair, peer, team, adult or more varied situations;

Psychological: perception, intake, time and mobility;

Psychological based on analytic mode, left/right brain and action.

This model has now been further developed as an online self-evaluation questionnaire (Learning Styles Analysis) by Barbara Prashnig, who has written about it in her book *The Power of Diversity*.

You have already met Honey and Mumford's learning styles (page 38) which draw on the David Kolb's experiential model of learning:

Activists

Reflectors

Theorists

Pragmatists.

As well as MBTI®, Dunn and Dunn, and Honey and Mumford, there are other widely used versions including:

Allinson and Hayes' Cognitive Styles Index, Apter's Motivational Style Profile, Entwhistle's Approaches and Study Skills Inventory for Students, Gregorc's Styles Delineators, Hermann's Brain Dominance Instrument, Kolb's Learning Style Inventory, Rider's Cognitive Styles Analysis, Sternberg's Thinking Styles Inventory and Vermunt's Inventory of Learning Styles.

Of these, recent research has found Allinson and Hayes, Apter and Vermunt to be the versions which meet tests of internal consistency, reliability and predictive validity best. While in terms of popularity in the UK, Honey and Mumford, and Myers–Briggs are probably most used.

Another, and in many ways the simplest, way of viewing learning styles is increasingly known as VAK: drawing on the idea that we prefer to take in data in different ways, for example visually, auditorily and kinesthetically. VAK has become popular largely as a result of the efforts of those advocating NLP and accelerated learning.

Whether you prefer to use your eyes or your ears or to get up and experience an activity is not something that is in any way fixed. Indeed effective learners seek to improve their confidence in each of these three modes. It can, however, be helpful to know more about your current preferences. This can be especially true if you are embarking on some learning which you know you are going to find difficult. In this case, you may be well advised to go for a method of taking in data which you feel confident about.

This is not really a learning style in the sense that the others described here are. Rather it helpfully reminds us that learning involves the senses and that some people develop preferences for different means of taking in data, using their eyes, ears or other senses.

Once you have used one or more of these approaches, then you may begin to understand more about yourself as a learner, knowing which methods you may instinctively prefer and, therefore, gaining insights into how you can keep going when the going is tough or when the learning itself is particularly difficult.

How to understand your own preferred learning style

1. Explore one or more of the different approaches to learning styles.
2. Examine the data you have about yourself as a learner. Where are you most confident? And where are you least confident?
3. Plan some experiences which allow you to develop or strengthen those areas about which you have less confidence or prefer least. You could incorporate this into your Personal Plan (see pages 62–66).

The learner as customer

In most walks of life we are increasingly treated as a customer, so why not in learning too? In fact this is already happening, with employers recognizing that their employees may not want to be 'dragged' away from work and sent on a training course, and universities, colleges and schools seeing that it pays to be learner-centred and go where the learners are.

A customer-centred approach ensures that the content and method of the learning closely match the needs of the learner.

When it comes to planned learning, there are, broadly speaking, three very different types of preferences that learners have:

1. Structured programmes, courses or lectures in which the learner is largely dependent and taught.
2. Structured programmes which are collaborative, for example using discussion, role play, simulations and case studies, in which the learner is actively engaged.
3. Learning experiences which are entirely shaped and managed by the individual learner.

Being aware of the kinds of choices that you can make whenever you are planning your learning may help you to feel more in control.

Staying motivated

Motivation to learn is an extremely complex area, both because learning is so intimately bound up with your self-esteem and confidence, and also because the experience of each learner is unique.

Why bother to understand your motivation?

It will help you to keep going.
It is really important if you want to achieve your goals.

Without motivation you are unlikely to be able to concentrate for long enough to gain the full benefit of whatever you are learning.

Most learners find that they need to learn how to increase the span of their attention – the amount of time that s/he is able to concentrate on an activity. There are many myths about this. For example, it has been said that a child can concentrate for about as many minutes as they are old in years. Or that you can only concentrate for 20 minutes at any one time. Neither one is true, although both contain an element of sense.

> "People who are unable to motivate themselves must be content with mediocrity, no matter how impressive their other talents."
>
> Andrew Carnegie

Many adults do, indeed, find that they can naturally concentrate for about 20–30 minutes, unless they are particularly engaged. But there are many factors that influence your attention span. These include the amount of sleep you had the night before, your general state of health and well-being, your interest in the topic, the environment in which the learning is taking place, the other human beings involved, the methods being used and, of course, your own resilience.

Most importantly, it is possible to increase your attention span as you become a more confident learner. It is also possible to improve the quality of your attention. Concentration is attention which is focused. At moments of high concentration, you become almost oblivious to what is going on around you, so intent do you become. This is sometimes referred to as the state of flow, see page 93.

When considering motivation, research suggests that there are four elements to consider – readiness, anticipated value, probability and impact.

You could look at it like this:

$$R \times V \times P \times I = M$$

R is the amount of readiness to learn. You need to be curious enough, comfortable enough and emotionally happy enough.

V is the anticipated value of the learning. This could be financial, social or cultural. It could get you a better job, for example.

P is the probability of the learning being successful. So, for example, if you have failed your driving test five times, you may not rate the probability of your passing it as being very high and consequently will not be well disposed towards learning to drive.

I is the likely impact of the learning on your life. This could be in terms of the opportunities it will create, the likelihood of dealing with some external change or the degree to which, if you can acquire the learning, you will be markedly more fulfilled as an individual.

> Most folks are about as happy as they make up their minds to be.
>
> Abraham Lincoln

M is the amount of motivation you have towards a particular learning opportunity.

How to motivate yourself

Here are some suggestions which you might like to consider:

1. Give yourself a reward.
2. Stop what you are doing and take some physical exercise.
3. Take a break.
4. Check that you have really got the big picture. It may be that you cannot see the wood for the trees.
5. Work out a different way of breaking up what you are learning into smaller chunks.
6. Try getting the information in a different way.
7. Celebrate what you have done so far.
8. Find something to laugh about. There is evidence that when you laugh your brain releases endorphins which act as relaxants.
9. Ask a friend or member of your family for help.
10. Stop and think what you did last time you felt like this.

Staying positive

At the heart of most successful and resilient learners is a positive outlook. Your attitude of mind – the degree to which you are able to be positive – is a major component of your likely success in life and learning. The good news is that, like almost all aspects of learning, it can be learned. Interestingly, positive thinking and negative thinking are 'contagious'. So you may like to think carefully about who you spend your time with!

Why bother with positive thinking?

Mind set really matters in life and in learning.

By using positive thinking you can improve your performance.

It will make you feel better.

How to be positive

The following are some approaches with which you may like to experiment:

1. Whatever you do, always spend a moment imagining what success will feel like. 'Fast forward' in your mind to a time when you have finished whatever activity you are contemplating and really immerse yourself in imagining yourself being successful at it.
2. Be clear about your goals, Commit to them by writing them down and sharing them with some of your close friends or family members.
3. Get into the habit of turning negative statements into positive ones.
4. Praise at least three times as many times as you blame people (including yourself).
5. Avoid making statements which are in the present tense and imply that things are fixed, for example 'I am no good at this'. Instead use the past tense and change it to 'Once I used to be no good at this but now I can'.
6. Choose to hang out with people who seem to you to be positive people and avoid spending time with those people who you regard as life's cynics.

Allied to a positive mind set is a good sense of humour. Humour is extremely helpful in learning (as in life). For when you are happy, your brain produces chemicals called endorphins which help you to relax. The smile which generally accompanies humour also acts as a powerful model for other learners.

> "Humour is by far the most significant activity of the human brain."
>
> Edward de Bono

According to the British Association of the Advancement of Science, the following is the funniest joke selected by 100,000 people from 10,000 entries from more than 70 countries in 2001:

> The well-known detective Sherlock Holmes and his friend Dr Watson go camping together and pitch their tent under the stars. During the night Holmes wakes Watson and says 'Watson, look up at the stars and tell me what you deduce'. Watson replies 'I see millions of stars, and, even if only a few of those have planets, it's quite likely that there are some planets like Earth out there and there might also be life.' To which Holmes says 'Watson you idiot. Someone stole our tent.'

Why bother seeing the funny side of things?

You will get bogged down if you do not.
Inevitably some learning is mechanical and a sense of humour will help you to keep this in perspective.

Being able to see the funny side of things is a key aspect of resilience.

How to see the funny side

Surprise surprise, there is no one simple suggestion for doing this!

You might like to:

- Get your friends to tell you when you are getting too serious.
- Note when you seem to get into a mood where nothing is funny.
- Develop a few simple ways of making fun of yourself.

At the practical level, your motivation is intimately linked with your ability to set achievable goals for yourself. Goals are essential for any learning. One of the many interesting things about the way that your brain works is that when you focus on something your brain starts to notice it.

Why bother setting goals?

We all need them.
You are more likely to make best use of time.
Setting a goal creates the right mind set to achieve it.

So, if you are focused on a goal, your brain starts to explore items which might be of interest to you and find connections with your interests. (A simple example of this is when you buy a new car you suddenly begin noticing other cars of the same make because your brain is tuned into this.)

We tend to learn well when we have a goal that involves us in exploring things which are at the edge of our comfort zone; also see page 41.

How to set goals

1. Work out what your goals are.
2. Decide which are the most important.
3. Be precise.
4. Be realistic. Do not aim too high but, equally, do not aim too low.
5. Set a timescale.
6. Write your goals down.
7. Share some of them with a small number of people who you trust.

> There are two tragedies in life. One is not to get your heart's desire. The other is to get it.
>
> George Bernard Shaw

Goal setting is important. So, too, is the ability to be uncertain about which the best direction may be in attaining your goal. In a world that hardly changes it may be smart to be sure about things. But in a rapidly changing environment, like the one in which we find ourselves in the twenty-first century, we need to be able to deal with uncertainty.

Why bother getting better at dealing with uncertainty?

Life is getting much more uncertain.

It will help you to come up with better ideas.

It will help you to work out solutions to complex problems.

Research into learning makes it clear that the capacity to be able to live with uncertainty is an important one. Interesting questions frequently arrive in an unclear state. Tough problems are often too complex to take in quickly. The experience of entertaining an unclear question, or trying to get your brain round a complicated problem, or not knowing what to do because what you confidently thought was going to work did not; that experience is called 'being confused'. When life is difficult, it may be smart to be confused.

How to deal with uncertainty

1. Practise saying 'I don't know'.
2. Make a list of all the things in your immediate life about which you are currently uncertain. Rather than fretting about this, try to enjoy at least some of them!
3. Next time you are confused or uncertain make a note of the feelings you are experiencing. Give these uncomfortable intruders names so that they will gradually exert less pressure on you to become certain in your view.

> Education is the path from cocky ignorance to miserable uncertainty.
>
> Mark Twain

Sometimes it pays to wait and defer your judgement. If you cannot do this, although you may be fast off the mark, what you say or think may be shallow, ill-advised or wrong. You may also lose friends along the way if you curb their creativity by jumping in too soon. If you can wait a bit, then the evidence suggests that you may be able to generate more creative ideas and better solutions.

Why bother learning to defer your judgement?

It is a useful technique if you are trying to come up with good ideas.

It helps you to analyse complex issues.

It encourages other people.

There is evidence that it will help you be more successful in life.

There is a famous indicator of this ability called the marshmallow test. Given to four-year-olds, a child is offered one marshmallow or two if they can wait for a moment. Subjects in original tests carried out in the 1960s were tested later in life and those who were able to defer their pleasure had done better in almost all ways in their life than those who had to have instant gratification. Deferring judgement is a bit like that.

How to defer judgement

Deferring judgement involves getting better at 'reading' those situations when you need to be patient. These include:

- any moments when someone else offers you one of their ideas
- difficult problems which need to be explored from a number of different angles
- situations where emotions are running high
- any time you are feeling confused.

Of course, learning is not a neutral activity. It can engage and transform you, causing both pleasurable and uncomfortable feelings. Becoming a more resilient learner will involve your becoming more comfortable with dealing with the feelings of frustration and the distress you get when you are stuck and at the end of your tether.

> 'You can develop good judgement as you do the muscles of your body – by judicious, daily exercise.'
>
> Grenville Kleiser

Why bother managing stress?

Getting in the right state for learning.

Staying healthy.

If the feelings you experience as you learn become distressing, then you are likely to find yourself becoming stressed. This, in turn, may impact negatively on your ability to keep going.

It is really a question of balance. To learn effectively you need to have a certain level of arousal. However, if you are too aroused, you will not be in the relaxed alert state that you need to be for effective learning. When you are under stress, your adrenal glands release adrenalin and if the threat continues they release cortisol, which takes longer to dissipate. Too much cortisol adversely affects brain functions. However, not all stress is bad; we all need a certain amount to ensure that we are sufficiently aroused to function. If we had no stress at all we would be under-stimulated and bored!

Recently, through the work of people like Candace Pert and Sue Gerhardt, we have begun to see how certain kinds of stress in the very early years can have a particularly damaging impact on the developing brain.

In situations of high stress – giving a speech, having a difficult meeting with your boss – effective learners acquire techniques to help them lower and manage their level of stress, for example taking deep breaths or using creative visualization.

How to manage stress

You might like to try some of these suggestions:

1. Have a regular programme of physical exercise. You might also like to learn yoga, try autogenic training or meditation. Or find out about better sitting posture, breathing and other useful techniques.
2. Treat yourself to a massage once a month.
3. Talk about things that are stressing you rather than bottling them up. Get an LP (learning practioner) to help you work through ideas which are causing you stress.
4. Tell jokes, encourage laughter and actively seek to find the funny side in all that goes on at home and work. Keep a few videos/DVDs to hand that are always guaranteed to make you laugh whatever your mood.
5. Spend the last hour of the working day on the least stressful things, for example, making some enjoyable telephone calls, thinking about the next day or tidying up. Then give yourself a few minutes of quiet reflection before you return through your front door at home. Avoid leaving that one last call so that it has to be done in your first minutes back home.
6. At work, try and create conditions where people have maximum control over their working lives, for example by sharing as much information as possible or by encouraging teams to manage themselves.
7. Ensure that you think about your goals for the week ahead a week before and your goals for tomorrow the day before or early in the day in question.
8. Ask for help throughout the day if you are unable to prioritize your own workload.
9. Encourage everyone to share their own favourite stress busters and display these as posters or on your intranet.
10. Have an old cushion or pillow to hand at home if life ever gets too tough and use it to take out your frustrations! Pummel it, shouting out what is on your mind as you do so. (Close the door if you do not want other family members to hear!)
11. Have a regular family meeting where you take it in turns to share what is on each of your minds and offer each other help in the coming weeks.

> Mens sana in corpore sano.
>
> Popular motto

As the saying goes, a healthy mind in a healthy body, for all aspects of learning health matters (also see pages 34–35). That is why many schools use the motto in the margin. It is simply a matter of common sense that resilient learners need to be generally in good health.

Why bother to stay healthy?

You will feel much better.
Your memory will be more reliable.
You will be able to concentrate for longer.

How to stay healthy

You might try these simple tips:

1. Eat a balanced diet, including at least five portions of fresh fruit and vegetables and plenty of fishy oils.
2. Stay well hydrated by drinking a couple of litres of water a day, more if you are being very active.
3. Take regular exercise.
4. Get enough sleep (seven or more hours for most adults).
5. Make sure that you know how to relax and do so daily.
6. Make sure that you know what matters to you and have a plan to get it.
7. Make sure you have an LP (someone who can act as your critical friend and buddy and adviser – see page 200).

Being persistent

Patience is essential in life and in learning. With patience you can wait for the really good ideas to bubble up. You can keep working at a tough problem, turning it over in your head and then putting it away for a bit. You can come at something from different perspectives. If you jump in too quickly it is all too easy to squash other people's ideas.

> Genius is eternal patience.
>
> Michelangelo

It is a myth that the first answer is always the best or that to have a low boredom threshold is necessarily a smart thing. Often it is through the more difficult period of testing an idea or a new approach that you really work out what is best or what is right.

To be persistent in learning it is also essential that you get better at managing distractions so that you can see things though. A distraction is anything that takes you away from what you want to learn. Effective learners know how to become absorbed in an activity and to stay in this state. Inevitably this means that they become good at managing distractions otherwise they would never see things through.

Why bother learning how to deal with distractions?

To help you to develop persistence.
So that you stay motivated.
To help you to stay focused when dealing with difficult challenges.

If you are a parent, then helping your child to minimize distractions when they are doing homework will be particularly helpful. (You could adapt the suggestions below to help you with this.)

How to deal with distractions

You might like to try the following:

1. You need to learn how to recognize distractions. Why is it suddenly a good idea to start vacuuming just when you know that a task involving concentration beckons? Do you really need to make a cup of coffee every ten minutes? Sometimes a break is a good idea. But not too often!
2. Set yourself realistic targets. You are going to work uninterrupted for, say, 60 minutes.
3. Take practical steps to minimize temptation. Set your voicemail. Turn off your mobile phone. Shut your door. Ask those around you not to disturb you.

More than this, you will find it helpful to say no to many of the requests that come your way.

Why bother to say no?

So that you can stick to your own priorities.
To avoid wasting time.
To avoid disappointing other people.

> ‘At painful times, when composition is impossible and reading is not enough, grammars and dictionaries are excellent for distraction.’
>
> Elizabeth Barrett Browning

There are only so many hours in the day. If you cannot say no, you will end up caring more about others than you do about yourself and never having enough time to develop yourself as an effective learner. You may also find yourself becoming unnecessarily emotionally dependent on others.

How to say no

You might like to try the following suggestions:

1. Recognize your feelings when you are asked to do something that you do not want to do. These could include: not wanting to hurt someone, worrying that the relationship will not work if you do not agree, anger that someone more powerful than you is asking you to do something that they should be doing for themselves.
2. Once you have recognized the feeling, stop and think whether it is an appropriate one. Think carefully about the negative consequences if you do not say no.
3. Say no! This may be difficult if you normally say yes. You may need to practise this or you could use some mental rehearsal.

Remember that you are not responsible for other people's feelings!

Often saying no will mean that you have to depend on your own inner resources and become more self-reliant. Self-reliant learners are able to learn on their own when appropriate and ensure that they have the motivation to keep going. Self-reliance is, consequently, an important attribute to acquire.

> "A man does not know what he is saying until he knows what he is not saying."
>
> G.K. Chesterton

Why bother with self-reliance?

It will help you to keep going.

You will develop in confidence.

How to be self-reliant

Self-reliance is part state of mind and part having a good general range of techniques.

The kinds of techniques which help include:

- Knowing how to use a variety of learning methods.
- Knowing how to find out things for yourself.
- Being well enough organized that you can find things you need to learn.
- Being able to recall previous occasions when you managed to work things out for yourself.

Being self-reliant does not mean doing everything on your own! Sometimes it is much smarter to learn with others.

Unless you are prepared to take risks you will never fully develop your creative self. All real learning involves an element of risk because it will inevitably take you out of your comfort zone. You may learn something, for example, which radically changes your view of the world.

Human beings have always had risk in their lives. Arguably, in today's society we are becoming more and more conscious of risks to such an extent that we may be denying ourselves the challenges we need to develop and grow. As a simple example: 30 years ago most children walked to school and were healthier partly as a consequence of this. Today it is the minority who walk, partly out of parental fear of the risk to walkers from cars or strangers.

Resilient learners need to be skilled at the informal process of risk analysis, able to work out which are real risks to be avoided and which are the kinds of risks they ought to take, possibly with some kind of personal support.

Why bother learning how to take risks?

You cannot grow and develop personally if you are not willing to move out of your comfort zone.
You will start being more creative.

Some factors in taking risks

Your personality	Enjoy risks	↔	Prefer certainty
The situation	Big benefit from success	↔	Small gain
	Real personal danger	↔	No actual personal danger
	High likelihood of success	↔	Little chance of success

How to take risks

A decision to take a risk involves assessing a number of factors, see the diagram above.

If you are someone who finds taking risks challenging, you might like to set yourself some very modest goals and gradually increase them.

You might start with very small things, like trying a new food. Then move on to trying a new style of dress, gradually working up to the bigger issues involving choices about life.

Reflectiveness

Chapter 9

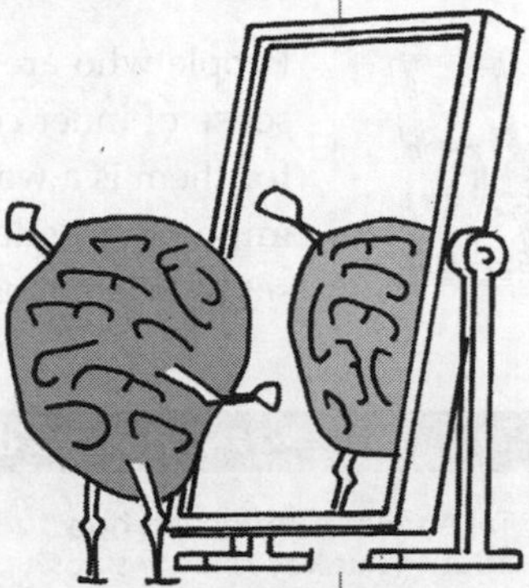

> I prefer thought to action, an idea to an event, reflection to activity.
>
> Honoré de Balzac

Effective learners know how to be reflective. They value mistakes for what they can learn from them and see them as a wholly natural and worthwhile part of their development. They constantly process their experiences, whether planned or accidental, so that they can learn from them and do better the next time around. Of course, reflection is not really an alternative to action, as Balzac suggests, but a complementary part of it.

Reflectiveness involves *noticing*, *questioning* and *distilling experiences*.

Much of what you have to learn is dictated by your needs – you want to get promoted; you are expecting your first child; your child has a learning disability – so you learn what is required.

Why bother discovering your passions?

You learn best when your emotions and thoughts are combined.
You are likely to stick with things you really care about.

In order to really develop you may want to enjoy learning about those things which you care a lot about: your passions.

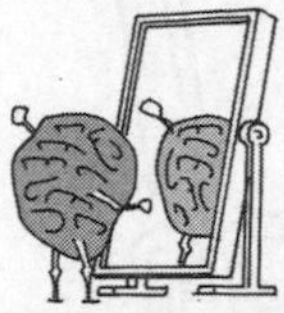

People who are in touch with what they care about seem to derive a sense of inner confidence and stability as a result. It is as if reflection for them is a way of being and they are constantly tuned in to what is important. Reflectiveness has become a way of thinking rather than a set of techniques.

How to discover your life passions

1. Take time to reflect on how fulfilled you currently are in your life and work. What about your key relationships?
2. Think about the things you really enjoy doing but never seem to have time for. What are they? Make a list of them.
3. Draw a line down the middle of a piece of paper. Head one column 'More of' and the other 'Less of'. Make a list of all the things you would like to do more of and vice versa.
4. Using the data you have gathered, make a plan to do at least one thing in the next week that you are really interested in. Then gradually develop your plan as you see how this fits in with your life.

Noticing

It is easy to go through life without really noticing, especially if you are working hard. But observing yourself and others helps you to develop new ways of doing things. Being able to observe changes in the environment is an important reason why human beings have evolved so successfully over the years. Your brain has a very effective tendency to copy and imitate others (as demonstrated on page 284), so you might as well follow your instincts as they are probably based on previous knowledge.

> ' There are no new truths, but only truths that have not been recognized by those who have perceived them without noticing. '
>
> Mary McCarthy

Why bother to observe the world?

It is a great way to learn.

It will help you to avoid making the same mistakes that others make.

How to observe others

You might like to try some of the following different kinds of techniques:

1. Try observing something in a very focused way, really attempting to search for the meaning. Then let your mind go into soft focus mode, with your eyes almost going out of focus. Do you see anything differently?
2. Try imagining what people and situations might look like from different perspectives, for example from above.
3. Put yourself in someone else's shoes. What might they be seeing?
4. Focus on each of your senses in turn. What does your world look like, sound like, taste like, feel like, smell like and so on?

When you were a child, you noticed everything around you. You were probably full of questions about your new experiences. But as you grow older your noticing sense seems to get dimmed through familiarity. To get back into the habit you might like to keep a diary for a week or be more focused on your learning and keep a learning log.

> "Knowledge is the intellectual manipulation of carefully verified observations."
>
> Sigmund Freud

How to keep a learning log

1. Get yourself some blank paper or create a new file on your computer. Create a number of pages each with four columns or four rows per entry titled: Date, Description, Key learning points and Plan.
2. Think back over a recent experience of learning. What happened? Try focusing on a small part of it. Write out a description of what happened without yet thinking about what you learned.
3. Now explore what happened. What were the key learning points?
4. Make a plan covering what you are going to do differently and how you are going to do it.

Questioning

Asking good questions is at the heart of what it is to be a good learner. You are really learning when your mind is seeking answers and your curiosity is engaged. Also, you can get better at asking (and answering) questions.

> I keep six honest serving-men,
> (They taught me all I knew);
> Their names are What and Why and When
> And How and Where and Who.
>
> Rudyard Kipling, 'The Elephant's Child'

Different situations call for different types of question. If you need a simple factual answer, without extra explanation, then asking questions beginning with words like: Did ..., Have ..., Will ..., Can ... and so on will help. Or, taking four of the key words suggested by the names of Kipling's honest serving-men, 'Why ... What ... When ... Where ...' will help.

Yes/no questions are sometimes known as closed questions. They are closed because they can only be answered shortly and simply, often by yes or no. Open questions, by contrast, invite longer and more detailed exploration. They often start with 'Why ...?' and 'How ...?' Open questions are also known as divergent questions, in other words they seek to diverge or open up an issue.

> The only real object of education is to leave a man in the condition of continually asking questions.
>
> Leo Tolstoy

There are three main types of questions:

Questions of fact These tend only to have one correct answer. Examples include: 'What is the name of your sister?' 'What did you do yesterday?' The more complex the area, however, the more complex the answer will be even to factual questions, for example: 'Why do objects fall to the ground?' While you may know that it is do to with gravity, you may well not be able to (or not want to) give the full details.

Questions of interpretation These normally have more than one answer, for example: 'Why did England win the rugby World Cup in 2003?' These kinds of questions are very important for learners who are exploring literature or science where there are many different perspectives. There may be right or wrong answers, but these kinds of question encourage points of view.

Questions of judgement These deliberately ask for some kind of opinion, belief or point of view. They have no wrong answers. 'Who is your favourite TV soap character?' 'What is the best way of improving at sport?' This last category of question gives the learner most scope to explore his or her views.

There is also a special kind of question called a leading question where the answer is being deliberately suggested. (The Romans had a smart way of dealing with this, deliberately signposting those questions expecting a 'yes' answer with the word 'nonne' and those with a 'no' answer with 'num'.)

'Would you allow your child to be taught at a school that does not believe in discipline?' is an example of a leading question, one in which you are being strongly guided as to how you should answer. Effective learners get smart at spotting such questions and avoiding the direction of their questioning!

> It is better to know some of the questions than all of the answers.
>
> James Thurber

Why bother asking good questions?

It will help you to define problems.

You can work out where you are going.

You will be better at developing relationships.

How to ask good questions

The following are some questions to help you ask better questions:

- Are you looking for a yes/no answer?
- Do you know the answer yourself?
- Why are you asking the question? Is it because you genuinely want to know the answer (which you do not currently know)? Or is it as a means of testing someone else's understanding?
- What kind of question is it?
- What would be the best word to start your question?
- What follow-up questions could you have ready to ask?

It often helps to practise your questions beforehand.

As well as asking questions, we are constantly answering them, whether as simple as 'What time is it?' or in response to complex questions like 'What is the meaning of life?' Sometimes answers can be 'yes' or 'no', in which case that is an end to the question. But the more interesting questions are more complex than this.

How you answer questions will vary, not only depending on the type of question but also on whether it is spoken or written. While spoken answers need to be given more quickly than written ones, the broad principles of answering are the same.

> The answer to the meaning of life, the universe and everything is 42.
>
> Douglas Adams, *The Hitchhiker's Guide to the Galaxy*

Why bother learning to answer questions?

Questions are an inevitable part of examinations and tests.
Every day you get asked questions, so you might as well be smart about answering them.

How to answer questions

1. Check that you have understood the question, either by asking for it to be repeated or by reading it again carefully.
2. Think of your possible answers.
3. Select the one which seems most appropriate to the situation. (In exams it is often important to give a full answer, writing in complete sentences.)
4. Check your answer. (If you are having a conversation you may want to go on and further explain or clarify what you have said in the light of the response you get from your questioner.)

Of course questioning works even better when you can do it in a pair, one asking questions of the other. This has given rise to one of the fastest growing kinds of learning: coaching.

Being willing and able to be both coach and coached is a key element of what it is to be an effective learner. This does not need to involve the formality of hiring or being hired as a coach (although you may want to read pages 230–231 for more on how this may be an option at work). It is more about acquiring the skills both of the coach and those of being able to be coached.

Coaching is a one-to-one method of learning, used in the workplace, in sports (from where it originally came as an idea) and, increasingly, in personal life. In the great scheme of things, coaching is not new. You can imagine it taking place around the fire in early civilizations as the lessons of the day's failed hunt were shared. Or when apprentices were commonplace it was simply part of the process of learning a craft. And within families one-to-one advice has a long tradition.

Why bother to understand coaching?

It helps you to explore personal learning needs.
It provides ongoing support rather than one-off advice.
It encourages continuous development.

How to be a successful coach

There are two aspects to being a successful coach. One involves developing certain mind sets and the other focuses on the development of certain key skills.

1. Attributes

A successful coach needs to learn to become: positive, creative, respectful, goal-focused, questioning, observant, creative, supportive, patient and comfortable with uncertainty or ambiguity.

2. Skills

The key skills required include: listening, asking good questions, giving feedback, goal setting, clarifying, making suggestions, analysing and exploring.

How to be coached successfully

As with coaching there are two elements to this, attributes or mind set and skills. The more important of these is mind set. You cannot force someone to be coached, just as you cannot make any individual learn.

1. Attributes

Attributes include: wanting to learn, being willing to receive feedback, commitment and resilience.

2. Skills

These include reflecting, analysing behaviour, trying new methods, listening, planning and goal setting.

Distilling experience

Your senses notice what is happening to you and your questioning instinct helps you to challenge any inconsistencies or uncertainties. It is now left to you to make sense of your experiences, to distil the meaning from them.

Naturally, some things and incidents are more important than others. And there are only so many hours in the day. So, as you reflect on what you have learned, smart learners select those episodes from which they are likely to extract most meaning and concentrate on them.

Why bother getting better at selecting?

You will be more focused.

People will like working with you because you will manage your time effectively.

How to select more effectively

To be able to select effectively you need to know where you are going and what is important to you.

So, assuming that you do:

1. Choose experiences that are most likely to help you to develop.
2. Focus on those experiences which you found most challenging to review.
3. Ring the changes, in other words if you concentrated on being a more effective communicator last month pick something else for the month ahead.
4. Talk to your friends about it; two heads are often better than one.

In a complex world it is not always clear what is important! Frequently this will need to be clarified. Clarifying involves investigating something to make it clearer or more distinct. It is a necessary skill to use when you are moving from a general concept to a more specific one, or trying to define more carefully exactly what something means.

The more a learner can clarify the faster and more efficient s/he is likely to be. To think effectively, it is essential to be able to have ways of seeking clarification.

The main way of clarifying is by asking questions.

Why bother to get better at clarifying?

It helps you to think more effectively.

You will learn faster.

You avoid wasting time.

How to develop techniques to help you clarify

You might like to try the following:

1. Keep asking questions beginning with 'Why ...?'
2. Compare what you are trying to clarify with something else. How is it similar; how is it different?
3. Try and explain what you are clarifying in the simplest possible terms.
4. Ask yourself what the one essential feature is.
5. Try and draw a simple picture or diagram of whatever you are seeking to clarify.
6. Get someone to ask you questions about it.

Only by reviewing experiences can you extract learning from them. Reviewing and reflecting are therefore key techniques for effective learners.

Why bother reviewing your experiences?

It is the best way of extracting their meaning.

You can learn how to do things better as a result.

How to review experiences

You can review:

- in your head
- by talking to someone else
- by writing some things down

and in many other ways.

You can have regular or occasional reviews. In some circumstances (such as after a difficult meeting) you may want to review it immediately. Sometimes it is better to let the dust settle (for example, if you have been involved in a very emotional situation). Most organizations find that monthly review meetings with managers are helpful, with a longer and possibly more formal review session once a year.

Whichever method(s) you choose to use, it is helpful to focus on specific incidents or areas of your life, rather than on general feelings. Try asking yourself questions:

What went well?
Why? How did you make it work?
What could have been better still?
What might you do better as a consequence?

A slightly more formal version of reviewing is evaluation.

Why bother with evaluation?

You need to measure what you do.

It is helpful to find out what works and what does not.

It helps to establish the value of an experience.

How to evaluate learning experiences

Remember there are four elements to think about:

- what you are learning;
- who you are learning with;
- how you are learning;
- where you are learning.

You might like to try one of the following approaches:

- Create a short list of questions about any learning that you undertake: a mini-questionnaire. (Did it meet my needs? What worked well? What could have gone better? Which methods did I prefer? And so on.)
- For each activity come up with a simple three-point scale (1 = worked well for me, 2 = worked well enough for me, 3 = did not work well enough for me – need to change something. If you are helping your child to evaluate his or her learning, then you might like to use a smiley face, a neutral face and a sad face instead of numbers). Use this simple tool as a means of being more precise about the elements of your learning.
- Often a conversation or interview with whoever is arranging the learning is a good means of evaluating an experience.
- If you are undertaking a longer piece of learning – a course of study, for example – then you may find it helpful to keep a journal of your reactions.

The last cluster of techniques, although potentially of use in groups, is largely envisaged for solitary activities.

However, as much of life and learning is social and sociable, you will undoubtedly need to work with a whole range of different people.

The ability to give and receive feedback is one of the most important skills to learn, and yet it is one which many learners find surprisingly hard to do. Feedback is information and opinion about how you have been doing. Effective learners love to give and receive feedback. It is one of the main methods by which they improve and grow.

Why bother with feedback?

It helps you to learn from mistakes.

Essential if you want to become more self-aware.

How to give and receive feedback

When giving feedback, make sure that you focus on behaviour and not on personality. Before you offer feedback, check that the recipient is ready and able to receive it. (If they are about to dash off to a meeting, it may not be a good moment.) *Before* you say things that may be seen as critical, find at *least two* specific things that you can compliment the recipient on.

When receiving feedback check that you are ready to receive it. Try to listen and absorb rather than jump in with an immediate explanation or justification. Thank the person for giving you the feedback – it may have been hard for them, too.

You might like to try my **SAQ** approach

S – Be **S**pecific. Concentrate on a particular moment or incident. Focus on what it was that you observed. Describe what you saw or thought or felt. Be constructive. Suggest some ways in which the person might like to think about it and deal with it.

A – Make sure what you say is **A**ctionable. Ensure that the recipient is capable of putting your feedback into action. It is not much good telling someone to get better at dealing with email, for example, if they do not have access to a networked computer.

Q – Be **Q**uick. Try to give feedback close to the event. If too much time goes by, it can seem irrelevant or irritating or petty. Also the memory fades.

Increasingly organizations which value the learning to be gained from a free flow of feedback are introducing an approach called 360-degree feedback.

> 'Make sure you have someone in your life from whom you can get reflective feedback.'
>
> Warren Bennis

360-degree feedback

Taking its name from the number of degrees in a circle, this idea involves collecting perceptions about a person's performance and behaviour and the impact of that behaviour from all round them, from as many people as possible.

Normally used in workplaces as part of a commitment to everyone's development, this might typically involve getting opinions from the person's boss, the people who work for them, colleagues, fellow members of project teams, internal and external customers, and suppliers. To be effective 360-degree feedback, the process needs to be managed sensitively.

But whether you are using feedback approaches like this or not, the essence of a good learner involves learning from mistakes. As Charles Darwin showed, species that do not adapt and learn from their mistakes ultimately die out. The smart thing to do is to analyse the cause, effect and necessary corrective action of any mistake.

Sadly, the prevailing blame culture in which we live today means that people are quick to judge, even to take out a law suit when things go wrong. Not surprisingly, this leads many people to see making mistakes as a form of weakness when, for a developing learner, it is a sign of strength. Although obviously making the same mistake over and over again is not helpful for you or those around you.

All successful learners make mistakes. Indeed mistakes are the raw material of learning. If you never tried to do something that you might not be able to do you would never improve.

Of course making mistakes can be uncomfortable and embarrassing. Make lots of them and you may suffer from a loss of self-esteem and confidence. But effective learners know that getting used to the uncomfortable feelings associated with making mistakes is a smart thing to do. All the great leaps of progress have involved making mistakes along the way and learning from them. Think of the Apollo Moon mission, the invention of the computer or the discovery of DNA (deoxyribonucleic acid).

Why bother to learn from your mistakes?

You will improve if you do.

You will lose friends if you do not.

How to learn from your mistakes

1. See mistakes as something to learn from rather than be ashamed about. Ask yourself 'How could this be an opportunity?'
2. Get into the habit of saying that you have made a mistake when you have. Try and say sorry if it involves other people. Contrary to what you might think, this will be seen as a sign of strength and maturity by others rather than as an indication of your weakness.
3. After any intensive learning (or life) experience, review what you have learned. Stop for a moment and jot down some of the key points.
4. Get into the habit of keeping a learning log.

Once you have mastered the idea of learning from your mistakes as an individual, the next level of challenge involves all of those around you doing the same, too.

Double-loop learning

Invented by Chris Argyris, double-loop learning involves understanding the underlying system rather than dealing with incidents as if they were unconnected (in other words, single-loop thinking).

It is a powerful kind of systems thinking. In double-loop learning, assumptions underlying current views are questioned and hypotheses about behaviour tested. The end result of double-loop learning is increased effectiveness in decision making and better acceptance of failures and mistakes.

Even a domestic example can make the point. Say your child is constantly forgetting to do his or her homework. A single-loop solution would involve sitting over him or her each night and checking that s/he has done it. A double-loop approach would have you come up with a method by which your child could plan homework commitments on a weekly basis, perhaps with a simple chart on the bedroom wall for each week.

You might like to try this approach on an issue in your own home or work life. If so, start by thinking of a number of issues. Then choose one that is a middling one not, too serious or emotional, but equally not too insignificant – so that you do not care about the result. Begin by thinking of some single-loop solutions.

For example, if your teenage son is watching too much television, a single-loop solution would be to confiscate or ban the television. Now try and come up with some double-loop ideas. For this example, it could involve a serious discussion to agree a maximum number of hours to be watched on a daily or weekly basis and certain other voluntary rules for the use of the television.

> A life spent in making mistakes is not only more honourable but more useful than a life spent doing nothing.
>
> George Bernard Shaw

A continuously reflective view of learning underpins what is generally called formative assessment. Most universities and colleges use this as do some work-based courses and schools. Its purpose is to provide learners with regular feedback on their progress throughout any episode of their learning. This could be in oral or written form. Formative assessment encourages learners to become more reflective. It allows learners to adapt their approaches, developing tools and techniques as necessary. It helps teachers to adapt their teaching in the light of the information they receive. Examples of effective approaches include interviews, peer review, diaries, journals, learning logs, profiles, records of achievement and various other self-assessment approaches. Researchers have found that regular formative assessment improves performance by a measurable amount.

You can find out more about different kinds of assessment in Chapter 11.

10

Responsiveness

Chapter 10

❛ It is not the strongest of the species that survive, nor the most intelligent, but the ones most responsive to change. ❜

Charles Darwin

Effective learners know how to be responsive, changing and adapting as circumstances demand. There are three elements to this: 'Accepting change', 'Adapting and flexing', and 'Life planning'. The fifth R (responsiveness) includes some of the most challenging aspects of effective learning as it requires the ability to be constantly altering behaviour, something that many of us find easy to describe but much more difficult to actually do in practice.

Accepting change

Being able to deal effectively with the inevitability of change is essential if you are to survive. Learning is the key to dealing with change, whether in your personal circumstances – you are given a new job or you move house – or a more global issue such as the arrival of the internet which has provided new opportunities and challenges in every aspect of life. The faster the world around you is changing the faster you need to learn in order to be able to keep up with it.

Why bother learning to deal with change?

Everyone needs to adapt to new circumstances.
It is the key to surviving and thriving.
There is a lot of change about.

While it is possible to be rational about change ('It's only natural that now I am older I should stop working') it is often the emotional component of change that is the most difficult to deal with. This is particularly the case when change is thrust upon you before you are ready for it. In such cases there is an almost inevitable series of feelings that you are likely to experience.

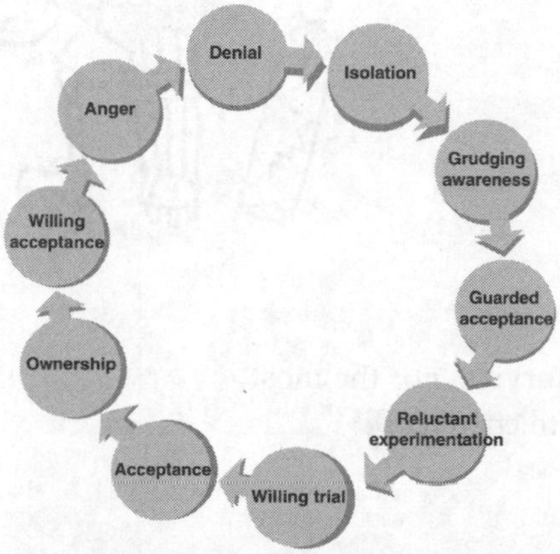

This chart shows some of the typical feelings; often, the first of these is anger.

The most helpful skill you can learn is to cultivate a mind set that welcomes change, assuming that you will always be able to benefit from it rather than finding it threatening to your lifestyle.

How to deal with change

Here are some approaches you might like to try out for yourself:

1. Notice what has changed.
2. Describe the change you are experiencing carefully to yourself.
3. Write it down. (Simply putting a name to something you are worried about can help; it will also force you to be specific.)
4. Consider what the worst thing it could bring would be. (It may not be as bad you feared it could be.)
5. Consider how it might improve your life. (You may only have looked at the negative side so far.)
6. Think of all the times when you have dealt with something like this before and make a list of all the things which might help you in your current situation.
7. Ask for other opinions and consult widely.
8. Gather up all the positive ways ahead you can think of and choose the one or ones which seem most likely to work.
9. Do not be afraid of unpleasant feelings – uncertainty, fear and so on. Let them bubble up and talk openly about them.
10. Once you have decided on a course of action, get on with it. There is no point in spinning things out unnecessarily.

There has never been more uncertainty than there is in today's fast-moving world. Even as we solve one mystery – take the unravelling of DNA – we discover another, like the impact of genetically modified foods. Our grandparents would hardly know what to do in today's world if they were young again now.

> There is nothing like returning to a place that remains unchanged to find the ways in which you yourself have altered.
>
> Nelson Mandela

According to thinkers like Alvin Toffler, a 'totally new social force, a stream of change so accelerated that it influences our sense of time', has been unleashed upon us. The tempo of daily life is such that everything looks and feels different.

A paradigm shift

A paradigm is a framework or pattern, a way of seeing the world. Thomas Huhn is credited with creating the concept of a paradigm shift which describes a moment of dramatic change and the new theory which explains it.

Examples of this include:

the discovery that the Earth was round and not flat;
the discovery of DNA;
women becoming eligible to vote;
Moore's law which says that computer power doubles every 18 months;
fathers staying at home to look after their children;
the way that email and the world wide web have transformed the way we communicate;
the discovery of the human genome.

Just think how profoundly different the world must have looked after the discovery that you could not fall off the edge. Yet at the same time, life still moved with the predictable rhythms of the Earthly seasons. We are experiencing so many dramatic changes of similar drama on a regular basis today that the way you view change is, arguably, much more important now than it ever has been.

Not surprisingly, change causes many people to be fearful. And so can the act of learning itself. One moment you are moving in one direction and the next you find yourself promoted at work.

Everyone feels fear from time to time. It is an inevitable and entirely normal part of living. But fear and learning do not go well together. Some people, for example, have such strongly negative memories of their schooldays that the thought of doing any learning as an adult makes them feel awful. If you are such a person then you are very likely to want to deal with your fears. For, when you are afraid, unbeknown to you, certain parts of your brain which would normally be available to help you figure out an answer are not available. For fear signals threat to your brain and the instinctive response of a human being under threat is to fight or flee – neither of which are very helpful in learning.

In truth, we all need to do this on a recurring basis. In a fast-moving world, many of us face the fear of change on a daily basis, especially when it affects our life or work directly.

Why bother to deal with your fears?

You may want to deal with bad learning experiences from the past.

You will be able to try difficult things.

You can help your child to overcome fears about school.

How to deal with your fears

Whether you are dealing with something that happened a long while ago or something that has not yet occurred, the starting point is recognition. You need to give your fear a name and be as clear as you can about what it is.

Once you have done this, there are a number of approaches you might like to try:

- Before you start to work on your fear, close your eyes. Think of your favourite places. Think of the times in your life when you have been happiest and most successful. Enjoy them. Feel good about them.
- Make a list of all the other times you have faced something similar in the past and found a way of dealing with it. See if this helps you.
- Take a look at your fear from another perspective. Imagine you have a portable stepladder. Place it beside you and the situation you are afraid of and lean it against an imaginary wall. Climb up and look down from it. What do you see? Who is doing what? Could you do anything differently?
- Use the idea of a ladder in this way. Make a list of little things that you could do to overcome your fear in order of their scariness. (Say you want to go to an evening class but are afraid to. Your list might start: a) walk past the college; b) walk into the college and get a course brochure; c) find someone who has been to the class and chat to them; d) ask the tutor if you can come to a class with a friend on a trial basis; d) go along to the class with a friend; e) enrol in the class; f) try the class yourself.)
- Imagine you have solved your problem. Jump forward in time. It is a week after the fear has been dealt with. How are you feeling? What did you do?
- Make a mini-film in your head of your fear. Run it through from start to finish. Now do this again, only this time, start from the end and work backwards quickly, not dwelling on the nasty bits. Has that helped?
- Explain your fear to a trusted friend. Ask them for their advice. Ask them to suggest some possible things that they might do to overcome it.

One of the most challenging aspects about change is that, especially when it is most rapid, it can present you with apparently contradictory courses of action. This is where reflection is especially important in helping you to deal with conflict.

> Courage is a special kind of knowledge: the knowledge of how to fear what ought to be feared and how not to fear what ought not to be feared.
>
> Plato

Luckily, when we are presented with conflict in its most extreme form, the human brain is wired so that we will survive. We will either fight or flee. Effective learners rarely have to use either of these two strategies, successful as they may have been in our evolutionary past.

However, they frequently do have to deal with intellectual and emotional conflict. Doing so effectively is a key element of putting your learning into practice. So, you may have resolved that the next time someone starts chairing a meeting without an agenda, or any sense of what is to be covered, you will intervene. But in reality such a (sensible) tactic is fraught with potential conflict and you may feel intimidated. Or you may want to change some aspect of your own behaviour, but find that there is a real internal conflict as your thoughts clash with your feelings. Or it may just be smart to live with a number of statements which seem, on the surface, to be contradictory.

Dealing with conflict without being aggressive while still ensuring progress is made is a key attribute to acquire.

Why bother to deal with conflict?

It will stop you getting into unnecessary arguments.
You will be able to deal with complex situations better.
You will learn more about yourself.

How to deal with conflict

You might like to try some of the following approaches:

1. Accept that conflict is an inevitable and necessary part of life.
2. Try to distinguish between conflict which is helpful – for example, when you are dealing with a difficult issue where there are no right answers – and that which is unhelpful – where people's behaviours are causing aggressive responses.
3. Watch out for early signs of conflict. For example negative body language, raised voices, over-defensiveness, unnecessary secrecy, open disagreement and so on.
4. Try:

   listening to all sides
   finding the common ground
   recognizing the feelings of other people
   focusing on what really matters
   taking a break and coming back later
   agreeing to disagree
   using a neutral facilitator or chairperson.

Adapting and flexing

The world continually changes. Situations alter. And effective learners need to be flexible so that they can adapt to meet the new challenges and opportunities which life throws at them. But how do you do this? Is it easy?

> The test of a first rate intelligence is the ability to hold two opposed ideas in mind at the same time and still retain the ability to function.
>
> F. Scott Fitzgerald

When was the last time something made you really re-think the way you see the world? What was it that persuaded you? Did you change everything as a consequence or just adapt your philosophy to accommodate the new data? Or was it something completely different from this?

Accommodation or assimilation

Psychologist Jean Piaget suggested that we learn through a process of adaptation. You notice something, adjust your thinking and, as a consequence, adapt the way you act. In practice, you either fit your theory to your experience – accommodation – or fit your experience to any theory you have already formed in your head – assimilation.

So, if your theory of children was that they were always naughty and you met a child who was well behaved, you would accommodate your views by adjusting your theory. From then on children would become capable of good or bad behaviour. If you chose to assimilate this data, then your view of children would remain the same and your mind would explain away your experience by thinking of the nice child as an odd exception to the rule.

Of the two kinds of adaptation described by Piaget, accommodation is the more challenging. For it requires you to re-think the way you view the world. Effective learners recognize that accommodation is a way in which they can change and adapt their world view in the light of new evidence.

Assimilation occurs when you are able to fit your experience to a theory you have developed. So, for example, as you grow up you discover the force of gravity. You push your milk bottle off your high chair and it falls to the floor. The same happens for bits of fruit. Then you play with a hose and see the water arching downwards. Footballs, glass, even human beings all gradually get assimilated into your initially sketchy sense of the force of gravity.

You may like to become more aware of when you are fitting your theories to what happens in practice and when you are adapting your theories in the light of your experience, in other words accommodating new views. How do you feel? Is it comfortable? What is going on as you try to adapt your mind set? What kinds of things help you though this process?

Or perhaps you could be aware, when you are learning more about a theory, that you already have experienced similar events in different environments. Let us say that you believe people are more likely to help you if you help them. See how many different examples of this you can gather – with a colleague, at work, in a shop, at home and so on. See what you learn each time.

Just because you are living in a fast-moving world does not mean that you cannot stay true to yourself. In fact the opposite is true. The more your own behaviour and beliefs are aligned, the more you are likely to need to be confident in your self.

Why bother to align your behaviour to your beliefs?

You will feel much better if you can 'walk the talk'.
People will trust you more if you do what you say you believe.

Ensuring that the way you conduct yourself – your behaviour – is in line with what you believe is an important aspect of being an effective learner. It involves self-understanding and continuous practice. It is all too easy to allow an occasional lapse of self-control to become a habit or engrained behaviour.

How to align your behaviour with your beliefs

You might like to try some of the following ideas:

1. Be clear about which of your beliefs are most important to you. These might be things like always trying to be open; the value of patience; the importance of listening.
2. Share your beliefs with those around you and encourage them to give you feedback.
3. Notice when you are out of alignment. For example, if you said that being patient was important, then notice what makes you lose your temper.
4. Pick one or two simple things to do when you sense that you are about to behave in a way that does not seem right. These might be as simple as stopping and counting to ten or taking deep breaths and starting again.

But can you really change? Is it possible to alter the way you behave? Psychologists used to think that it was not. Indeed a group of them, of whom Ivan Pavlov and B.F. Skinner are two of the most famous, became known as the behaviourists precisely because they argued that the environment in which you operated was a more powerful influence than you could be as an individual.

We now know that this is not the case. It is more complex than this. And it is possible to change the way you behave very significantly. One of the most powerful elements in this, as it is in so much of your learning, is your mind set.

Learned optimism

Invented by Martin Seligman in the 1990s, learned optimism describes the positive mind set that learners need cultivate to help them achieve success. Seligman suggests that the world is divided into two kinds of people. One group are optimists, the other are pessimists. It all comes down to the way you account for things that happen to you, your 'explanatory style'. Seligman describes this as having three elements: permanence, pervasiveness and personalization – the 3Ps.

Have you ever wondered why people who seem to be very similarly talented can have very different dispositions towards what needs to be done? Some are 'half-full' people, always seeing the bright side of a problem, while others are 'half-empty', seeing the worse side. Some are only knocked back for a few moments when something goes wrong and rapidly evolve a way of seeing it as an isolated misfortune, where others immediately make it part of a pattern of failure and bad luck. The 3Ps help to explain this.

Permanence When something goes wrong optimists see this as a one-off setback, pessimists as something that always happens. A pessimist would say: 'Things like this ALWAYS happen to me and the effects go on for ever.'

Pervasiveness When something goes wrong, optimists realize it was because of a particular situation, pessimists see it spreading right through their lives. A pessimist would say: 'Things like this ALWAYS happen to me and that's typical of anything I do in my life.'

Personalization When things go wrong, optimists take control of events, pessimists sink into a depression imagining that the whole world is against them. A pessimist would say: 'Things like this always happen to ME.'

Behaviourist theory suggests that you are a victim of your environment and situation. The concept of learned optimism and its associated techniques show that this need not be the case.

American researcher, Carol Dweck, has gone further still, suggesting that some children become victim to an extreme version of the pessimistic mind set through being 'spoon-fed' at school. She calls this 'learned helplessness', a condition in which the young learner has come to depend so much on those around that he or she has, in effect, become an ineffective learner.

So if you were going to try and put some optimism back into your life you might like to follow the following steps:

1. Look back on the previous week. Make a note of all of the 'events' that happened to you (for example, you missed your train because you spent too long over breakfast, the photocopier broke down and so on).

2. Examine each one carefully. Using the 3Ps, make up a statement to describe your explanation under each heading.
3. If your statements are anything like the pessimistic examples above, reframe them so that you see the event as a one-off example of something that happened because of good reasons that were nothing to do with you and your life. For example, if the photocopier has broken, your optimistic explanation could be: 'Oh dear the machine's broken. I can see it's because someone jammed it with paper earlier. I'll walk down the corridor and use the other one.'
4. You might like to notice how often an optimistic statement avoids the present tense (which implies things are fixed and stuck) and prefers to use the past tense (it's happened and over) along with the future tense (outlining something positive that you can do to put it right).

> The point of living, and of being an optimist, is to be foolish enough to believe the best is yet to come.
>
> Peter Ustinov

At the heart of being an effective learner is the ability to change your behaviour in the light of circumstances. It is what has ensured that human beings have thrived where other species have not.

Why bother altering your behaviour?

You are more likely to get on at home, at work and at school.
You are more likely to have happy relationships.
You will get stuck in a rut if you do not.
The human race is doomed if individual members cannot adapt the way they do things.

From the earliest age, when we touch a kettle, realize it is painfully hot and decide not to touch it again, we learn to modify our behaviour. Of course this does not just apply to physical actions. It equally influences what we say, how we dress and every aspect of our reactions to other people.

Many of our most important institutions – schools and prisons for example – are founded on the assumption that it is possible to change behaviour. Advertisers, social workers, therapists, parents, politicians – all know the importance of seeking to change people's behaviour.

Until comparatively recently little was known about the significant degree to which it was possible to change behaviour. Indeed there was a school of thought that argued that certain kinds of behaviour were almost impossible to change.

Effective learners realize that they are doing something which is not appropriate for a particular situation, adapt their behaviour and start doing things differently. The most engrained habits are, of course, the most difficult to change. We get used to doing things in certain ways, (see pages 123–125 for more on the pattern-making tendency of our minds).

How to alter your behaviour

Really altering your behaviour is tough. It certainly involves all of the 5Rs, especially resilience, resourcefulness and responsiveness. You might like to try the following ideas and develop strategies which work for you.

1. The first and most important stage is to notice that you are doing something that needs changing.
2. Then you need to want to change.
3. The real action starts here. Decide how you would prefer to behave. Often an entrenched behaviour cannot be altered overnight. So it is important to set a timescale that is realistic.
4. It may help to analyse your behaviour further so that you understand more about it. When do you do it? What is the trigger for it? What helps you behave differently? Make some notes to help you.
5. You might like to ask for help, especially from someone close to you who can gently prompt you without making you annoyed.

If there are significant changes in the animal or plant kingdom then a new species is born or an old one dies out. Or a species changes so that, where it once swam in the sea, it now crawls on the land. The hedgehog which had an 'avoid car headlights' mentality, for example, would survive more effectively than its poor car-squashed brothers and sisters. Individual members of one species imitate each other and new patterns of behaviour emerge. And the result of all this is that new combinations of genes are created.

Through the incredible scientific breakthrough which has allowed scientists to map the human gene bank, we can see the evidence of our development. We can see that we share many genes with the humble mouse! We can see how evolution has made sense of the great soup in which we once all swam.

But what about ideas? What about changes in culture? Can these be measured in the same way as human evolution can? Some scientists think they can.

The meme

A meme is a new word coined by Stephen Dawkins in the 1970s to describe the essence of new ideas. Sounding like a gene, a meme is a single unit of cultural transmission. A meme is at the heart of the way we evolve ideas (like the gene is the smallest unit of the way our bodies evolve).

Examples of memes include catch-phrases, new ideas like 'going organic', melodies, fashions – any new way of doing something can be broken down into small items that one brain can copy from another and so on.

Life planning

There is much talk today about work–life balance. This phrase assumes that you are in work and that, if life and work are in balance, all will be fine. While there is much truth in this, it is of course much more complex.

Why bother to plan your life?

People who plan normally get what they are planning.

If you do not plan your life may take you over.

It will help ensure that you spend your time with the people you love and like.

At the start of *Discover Your Hidden Talents* you explored the difference between unplanned and planned learning; see pages 12–15. Throughout your life you will undertake both kinds and most of either kind will be informal – the business of reflecting on and responding to the experiences that come your way.

But as you become more confident as a learner, it is almost inevitable that you will realize the huge advantages which flow from organizing your life so that you plan for an increased amount of learning. To do this requires more than just setting aside time for learning. It almost inevitably requires you to plan your time collaboratively with those around you who are most important. For many people this means involving your partner.

How to plan your life

All relationships are individual, so this may or may not work for you. You might like to try this with your wife/husband/partner or adapt it for use with a close friend.

1. Set one whole weekend aside when you will not be disturbed by family or friends.
2. Plan to do some of the things you most enjoy doing together and, while you are doing these things, make lots of time to talk, listen, learn, feel and think.
3. Start by looking back over the highs and lows of the last year and taking stock.
4. Talk about and agree where you currently think you want to get to in your lives and what you need that you do not currently have.
5. Focus on what you want to do in the next 12 months.
6. Focus on how you can do what you want to do in the next 12 months.
7. Produce some kind of written or pictorial record of how and when you are going to do what you have agreed that you want to do. What kind of learning will you need to plan to do in order for you to achieve your goals?

Sometimes what you may need to do is not more of the same but something completely different. What is called for is not so much learning as unlearning. Being able to let go, change and do things differently are important aspects of learning. Given that the brain loves connections and patterns (see pages 96–97), this can often be difficult. Successful people have a habit of regularly re-inventing themselves, re-thinking the way they see the world.

Why bother learning how to unlearn?

It is all too easy to get stuck in a rut.

Sometimes thinking moves on and you need to change with it.

It is a key element in learning to be more adaptable.

How to unlearn things

You might like to start with the following ideas:

1. Begin by thinking about yourself and your habits. Make a long list of these down one side of a piece of paper. Now go through the list and think of the opposite. So, if you wrote tidy, write untidy next to it and so on. In the next few weeks systematically try unlearning a habit on the left-hand side of the page by learning one from the right.
2. Think of the world as you know it. Make a list of all the rules or inventions which have eventually been proved wrong or superseded. An obvious example would be the belief that the world was flat or that all the planets went around the Earth.
3. Think of your own family. Think of a behaviour of yours that you do not actually like much. Maybe you shout at one of your children or too easily become defensive with your partner. 'Run' a short video of a typical scene in your head. Now rerun it with you behaving in the opposite way as if you had unlearned the behaviour. Now put it into practice next time the situation arises.

Family learning

Chapter 11

Ten years ago the phrase 'family learning' was hardly used. But increasingly today, new research is showing the huge benefits of learning in terms of the educational performance of young people and the health of older adults; family learning is seen as an important concept.

In this and the following chapter you can find out about some of the issues relating to learning in the two most popular environments for adults: home and work.

The top ten places we like to learn	Per cent
1. Home	57
2. Work	43
3. Libraries	36
4. College/university	29
5. On holidays/travelling	22
6. Museums	13
7. Adult learning centres	11
8. School	8
9. Pubs/clubs	8
10. Other people's homes	6

Source: MORI poll for the Campaign for Learning (1998)

Families are not only our first and most important teachers but they also teach us many of the most important things in life. The values, attitudes and culture that we learn from our families can stay with us throughout our lives. We acquire knowledge from school but that knowledge is given a context by the family. For example, children learn to read at school but it is often the family that nurtures a love of reading. History can seem remote in textbooks but a grandparent's stories of the Second World War can bring it to life.

Without family support, a child's formal education can be an uphill struggle. There is evidence that family learning can overcome difficulties associated with a disadvantaged background for both parents and children.

Family learning covers all forms of informal and formal learning that involve more than one generation. For most people it is largely informal.

There is clearly some way to go in becoming a learning society. In the National Adult Learning Survey conducted by the Department for Education and Skills in 2001, 26 per cent of adults said that they had not taken part in any learning in the previous year, classifying themselves as 'non-learners'. (Luckily we know that the category 'non-learner' does not really exist as the vast majority of us are learning all the time – informally!)

Informal opportunities

Whatever your own family situation, assuming that you spend some time at home with either family or friends, there will be a social dimension to your learning here. The values that you hold will be particularly important. They are what make you say yes or no when faced with a difficult choice. If you swear all the time, it is likely that your children will imitate you, seeing it as acceptable behaviour. It has even been suggested that there is a specific intelligence called spiritual intelligence.

Spiritual intelligence

First suggested by Danah Zohar and Ian Marshall in 2000, spiritual intelligence is intimately linked to the human search for meaning in life. It is what we use when we explore beliefs. Of the multiple kinds of intelligence described in *Discover Your Hidden Talents*, this is one of the most contested.

If you have a well-developed spiritual intelligence, you like to deal with the fundamental questions of existence. You are the kind of person who, when faced with difficult issues, will want to act according to your principles, possibly questioning the normal ways of behaving in the situation you find yourself in. You seek constantly to explore your whole self and to heal those bits which seem not to be well. You are interested in values. You will probably hold particularly well-developed beliefs but may or may not practise any particular religious faith. You think about issues of duty. You tend to see some value in different sides of an argument. You may well be involved in some kind of community service. You would be ready to stand up and be counted for what you believe in.

Whether or not you like this idea, it is worth being aware of how your own values will almost inevitably transmit themselves to your children. So, if you are negative about the value of learning so may they be.

There will always be exceptions to this rule – children who turn into wonderful adults despite their parents' worst attempts – but these tend to be the exceptions!

Modelling

Modelling is the process by which you learn by consciously or unconsciously imitating others. It is a powerful way of learning. It explains why it really does matter how parents and teachers behave as, contrary to what we sometimes think, children are influenced by what we do. (So, if you start panicking when a wasp comes near you as a parent, do not be surprised if your children do likewise.) The same is equally true of the relationship between managers and the people who work for them. Role models are powerful!

Research suggests that we are more likely to be influenced by models where they are very competent, where we identify with them (for example, as a sporting hero or because of something they have achieved) and where they really do what they say they do, in other words they are authentic.

> I believe in recovery, and I believe that as a role model I have the responsibility to let young people know that you can make a mistake and come back from it.
>
> Ann Richards

For many people (some eight million families in the UK) family learning involves parenting children. But, having said this, it is important to recognize the many very different kinds of family units, with a growing number of children (some two million currently) living in single-parent families. The role of the step-parent is also growing in importance, and the influence of fathers is increasingly acknowledged. It is difficult to be precise about any of these statistics, because many family units are flexible. Another significant factor in any exploration of family learning is the different emphasis which various cultural groups place on learning.

Being a parent

> Parents can only give good advice or put them on the right paths, but the final forming of a person's character lies in their own hands.
>
> Anne Frank

Bringing up children has always been a daunting challenge. Today it is particularly the case, with relentless pressure from television, the web, the music and fashion industries, and the media in general to conform to the view of yourself that others would like you to have.

If you have children, what kind of a parent are you? How do you deal with all of these pressures? In the next few pages you will have the chance to explore some of these issues.

Parent types

You have already found out about the idea of learning styles, but what about parenting? Are there certain predictable styles and preferences?

I believe so, and have developed a simple way of looking at parent types which is based on research into parenting and learning. You might like to see where you sit if you are a parent. There are no right or wrong behaviours and most parents will need to be able to adopt all the different views at some stage. However, if you only adopt one of each alternative it will undoubtedly affect the way that your child learns and grows.

For example, if you only ever tell your child things, then s/he may find it much more difficult to engage in complex issues because s/he has been conditioned into thinking that your answer is always the best one. Or if you only ever blame and never praise, then your child may feel undervalued and criticized and have low self-esteem.

Stay close	v.	Hang back
Optimist	v.	Pessimist
Big picture	v.	Detail
Relaxed	v.	Anxious
Fun loving	v.	Serious

Like variety	v.	Like routine
Show emotions	v.	Keep emotions hidden
Like to say yes	v.	Prefer to say no
Praise	v.	Blame
Coaching	v.	Telling
Adults always know best	v.	Adults sometimes know best
Comfortable with conflict	v.	Avoid conflict

> The most valuable lesson my children have taught me is that the best start in life is being loved.
>
> Iain Banks

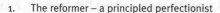

You might like to consider each of these pairs in turn and work out where you are as a parent. Do you change depending on where you are or what mood you are in? Are you comfortable with your current approaches? If not, you may find implied suggestions as to how you could do things differently if you wanted to.

Earlier in *Discover Your Hidden Talents,* on pages 142 and 145, you explored the idea of learning styles and now you have considered the idea that there may be certain kinds of parenting. Here is one more approach for you to consider.

An enneagram

Based on an ancient symbol, the enneagram has been developed into a theory of personality type which some learners find helpful. Although not grounded in any specific science, the 'types' can help to stimulate reflection. There are nine personality types:

1. The reformer – a principled perfectionist
2. The helper – generous and keen to please
3. The achiever – adaptable and driven
4. The individualist – dramatic and temperamental
5. The investigator – innovative, provocative and often secretive
6. The loyalist – responsible, engaging and sometimes anxious
7. The enthusiast – spontaneous, versatile and sometimes easily distracted
8. The challenger – self-confident, decisive and sometimes confrontational
9. The peacemaker – reassuring, agreeable and sometimes complacent.

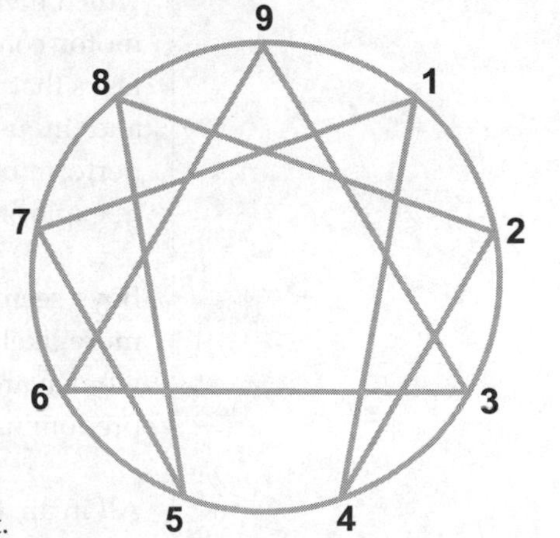

Most people recognize little bits of each of these in them and most can select one which is their basic personality type. The chart in the margin shows how types tend to be connected.

These kinds of labels are only helpful if seen as a prompt to further reflection and should not be taken too seriously. Some people find them a bit easier to use than the language of another popular personality–type indicator: the MBTI® (see page 143).

An immediate issue for many parents is the different needs of boys and girls. The popular stereotype is that boys will be boys and girls will be girls. Boys will turn any object into a gun and be nasty and aggressive while girls will be gentle, studious and mature earlier.

While there are some grains of truth in all of these ideas, it is, of course, much more complex than this.

Do boys learn differently from girls, men from women? Are their brains different? Many teachers and parents would say that boys and girls are different. But, scientifically speaking, it seems that the brains of boys and the brains of girls have more in common than they have difference. Much of the research that exists can be interpreted in many different ways and is often very loaded. The popular press has latched on to a simplistic idea that men are from Mars and fight a lot, while women come from Venus and cannot read maps.

Here are a few baseline facts. The male brain is slightly bigger and heavier on average, although the density of cells in women's brains is higher. Men tend to perform slightly better than women on tasks which involve spatial awareness, but women seem to have better fine motor control. It seems that, in general, women tend to do better in tasks that involve matching items together, in most language activities and in using landmarks for navigation. Men, on the other hand, perform better in mechanical skills, in simple repetitive activities and in exploring abstract ideas.

Boys seem to be more vulnerable to conditions like dyslexia and are more likely to stammer than girls. According to Myers–Briggs MBTI®, women are more likely to have psychological profiles in which feeling predominates and men more likely to have thinking as dominating.

All in all, there is much less variation in learning ability between boys and girls than there is between boys and boys and girls and girls.

Helping your child to learn

There are many things which you can do to help your child to learn. But the three most important are:

- showing in everything you do that you really care about learning;
- creating a learning environment that is stimulating;
- helping him or her to become an effective learner by showing that learning is learnable.

Stimulation is essential. Stimulation is the process of rousing you to action. We all need to be stimulated, and we now know that stimulation is particularly important for the growth of a healthy mind in the early years. Equally, it is important in later years to ensure continued health in the latter stages of life.

Praise is essential too. All learners need to be praised. Praise improves motivation and raises self-esteem where blame has the opposite effect.

> Since we cannot know what knowledge will be most needed in the future, it is sensible to try to teach it in advance. Instead we should try to turn out people who love learning so much and learn so well that they will be able to learn whatever needs to be learned.
>
> John Holt

Source: Bill Lucas and Alistair Smith (2002) *Help Your Child to Succeed*, Network Educational Press

But constant praise which does not discriminate does not help much. Learners need feedback which is specific and actionable.

Much of what you do is likely to revolve around play. Play, the act of enjoyably exploring people and places, is essential in learning and especially important in the early years of childhood. Indeed, with the current emphasis on tests and exams in schools and the pressures on time of schools, there is an argument that play is even more important than it has always been. This argument is further strengthened by statistics showing the large number of hours that young people (and adults) spend in relatively passive activities in front of computers and televisions.

Play has come to mean the opposite of work. So if you are working long hours the word has an attractive meaning. However, in many educational circles it has acquired a negative association. It is as if a teacher were saying, 'Class, stop playing around and get on with your work now, please.' Play has somehow become detached from learning, when we know that it is intimately a part of it. This view even persists into adulthood. Research has shown that, for example, if you ask a group of adults to perform a task and tell them that it will be fun and playful they will enjoy it more and do it better than a similar group who, given the same task, are told that what they have to do is a serious job of work.

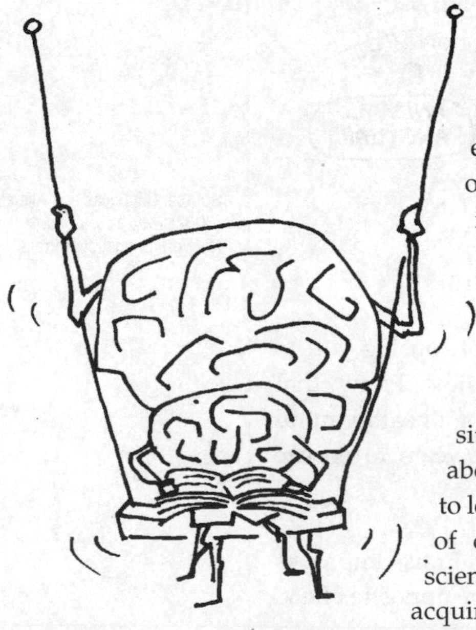

In the early years of childhood your brain develops most rapidly as a result of the external stimulation received, and research suggests that this is largely a function of the amount of play in which a child engages. Play almost inevitably involves many or all of the senses and consequently is likely to engage many different parts of the brain. Research also shows that children who are encouraged to use their imagination and make-believe cope with stress better later in life.

Play allows children (and adults) to imagine, rehearse situations, practise, test out boundaries, explore, learn about give and take, and take on roles. It allows children to learn how to take risks. It encourages the development of curiosity. Many of the most successful inventors, scientists and artists can point to insights that they have acquired while being playful. A playful mind is a what-if mind where a mind dominated by work can so easily find itself caught up in its own predictable patterns of stressed living.

Games are enjoyable activities in which one or more players participate in some kind of structured activity. They can be an excellent way of engaging learners and of having fun when learning. Of course, the more competitive games will have losers and not everyone likes losing even in a game! Also, there are certain topics which games might seem to trivialize.

Many games have been designed specifically to help you learn something and some games of learning specifically exist to test individual's knowledge; *Who Wants to be a Millionaire?* is a good example of a popular television version. Incidentally, the three options given contestants on the show – asking the audience (consulting your peers), phoning a friend or going 50:50 (narrowing the odds) – are good lifelong learning strategies.

> ‘It is requisite for the relaxation of the mind that we make use, from time to time, of playful deeds and jokes.’
>
> Thomas Aquinas

Equipping yourself with good books of family games and with lots of board and card games is as good a starting point as any.

As a parent you can help your child to learn a range of skills. Skills are expertises or competences acquired through learning. They can be mental, physical or social. In the early years it may involve learning how to hold a spoon, while much later on it progresses to learning how to say no to unwanted alcohol. Alongside skills, you are all the time helping your children to acquire knowledge and appropriate attitudes to life.

When your child reaches school age, you can continue to ensure that s/he engages in lots of informal learning by encouraging him or her to become involved with extra-curricular activities at school. These include activities such as drama, sports, chess and computers, outside of the normal school hours.

Increasingly, schools are running homework clubs. This is a special after-school club organized by teachers or other adults to help children with their homework. It is especially useful if parents have long working hours or feel that their child needs professional help. If you are choosing your child's school, you may want to ask about this. It may be especially helpful to you if you are a working parent.

The stages of child development

Children go though a number of key development stages, when their learning tends to be characterized by different approaches.

One of the most famous descriptions of the stages of child development was provided by Jean Piaget. Today these categories are useful guides; even though many psychologists believe that Piaget's categories are too rigid and do not take enough regard of social factors.

0–2 sensory-motor	Child recognizes objects as being different from him or herself and starts to act intentionally.
2–7 pre-operational	Child begins to use language although s/he can only use crude categories to describe objects. Child is still very much self-centred.
7–11 concrete operational	Child begins to be more subtle in his or her categorization of objects and can use number. Can think logically about people and events.
11+ formal operational	Child can begin to think more abstractly.

Knowing more about the learning needs of each of the key child development stages and what you can do as an adult to support children is very helpful.

While we now know that the stages of child development are not quite as rigid as Piaget implies, this kind of framework is potentially helpful to any parent. It suggests that you would not try to play a game involving abstract thought with a very young child, for example.

Often what a parent is doing is providing a safe context for exploration.

Scaffolding learning

Scaffolding learning is like scaffolding a house while you are rebuilding it. The scaffolding offers support and a means of accessing it.

Drawn from the work of Lev Vygotsky, the idea of scaffolding is a simple one. If a learner is stepping out of their comfort zone, then they need the help of an adult who can give them support, suggest techniques and so on to help them to achieve their goals.

Scaffolding in learning is essential. It allows us to grow and develop with support. If you were teaching your child how to ride a bicycle, then you might start with familiarizing him or her with sitting on the bike seat, then try riding with stabilizers, then set short targets for un-stabilized riding, with you holding the handlebars, and so on.

As your child grows older, you will find him or her increasingly influenced by his or her peers, often referred to as peer pressure. Children are very influenced by those in their class or friendship group. They are also influenced by fashion, as are adults. So, as a parent you may want to bear this in mind. There are ways in which you can influence your child's peer group, by taking the trouble, for example, to ensure that you invite a good range of children to your home so that your child can take part in activities which you can control or influence. The ideal will be for your child to be surrounded by other children who are curious, positive and determined.

Of course, pressure can work both ways. It can be positive, for example creating an atmosphere where everyone wants to share and learn. Or it can be negative, leading to a culture of racist name-calling. If you are a parent and are worried about the company your young child is keeping you might like to encourage your child to take up some new interests where he or she will mix with different groups or hold a special party or games afternoon to which you invite some new faces. Most importantly, you might like to remember to model the kinds of sharing and responsible behaviours you want to see in your child in everything that you do. That is the hard bit!

Another form of negative pressure can come in the form of favouritism. Favouritism is the unreasonable favouring of one person over another. Many of you will have memories of this from school, where the expression 'teacher's pet' describes this situation. Favouritism can continue into adult life and be damaging both in families and in workplaces.

If you think that you are the victim of this, then you may want to deal with it. Normally this involves expressing your concerns in as calm a manner as possible to the person concerned. If s/he is in a position of authority (your boss, for example) then you may want to take a colleague with you. If you are a parent it is particularly important that you show your love and attention as equally as possible to each of your children or they may well grow up with anger and hostility towards you.

Television can also be a challenge. Adults in the UK now watch an average of about three hours of television a night with more at the weekend. You do not need to be a genius to see that the time which is left and potentially available for other family activities is comparatively small.

Yet there is much that is educational and helpful on television. As well as the BBC and its websites, the Discovery channel and various other satellite channels are full of excellent material for learners.

Effective learners are smart about the use of the TV. They turn it off or use the video/DVD recorder so that it does not dominate their life. If you are a parent, you might like to think carefully about letting your child have a television in his or her bedroom and insist on some TV-free days and even weeks.

The same applies to computers, especially those with internet access. Computers can be enormously positive aids to learning, as you have seen on pages 89–90. A particularly contemporary skill which your child (and you) needs to acquire is 'searching'. Since the invention of the internet, the idea of a search has become more potent. Using search engines, like Google, a simple enquiry can throw up hundreds of possible answers on hundreds of different websites. Effective learners know how to:

- narrow their search by using keywords;
- use their common sense to check the status and reliability of the information they have found;
- check data by cross-referencing it to other sites.

Managing emotions

Much of parenting involves dealing with the emotions that inevitably fly around the home. Effective parents will constantly be explaining the boundaries within which their children can act. This will inevitably lead to conflict and, from time to time, tears.

As a parent you are also likely to be dealing with the emotional needs of your partner, too.

The emotional bank account

Everyone has heard of a bank account for money, but how about one for emotions?

The emotional bank account is a really useful concept invented by American writer Stephen Covey. As with a bank account, you can make deposits or withdrawals from an emotional bank account.

The central idea is that, in any human relationship, you need to keep each person's account adequately topped up so that they feel sufficiently loved and valued. So, for example, if you constantly make demands on your partner but never give support back to him or her, then the relationship may not work well.

If you like this idea, you might like to put it into practice in your life. If so, you could try the following steps:

1. Talk about the idea with someone who is close to you in your life.
2. Make an honest assessment about who has been making most 'deposits' recently and who has been making most 'withdrawals'.
3. Discuss the ways that each of you like to be appreciated emotionally by the other.
4. Try and put some of this into practice.

While verbal expressions of love are hugely important, emotions are equally easily conveyed through non-verbal communication. Non-verbal communication is the expression used to describe all the aspects of communication that do not involve words. Research suggests that how you say things is more important than what you say. Your tone of voice and body language are very important.

You might like to think about how often you look people in the eyes, whether there are times when people seem to be too close to you and how you use space generally.

When things seem to be going wrong

There are many times when parents fret that they or their children are 'going wrong'. Indeed, it is probably a normal condition of parenthood to feel a degree of anxiety.

A common concern that parents have is about whether their child is left or right handed.

Handedness

We do not yet know definitively why some people are right handed and others are left handed, although it seems likely that there is a strong genetic factor involved.

About 13 per cent of the population around the world are left handed. Often left-handed people seem clumsy when they are really just trying to cope with equipment (such as scissors) which was designed for right-handed people. Writing with a pen can be difficult for left-handed children as they tend to smudge their writing.

Most tools and equipment are made for a right-handed world. So your child may well experience more difficulty than their peers. What can a parent do? Rather than trying to do things in the opposite of what they know when teaching their children, in order to have the child see the hand movements in the proper direction, you might like to sit opposite your child rather than next to or behind him or her. A left-handed child is the mirror image of a right-handed one. So you can learn to be your child's mirror.

Most importantly, you can reassure your child that s/he is absolutely normal and special, as you would every other child.

Another common concern is spelling. English is one of the most complicated languages to spell. This is partly because it is a mixture of Anglo-Saxon and old French, each of which have different conventions, and partly on account of the way vowels changed during the Middle Ages, leading to many words ending in an 'e'. Then, with the invention of printing, for a long period there were many different possible spellings for the same words.

In the nineteenth century, with the publication of influential school grammar books, English spelling began to settle. Full of inconsistencies (i before e in believe, i after e in receive, for example) the oddities of spelling are best learned by rote (see page 206) and then practised in context.

With the growing importance of English as the global language of the internet, words are increasingly being spelled interchangeably in their American English and English English ways. Spell-checkers on computers can help you to a certain extent, but be aware that many are pre-set to American-English spellings.

How to help your child with spelling

The following are some things you might like to try:

1. Encourage your child to have a go and offer praise every time a word is spelled correctly.
2. Try not to over-correct your child's spelling. This can be very de-motivating.
3. If your child writes a story for you, concentrate on the story first and only later on the spelling.
4. Try to find at least four correct spellings for every wrong one.
5. Play word games like crosswords and I-spy.
6. Encourage your child to use a junior dictionary or spell-checker on the computer.

Another cause for concern is the way children speak, especially with regard to stammering. One of the most important things you can say to your child is that, however painful it is for him or her, what you say is much more important than how you say it. There are all sorts of practical tips which will help those who stammer to manage their condition.

How to help a child who stammers

You might like to try these suggestions from the British Stammering Association:

1. For five minutes at least three times a week, daily if you can manage it, arrange a time in the day when you can give your child your full attention in a calm and relaxed atmosphere.
2. Slow down your own speech when you talk to your child, as it will make it easier for him or her to follow what you are saying and help him or her feel less rushed. This can be more helpful than telling the child to slow down, start again or take a deep breath.
3. It may help to pause for one second before you answer him or her, or ask a question. This slow, less hurried way of speaking gives your child time before answering.
4. Use the same sort of sentences your child does – keep them short and simple.
5. Keep natural eye-contact when s/he is speaking. Do not look away when s/he stammers.
6. Reduce the number of questions you ask. Always be sure that you give your child time to answer one before you ask another. Children can feel under pressure when asked a lot of questions at once. Encourage everyone in the family to take turns to talk. This will reduce the amount that your child is interrupted and that s/he interrupts others.
7. Praise your child for things s/he does well. This will help to build confidence.
8. Respond to the behaviour of the child who stammers in the same way as that of a child who does not stammer. Discipline needs to be appropriate and consistent.
9. Try to avoid a hectic and rushed lifestyle. Children who stammer respond well to a routine and structured environment at home and at school.
10. Stammering can increase when a child is tired. Try to establish regular sleep patterns and a regular healthy diet.

If you are worried about these or any other matters, you need to see an educational psychologist. As the name implies, this is a specific kind of psychologist who specializes in understanding child development and in working with teachers and others to help children with specific learning conditions.

For specific information about conditions like dyscalculia, dyslexia and dyspraxia, see Chapter 18.

Your own family learning

Important as your family are, it is essential that you make time for your own planned learning at and from home. One really useful step you could take is to make sure that you have someone who can act as your buddy or critical friend.

An LP

Developed by the author as a concept, an LP or learning practitioner (like a GP) is a friend or colleague who does for your mind what your GP does for your body – gives you feedback and advice whenever you need help. In an ideal world everyone has an LP.

If you like this idea, you might wish to try the following steps to get yourself an LP:

1. Make a list of all your really close a) friends or family members and b) colleagues.
2. Study the list. Who would you like to discuss the progress of your own learning with?
3. Look back at the sections on coaching and feedback. Who on your list seems most likely to have the kind of qualities which would help you?
4. Gradually narrow down the list. It is important that anyone you approach is totally trustworthy and someone whose personality you think would complement yours.
5. Approach your top choice. Explain that you are interested in meeting up from time to time, calling on the telephone or emailing with a view to developing a mutually satisfactory relationship as 'critical friends'.

When it all gets too much for you, why not take yourself off into a quiet part of the house or garden and actively seek to relax (see also page 76). You might like to take up yoga or something similar.

Yoga is an ancient Indian practice, dating back to 2500 BC. It is a scientific system designed to bring people health, happiness and a greater sense of self. In yoga, the body and mind are linked to create a state of internal peace, helping an individual to be flexible, accepting and whole. There are a number of different kinds of yoga, each with slightly different techniques.

People who regularly use yoga report that it helps combat stress and helps circulation, movement and posture. Yoga employs stretching postures, breathing, and meditation techniques to calm the emotional state of the mind, and tone the body.

Ageing happily

There is no doubt that one of the best ways of staying happy and healthy is by learning throughout your life, especially as you get older, contrary to some of the popular myths. Exercise also helps, especially when, at around 50 years of age, many people experience a slowing down of brain activity.

Use it or lose it

You may well have heard of this idea, as it has become popular.

Is it true? Technically yes. From early on in your life your brain cells die away and this process, sometimes referred to as 'neural pruning', continues as you get older.

But the fact is that, with more than 100 billion nerve cells, you still have plenty of brain power and are capable of learning new things until the day you die. In any case, it is the connections between cells that matters most, and you still have plenty of possibilities left even when you are much older and have lost a few brain cells.

It is also true that, the more you use your brain the better (in fact studies have shown how good health in later years correlates with the amount of learning you do).

Is it helpful? Not really as it scares more than it encourages!

Formal opportunities

As you will have already discovered in your life to date, formal education is what most people associate with learning. But as *Discover Your Hidden Talents* has been at pains to point out, the two are not the same thing at all.

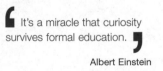

> 'It's a miracle that curiosity survives formal education.'
>
> Albert Einstein

Paradoxically, one of the main challenges for many effective lifelong learners is actually getting the best out of the formal system. For the very attributes that they have developed – all those suggested by the 5Rs – often run counter to educational systems which are very delivery oriented and often a bit too quick to use crude methods of assessment.

Lifelong learning is essentially about finding your personal best – discovering the hidden talents within you. Yet much of formal education is a thinly disguised competition – a trial of ability or an attempt to do better than someone else at something. Of course, in the great scheme of things, human beings are where they are as the result of a process of natural competition, and being able to deal with competitive pressure is undoubtedly an essential life skill.

In learning, competition can be a force for good if it provides motivation for an individual to improve. Or it can be a less helpful influence if learners end up seeking marks or grades rather than enjoyment and understanding. Worse still, it can be counter-productive contributing to low self-esteem and disenchantment with learning. And, of course, people respond differently to competitive pressures.

Sometimes it is possible to hit the target but miss the point.

> When you are content to be simply yourself and don't compare or compete, everybody will respect you.
>
> Lao-Tzu

Many parents have to take difficult decisions about the amount of competition they think will suit their child in his or her school. While it is tempting to assume that a school that boasts about its academic successes is a good school, it is equally important to find out how a school ensures that individuals achieve their potential. In terms of becoming an effective lifelong learner, it is undoubtedly more important for children to achieve their personal best than be better than someone else in their class.

It all starts with school. And then there is the whole apparatus of examinations and testing which are associated with formal education.

Types of school

There are, of course, many different kinds of school.

First there are state schools, all those schools provided by the state and funded indirectly through taxation. These schools are free in the UK. Some state schools are also church schools – having an association and being partly funded by the church.

There are then various levels of school from nursery (up to four years old), primary (four to eleven) and secondary (11 to 16 or 11 to 18). In some areas of the country there are sixth form colleges specializing in the 16 to 19 age range. In some parts you can still find middle schools, typically dealing with children between the ages of nine and 13. State schools dealing with pupils up to the age of 16 are divided up into local education authorities who have a role in providing certain services to them and overseeing their quality.

The local education authority, often shortened to LEA, is the name given to the function of local government in England, Wales and Scotland which has responsibility for running education in your area. If you are a parent, then you may need to contact the LEA when your child first goes to school, when your child is going to secondary school and about matters such as school term dates or, if your child has special educational needs, to find out about support from an educational psychologist.

Recently a body called the Learning and Skills Council (LSC) was given control of all educational institutions in the 16 to 19 age range, so although these may be in the same LEA as the secondary school your child goes to, a sixth form college's main allegiance will be to its funding body, the LSC.

As well as state schools there are private schools. These are schools which charge fees. They are not subject to the same controls affecting state schools and are consequently able to offer additional educational opportunities. 'Junior' private schools are often known as preparatory schools, sometimes abbreviated to prep schools. These normally cater for children aged four to 13. Schools for older pupils are known as public schools (like Eton, Harrow, Winchester and so on). The age of transfer to public schools is often at 13 not 11, which may present challenges to some pupils if they are moving from one system to another.

Two particular kinds of private schools are worth a specific mention:

- *Montessori schools* In 1907 an Italian doctor, Maria Montessori, opened a school for children living in the slums of San Lorenzo. She was convinced that young people learned best when engaged in purposeful activity rather than simply being fed information and that it was essential to satisfy the needs of the whole child. She inspired an international movement of schools based on these ideas. In many areas of the country there are Montessori schools, especially for younger children.

- *Steiner schools* Based on the approaches advocated by Rudolph Steiner, Steiner schools place emphasis on the whole development of the child, including a child's spiritual, physical and moral well-being along with academic progress. There is a strong emphasis on social abilities, with formal learning beginning later than in many schools. Learning is often themed so that it is less fragmented than in the subjects you would find in most schools.

There is always the option of private tuition. Parents have long bought private tuition to enable their children to learn a musical instrument or to go to dance or drama classes. There are a range of other areas for which a private tutor might be helpful, from dyslexia to foreign languages. Adults may also seek private tuition to help them learn something with which they have difficulty.

Most state schools are non-selective – admission is not based on ability – although there are many faith schools and a growing number of specialist schools (which seek to gain an expertise and reputation for specific subjects and which may operate selection procedures for pupils wishing to go to them).

Although, in theory, the government is committed to open enrolment (you choose where you want to send your child to school) in practice limited school places mean that many parents do not have much choice.

Any parent choosing a state school for their child would be well-advised to look around both within the LEA and beyond it, especially in urban areas where travel between LEAs is quite practical.

Factors to consider when selecting a school for your child

These include, in no particular order:

distance
transport
needs of your child
Ofsted report
local reputation
the headteacher
other teachers
the feel of the school
ethos – traditional or progressive
uniform
size
subjects available
diversity of students
extra-curricular opportunities
language provision
sports provision
how the school deals with you as a parent
your own child's views, especially as s/he gets older.

The organization of schools

UK state schools divide the statutory years of schooling into four Key Stages:

5–7	Key Stage 1	11–14	Key Stage 3
7–11	Key Stage 2	14–16	Key Stage 4.

There is also a growing emphasis on the provision of pre-school education in the three to five age group.

Much of learning is social and consequently takes place in groups. There are many different ways of grouping learners, both in formal and informal learning situations. Groupings could be by interest, age, ability or availability, for example. If you are embarking on a course, you may wish to find out the rationale behind any grouping decisions. Similarly, if you are a parent you may wish to understand your child's school's attitude towards groupings.

Children may be banded (broad ability groupings) put into sets (grouped by ability in individual subjects) or taught in mixed ability groups, sometimes in their class group (at primary school) or their tutor group (at secondary school).

Research has shown that, in any group, what tends to happen is that the group establishes its own norms of behaviour. This can be positive – for example if the group sets out standards of conduct – or less good if the group starts to 'dumb down' the learning.

All state schools are subject to the national curriculum. This was introduced in most of the UK as part of the Education Reform Act in 1988. The national curriculum specifies which subjects and what parts of these subjects should be taught in schools at each of four Key Stages.

All pupils need to learn English, maths and science, along with geography, history, art, drama, physical education, a modern foreign language, religious education, PHSE (personal health and social education) and, most recently, citizenship.

In the last few years there has been a considerable focus on literacy and numeracy (English and maths in the old language). In both cases there has been a deliberate attempt to use the best of the old methods along with the best of the more progressive ones. The teaching of reading has recently been re-analysed with a return to methods which include phonetics. (A phoneme is the smallest unit of sound that you can make, smaller than a syllable. So CAT can be sounded C – A – T.) There is much debate about the use of phonetic approaches in the teaching of reading, with the consensus being that phonetic approaches and those which simply enjoy stories without stopping to break up new words are helpful.

Rote learning

Rote learning, or learning by heart as it is sometimes called, is a useful strategy for certain aspects of learning. Using the principle that repetition and regular reinforcement of learning helps the learning to stick; going over something again and again can help things like times tables, tricky spellings or lists of facts to remain in the mind.

Rote learning will not be effective where what is being learned is ambiguous or complex. For in rote learning there can only be one answer and there is not much thought involved. This allows the learner to have only a fairly passive relationship with the 'fact'. Whereas if there are, for example, a number of possible explanations for something, then the learner's judgement and opinion-forming senses can become engaged.

The government's numeracy strategy in schools makes considerable use of rote learning.

The content of any curriculum was once thought to be the facts of whatever it was that you were learning. Of course it is much more than this, encompassing feelings, beliefs and experiences. Content is the word that you will find in the brochures of schools, colleges, universities and online providers to describe what you might choose to enrol in.

In some schools, partly as a result of organizations like the Campaign for Learning, the RSA (Royal Society for the Encouragement of Arts, Manufacture and Commerce) and a number of universities, there is a growing interest in the teaching of learning to learn – a recognition that the content of the 5Rs is as legitimate for pupils as it is for lifelong learners.

So, a recent UK Minister for School Standards, David Miliband, was emphatic about this point in 2002:

> For young Britons in the twenty-first century, teaching needs to serve three functions: the transmission of knowledge for a world built on information, the broadening of horizons in a country still scarred by disadvantage, and learning how to learn in preparation for a lifetime of change.

Thinking skills are intimately connected with learning and recently schools in England have realized that they are important enough to be taught to children. Techniques include analytical thinking, problem solving, questioning, creative thinking, conceptual thinking and practical thinking.

The science and art of teaching children – pedagogy – is changing. Our theories of what is going on have changed dramatically. Teachers used to think of children as little vessels to be filled up or empty slates to be written on. Most contemporary educationalists see this as a far more complex task of preparing to learn throughout their lives, just as is being described in *Discover Your Hidden Talents.*

> Facts alone are wanted in life. Plant nothing else, and root out everything else. You can only form the minds of reasoning animals upon Facts: nothing else will ever be of any service to them. This is the principle on which I bring up my own children, and this is the principle on which I bring up these children.
>
> Charles Dickens, (Mr Gragrind, *Hard Times*)

Waiting time

The tendency in many learning situations, especially in the classroom, is to encourage learners to contribute answers as quickly as possible. Research suggests that:

1. This may disadvantage quieter more introvert learners.
2. It can lead to simplistic answers where more thought would produce better ones.
3. It can create an overly competitive environment.

Allowing more waiting time in learning can be a useful approach.

Schools, colleges, universities and other not for profit organizations have a group of individuals – a governing body – who act as a board overseeing the strategy of the institution. If you are a parent you might like to consider becoming a parent-governor at your child's school. If you work in business and have an interest in education you might like to consider becoming a governor of a local school.

Very occasionally, things go badly wrong at school. Consequently there is an outside chance that your child might be excluded if s/he commits a serious misdemeanour. Exclusion, when applied to education, refers to the rare occasion that a school bars one of its pupils from attending. If your child has seriously misbehaved, then you will be required by his or her school's headteacher to attend a formal meeting. Children can currently be excluded on a temporary basis for up to 15 days, and in the majority of cases, after something of a shock, are readmitted. If your child continues to misbehave there is a chance that a temporary exclusion would become permanent and his or her education would continue in a pupil referral unit.

All schools are inspected from time to time by an organization called Ofsted – the Office for Standards in Education. This is the public body responsible for inspecting and publishing reports about state schools. If you are a parent looking for a school for your child you can look up the most recent report about any school on Ofsted's website.

Supporting your child

In the classroom it is the job of the teacher to teach in such a way that your child's needs are met. Increasingly, teachers may be helped by a teaching assistant. As well as being an extra pair of hands, teaching assistants may also have specialist functions, for example coaching reluctant readers or developing the school's use of computers.

Pastoral care is the more general term used in schools, colleges and universities to describe the kind of care that involves you as a whole person. Its focus is not your academic or vocational work, but your health and well-being. Schools have long been aware that the pressures of schooling can get to children. All schools have a pastoral system designed to support the all-round needs of children. If your child is not happy, then ask to speak either to his or her teacher (at primary school) or to the tutor or head of year/house (at secondary school). A few schools have a school counsellor, too.

It may be that your child has special educational needs, either because s/he is very gifted or because extra help is needed. Some children with learning difficulties receive what is a called a 'statement'. This is a statement of their special educational needs and is designed to ensure that extra funds are available to support your child. This process, known as statementing, is carried out by your LEA. Although it can be distressing for parents and children, statementing is designed to be a positive process and one which will produce more resources for your child's school to use to help your child learn.

But the phrase 'special educational needs' is a broad one, used to describe a wide range of issues which prevent learners from learning as effectively as others. These include ADHD, dyscalculia, dyspraxia and dyslexia, as well as more general conditions, all of which you can read more about in Chapter 18. Of course there is a real sense in which we all have special educational needs. It is good to remember this if you are feeling in any way that the phrase is itself a negative one.

All children will be set homework to complement the education that takes place during the school day. Ideally, homework involves exploratory activities that will further reinforce learning at school and more open-ended tasks that can better be done at home rather than at school. If your child is getting homework that s/he does not seem able to do, go and talk to your child's class teacher or form tutor.

As a parent, your assistance in getting your child to organize his or her time and your help as a coach will be necessary. Try not to do it for them!

> 'Doing your child's homework is a bit like believing that you can get into shape by watching someone else exercise.'
>
> Lawrence Cutner

Schools hold evenings – parent–teacher evenings – when parents are invited to speak to their children's teachers and review progress. If you are a parent of a primary-age child you might like to make a point of looking through all of his or her books so that you have some understanding of what has been taught. Make sure that you make a note of any important questions you want to ask a teacher. If you do not get enough time (parent–teacher evenings are often quite stressful occasions) then insist on a separate private meeting.

Alternative education

Home education is the long established legal right of parents to provide an alternative education for their children at home. There are currently some 90,000 (1 per cent) of children of compulsory educational age in the UK who are educated at home.

If you are a parent and thinking about becoming a home educator, then there are many specialist organizations from which you can receive advice. Of these, Education Otherwise is one of the most widely respected; see www.education-otherwise.org

In recent years students have begun to have to contribute towards the costs of their tuition at university (fees) and, in many cases, taken advantage of a government backed loan system which allows them to borrow money and only pay it back when they are earning later in life.

Going off to university

Once your child leaves school, s/he may well want to go to university. Indeed it is the current government's hope that 50 per cent of all young people will do this. And even if they do not, it will increasingly be very uncommon for a young person not to be in some kind of formal education between the ages of 16 and 19.

Your child's secondary school will be able to advise you and him or her as to how you choose and apply for a university during the autumn term of the last year at school.

Young people increasingly opt for what is known as a 'gap year', when they travel the world or get a job or undertake some voluntary work in an attempt to broaden their horizons.

Continuing your own formal education

Many adults choose to continue their own formal education throughout their life. This can be a life changing experience, as in the classic film *Educating Rita*. Or it can be a gentler one. It could involve courses of study at university, college or one of the many other organizations, some of which are online.

You may come across various terms:

Higher education The general term, sometimes called HE, for university-level education.

Further education Further education, or FE as it is often shortened to, is the term used to describe education beyond school which is not at university level, especially at colleges. However, in today's fast-moving educational world, the specific use of this term is becoming more flexible.

University Before the nineteenth century there were only six universities in the UK – Oxford, Cambridge, Aberdeen, Edinburgh, Glasgow and St Andrews. The early universities were usually linked to the Church and were established between the thirteenth and fifteenth centuries.

A number of universities were established in the nineteenth and early twentieth centuries as a result of the Industrial Revolution and the demand for highly skilled people. These universities were generally established in major industrial centres, such as Birmingham, Manchester, Newcastle-upon-Tyne and other big cities.

In the 1960s more new universities were created. This was largely due to the need for places caused by a boom in the birth rate after the Second World War.

In 1992, UK polytechnics were made into universities. Today you may also find the term'university college' being used as there are, at the time of writing, seven institutions in the UK that can legally call themselves that.

The Open University (OU) Founded in 1971, the OU is a very different kind of university. For, as its name implies, it is open to all. Its undergraduate level courses do not require any formal entry qualifications and more than a third of people starting these courses have qualifications below conventional university entry requirements. Despite this, around 70 per cent of all OU students successfully complete their courses each year. The OU is the UK's largest university, currently with over 200,000 students. Two-thirds of the students are aged between 25 and 44. It currently represents 22 per cent of all part-time higher education students in the UK.

Correspondence courses In the middle of the nineteenth century, in England, Isaac Pitman had a great idea. He would teach shorthand by correspondence. This idea was quickly adopted by universities in the UK, USA and Australia. So began the history of distance learning, in other words learning without having to go to a school, college or university, made possible by the phonograph, postal service, telephone, radio, television and now the internet. Distance learning is also known as flexible learning. Today's version of correspondence courses is a thriving industry, including the OU and the first government backed online learning institution – learndirect – set up in the UK in the 1990s, and many other private providers.

The Workers' Educational Association (*WEA*) The WEA is the UK's largest voluntary provider of adult education. Founded in 1903 to support the educational needs of working men and women, it provides access to education and learning for adults from all backgrounds, and, in particular, those who have previously missed out on education. Operating out of many local and regional centres, the WEA currently runs some 10,000 courses each year, providing learning for more than 110,000 adults of all ages and drawn from all walks of life. Courses are created and delivered in response to local need, often in partnership with local community groups and organizations. See www.wea.org.uk

Adult education You may also come across this more general phrase to describe learning opportunities. A helpful website is www.niace.org.uk

Finding your way around the examination and assessment system

If you go to school in the UK you are likely to sit more school exams than in almost any other country in the world. You will be examined at seven, 11, 14, 16, 17 and 18. Unfortunately, only some of this assessment is actually helpful to either the pupils or to the schools which have to administer it.

> Our theories determine what we measure.
>
> Albert Einstein

The true purpose of assessment is to help you to become a better learner by giving you helpful feedback on your progress so far. Assessment is measurement of some aspect of learning, for example knowledge, skills, progress and needs. Assessment can be carried out by an organization (such as a university, a school or an examination board) or by an individual (like a coach, a piano teacher or a parent) or, of course, by yourself. All effective learning involves feedback and taking stock. It follows that effective learners need to become good at assessing their progress.

Assessment is most effective when it is undertaken for the purpose of helping learners to learn more effectively by providing feedback which they can use. Such action might involve trying a different method, re-thinking an approach, finding out more and so on. It works well when the learner is fully involved in the process of assessment, understanding the language and approaches being used. Assessment is widely used as a means of ranking individuals or as a test of the effectiveness of a particular course. Often marks or grades are given as the result of the assessment process. In this case, it is helpful for the learner to understand as much as possible about the criteria being used for the allocation of these scores.

There are many different types of assessment, of which the most common kinds described are: diagnostic, formative, summative and self-assessment.

Diagnostic assessment The purpose of diagnostic assessment is to describe the abilities, potential or needs of a learner before s/he embarks on a particular learning activity. The diagnosis can then be used to match a learner to the learning on offer, to ensure that the learning is at the appropriate level, to put learners into groups or to ascertain any specific needs which a learner may have. This might include provision for those with visual impairments or auditory impairments.

Formative assessment The purpose of formative assessment is to provide learners with regular feedback on their progress throughout any episode of their learning. This could be in oral or written form. Formative assessment encourages learners to become more reflective. It allows learners to adapt their approaches, developing tools and techniques as necessary. It helps teachers to adapt their teaching in the light of the information that they receive. Examples of effective approaches include: interviews, peer review, diaries, journals, learning logs, profiles, records of achievement and various other self-assessment approaches. Researchers have found that regular formative assessment improves performance by a measurable amount.

Summative assessment The purpose of summative assessment is to mark, grade or describe learning which has been undertaken over a period of time. This could be as simple as a cook tasting the meal that s/he has produced or as complex as a university publishing the results of a three-year degree course. Summative assessment can involve grades or marks (as in examinations or tests) or passing or failing (when you take a driving test) or words (as in a citation for an award for an actor or actress). Dealing with the results of summative assessments of learning in which you have been involved can be a stressful process.

Self-assessment Self-assessment is the important process, essential in all effective learning, whereby the learner monitors his or her own progress. For this to be effective, you need to have clear indicators of your progress and a simple way of expressing those that you can understand.

How to use assessment to help you in your learning

You might like to try the following suggestions, either from your own point of view as a learner or in helping your child.

1. If you are undertaking a course, find out how it is being assessed and what that will mean for you.
2. Whenever you are trying to learn something, ask yourself: 'How am I going to tackle this?' and then 'How did I do?' followed by 'What could I do better next time around?'
3. Always ask for specific feedback in words, either written or spoken, as well as any grades or marks that you might be given.
4. Focus on your strengths – what you have done well.
5. Then look at your weaknesses – things you could do better next time around. Try to be specific about what you mean and how you could improve.
6. Find ways of reflecting on your learning that work for you.

Much of what goes on in schools is summative assessment. While this gives you some measure of your child's comparative achievement it does not necessarily help him or her to learn more effectively.

Most of the school and university system uses numbers or grades to measure progress. There are four main approaches:

1. Using numbers/grades where a certain proportion will always get As, Bs and so on regardless of how good they are.
2. Using numbers/grades where these are related to a set of criteria, so you get the grade if you have achieved a certain standard.
3. Pass or fail (like the driving test).
4. Using words, either written or spoken, to give you specific feedback on progress.

Research has shown that the last type of measurement is the most helpful to learners and also assists them in achieving higher results.

Assessment for learning

According to Paul Black and Dylan Wiliam, the two professors of education who founded much of the original thinking, assessment for learning is the process of seeking and interpreting evidence by learners and their teachers to decide where the learners are in their learning, where they need to go and how best to get there.

You might think that this is common sense and that all assessment should do this. But sadly this is not the case in many schools. Too often assessment is of learning and of learners. Its purpose is to check up on either the teacher or the pupil and to provide comparative data.

Schools which stopped giving marks or grades and instead gave pupils detailed helpful feedback on their work, either in writing or verbally, found that their pupils' exam scores went up!

Within this overall approach, it may be that your child is tested within specific subject areas. One of the most common of these is reading. Reading age is a measure used by teachers to describe reading ability in terms of the standard reached by an average child of that age. So, if you were a very good reader, you might have a chronological age of 11 and a reading age of 16 and vice versa. The main elements of deciding on reading age are lengths of words and complexity of sentences. (Many tabloid newspapers have a surprisingly low reading age when their stories are examined using this process.)

Other specific tests include: aptitude, CAT (cognitive abilities test), comprehension, intelligence, multiples choice and SAT (standard assessment test):

Aptitude tests Aptitude is a measure of an individual's ability to achieve and learn something, and can be used to describe skills in a range of different areas, from verbal to mathematical or interpersonal to design. Aptitude tests measure this potential. Good aptitude tests do not depend on what you already know, but seek to give you the chance to show what you could do in the future. Schools, universities and businesses increasingly use aptitude tests as part of their selection process. Almost inevitably, these tests do depend to a certain extent on what you already know, not least because most of them rely on language, sometimes on specific items of vocabulary.

Cognitive abilities tests (known as CATs) These are generally used with young people aged seven to 15. They seek to measure a broad range of 'thinking' abilities without becoming tests of particular subjects. Typically they will have questions dealing with verbal and non-verbal reasoning and involving numbers. CATs can help teachers find out more about their pupils' abilities and so plan teaching that will best suit them. Like all tests, however, they can simply be a means of ranking pupils. If you are a parent and your child is sitting CATs, you might like to find out more about the way these tests work by asking your child's teacher to explain them to you.

Comprehension tests Comprehension involves grasping or understanding a subject or situation with your whole mind. Often it is helpful to comprehend something not only technically (you know how to make an omelette) but also in the experiential sense (you know the taste of a fluffy omelette that is cooked but not over-cooked). Comprehension tests are a fact of life, whether at school or in the workplace. Consequently, it is worth learning how to give answers in the rather formal way that these tests often require.

Intelligence tests The most common tests of intelligence – the Stanford–Binet test and the Weschler intelligence scales – are derived from IQ. They principally assess linguistic and logical–mathematical intelligence. Recently various organizations have developed tests of EQ (emotional intelligence), which are much broader. A true intelligence test might measure intellectual and emotional learning power and give some indication of potential. It should not be a test of what you know or what you have experienced. As most intelligence tests involve language and figures and, in many cases, situations drawn from life, this is extremely problematical territory.

A more interesting thought might be: why do you want to use an intelligence test?

Multiple choice tests A kind of test or examination format developed because of its ease of marking which offers a number of possible answers for each question. Such approaches work relatively well for simple factual kinds of learning but do not work when complex areas are being considered or where there are a number of possible interpretations. If you are a parent, then you may want to be aware that your child will undoubtedly experience this form of assessment. If your child is anxious about it, you might like to make up some fun examples from your home life to help them gain confidence.

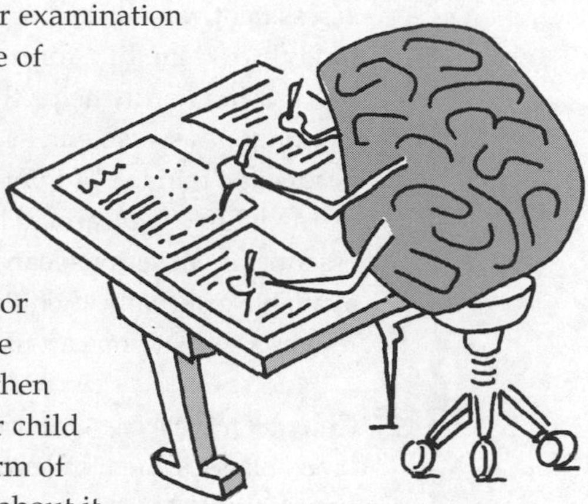

Standard assessment tests (known as SATs) When children are seven, 11 and 14, they take tests known as SATs (which measure what all children can do when asked the same questions). The tests are designed to ask questions only about what a child has been learning at school. Whether it is a good idea to test children at age seven is currently under review.

For a parent, these times can be very stressful for both your child and you, mainly because, for schools, the results are how their places in local and national league tables are decided. But in terms of educational opportunity, unless you are moving from one sector to another, or moving house and choosing a school which uses SATs' results to create ability sets of children, SATs have no significant bearing on the education that your child will be offered.

Other terms you might come across in connection with assessment include: coursework, continuous assessment, criterion referencing and norm referencing.

Coursework Many examinations require work to be produced throughout the course. This can take a large variety of forms – essays, investigations, photographs and so on – depending on the nature of the subject.

Continuous assessment Once upon a time the only kind of assessment was the test or examination at the end of the course, module or term. But, for many learners, this comes a bit late in the process and hardly helps them pick up feedback along the way. Continuous assessment, as its name implies, is assessment which occurs at a number of intervals throughout whatever is being learned. Effective learners know that continuous self-assessment is essential in all serious learning activities and, if the same is available externally, then the essential thing is to understand how it works so that you can use it to benefit your learning.

Criterion referencing Criterion referencing is one of the two main kinds of assessment in learning (the other being norm-referencing). Assessment using criteria as its reference points compares the standards reached by learners against objective criteria rather than against other learners. So, for example, in a test of wearing shoes you might score one for being able to put your shoe on, two for putting it on and tying your laces with help and three for doing all of this unaided. It does not matter how many people can do each of these three steps. They are awarded marks on the basis of the criteria attached to each score.

Norm referencing Norm-referenced tests or examinations compare a person's score against the scores of a group of people who have already taken the same exam. Regardless of how good a particular test result is it will be awarded a grade according to the predetermined numbers of A or B or C (and so on) grades which are to be awarded.

If your child is going to public school, then s/he may have to sit the common entrance. The common entrance exam is used by independent schools in the UK – public schools – to assess whether or not a child has an appropriate level of ability to do well at the school. It can be taken at age 11, 12 or 13. Set by an independent examination board – the

Independent Schools' Examinations Board – it is marked individually by the school to which a pupil has applied for a place. There is no common 'pass' mark. More academically selective schools set a higher pass mark, less selective schools a lower one. Day schools often set their own entrance exam.

An A–Z of current qualifications

Qualifications are one example of tangible evidence of success in learning. They can be awarded for courses of study, areas of personal interest and, in many professions, as part of a licence to practise (for example doctors, nurses, lawyers, teachers, accountants and so on). There are many of them and the qualification system in the UK is confusing, often muddled and frequently full of jargonistic words.

Most qualifications are based around examinations. These are formal, often externally managed, tests of what you have learned. Of course it is not just at school (or college or university) that examinations occur. There are many vocational examples, too.

The following is a mini A–Z.

A level (See also AS level, A2 level) A levels are the examinations that most pupils take at ages 16–19. Most universities use A levels, or their equivalents, as the basis for selecting students. First introduced in the 1950s, A levels cover a range of subjects which may be taught at school or at college. They normally take two years of study. Most A levels are assessed by examination. Some have coursework typically accounting for up to 20–30 per cent of the marks. Pupils might tend to take between two and six A levels, with three or four being the norm.

In 2000, A levels were split into two separate qualifications, AS level and A2 level: AS level can stand alone as a separate qualification. It has three units and counts as half the value of an A level. It is normally assessed at the end of the first year of sixth form study. It tends to cover the less demanding half of the syllabus. A2 is the second part of a full A level. It covers the more demanding material. The grade awarded at the end of the examination depends on performance in both the AS and A2 parts. There are five pass grades, A, B, C, D and E.

AS level AS level is the first year of A level.

A2 level This is the last year of A level.

Baccalaureate The Baccalaureate is an internationally recognized qualification – broadly similar in level to A level – and achieved during the last years of school. It is particularly popular in some European countries, but also used across the world. Wales already has its own Baccalaureate, but England, Scotland and Northern Ireland do not. Individuals or schools wishing to take a Baccalaureate examination normally take the International Baccalaureate.

It is designed to offer students a limited amount of choice across six main study areas. These areas are: language, second language, individuals and societies, experimental sciences, mathematics and computer sciences, and the arts. As well as the six study areas listed above, students taking an International Baccalaureate also have to study the 'theory of knowledge', write an extended essay and take part in activities or social programmes.

Bachelor's degree Often described by the letter BA or BSc, this is the level of higher education typically achieved after three years of study. See also Master's degree.

Credits Credits are one of the 'currencies' of learning. They are scores or values given to different courses. As such, they are particularly useful in many higher education situations where they have two particular functions. The first is to enable learners with non-standard examination results to work out if they have adequate qualifications to start a course. The second enables students to move between courses on a degree and 'clock-up' credit for bits of study or modules which they have undertaken.

In an ideal world it would be like living in the euro zone, with all institutions recognizing all credits easily and fairly, just like they recognize the euro as a common currency. However, in practice the learning market is not as streamlined.

Degrees Degrees are qualifications awarded by universities, normally after at least three years of study. These include: Bachelor's degree, Master's degree, Post-graduate certificate and diploma and Doctorate. If you are considering undertaking study which you hope will lead to a degree, then check out the status of the qualification carefully, as the word 'degree' is increasingly being used for qualifications that will not necessarily be recognized as such by all employers.

Diploma A diploma is a certificate or document certifying the successful completion of a course of study or set of experiences that is below degree level.

Foundation degree Launched in 2001, a new kind of degree strongly linked to the world of work and awarded by both universities and colleges. Typically a foundation degree can be turned into a full degree within 15 months further study.

GCSE The General Certificate of Secondary Education, or GCSE as it is more popularly known, was introduced in 1988 as a replacement for O levels and CSEs. Normally taken by students at age 15 or 16 in at least five subjects, GCSE is the last formal examination of the period of compulsory education which ends at age 16.

HNC/D The Higher National Certificate or Diploma is a vocational qualification (less academic and more geared to the world of work) which was introduced in 1973. It is roughly equivalent to the level of a GCSE – a level three qualification – although recently an A level equivalent option has been created (level four). If you'd like to know more about the various levels visit the Qualifications and Curriculum Authority's website, www.gca.org.uk

Master's degree Often described by the letters MA or MSc, this is the level of higher education typically achieved after four or more years study and is one level up from a Bachelor's degree

NVQ *(National Vocational Qualification)* NVQs are qualifications which are geared to the world of work. The central feature of NVQs is the National Occupational Standards on which they are based. These describe what a competent person in a particular occupation is expected to be able to do. They cover all the main aspects of an occupation, including current best practice, the ability to adapt to future requirements and the knowledge and understanding which underpins competent performance.

O level Before GCSEs were introduced, O levels were the examination taken by most people at age 16 at the end of their compulsory education.

Postgraduate degree Any degree level qualification that you take after an initial Bachelor's degree.

Accreditation is what you get when your learning is officially recognized, often after some kind of formal test or examination. It comes in many forms, for example a degree, a diploma, a certificate, an award, a badge, a scroll or a licence. Most governments have a national body whose job is to oversee accreditation and ensure that there is consistency of standards across the country.

Increasingly universities are recognizing that many adult learners may be much better assessed by some other method than A levels or their equivalent and are introducing more creative approaches.

Accreditation of prior experiential learning (APEL)

APEL is an informal way of giving learners credit for the skills that they have already acquired. It is especially useful for adults wishing to enter a course of study for which they do not have the necessary formal qualifications. It was pioneered by a number of universities and colleges throughout the world, including, in the UK, the Open University, as part of an attempt to attract students who had not acquired examination grades in the traditional way.

If you want to accredit your own prior learning then you need to reflect on what you have learned and when/how you learned it. This will involve your thinking carefully about how you could 'prove' to someone else that you had a particular skill. Examples of the kind of evidence you might use would include reports, photographs, certificates, sketches, essays, diaries, references or testimonials. Say you wanted to study for a degree in English literature but left school at 16 or 17, then you might use some of your own recent creative work along with a reference from your employer to show a university that you possessed the abilities they were looking for.

Most universities and colleges are prepared to consider APEL as a valid alternative to formal accreditation. Sometimes this will be called APL, sometimes APEL. The E signifies experience as opposed to academic study.

Endpiece

> I was thrown out of college for cheating on the metaphysics exam; I looked into the soul of the boy next to me.
>
> Woody Allen

Two thoughts.

'Cheating' in learning has long been associated with passing examinations by deception, perhaps by copying another person's results or illegally taking in material. This was particularly important in a world where examinations were essentially tests of factual knowledge.

So what might cheating involve today?

In the commercial world, cheating can be a breach of copyright, the theft of a brand or the use of someone else's intellectual property.

It is a paradox of learning that one of the most powerful ways in which your brain 'learns' is through imitation. Imitating others is always going to be a smart thing to do, therefore. See more on this on pages 283 and 284. So when does imitation become cheating?

When learning becomes education or training we must guard against 'teaching to the test' or training for a narrow range of competencies.

Goodhart's law

English economist Charles Goodhart invented the idea that when a measure becomes a target it ceases to be a good measure. This is of some interest to learners and considerable use to teachers who may wish to challenge externally created measures of what is valuable in learning.

12

Learning at work

Chapter 12

After the home the workplace is the preferred learning environment of most people.

Informal learning opportunities

If all of the learning opportunities at work were represented by an iceberg, then the part above the water would indicate the formal opportunities to learn and the much larger section below the waterline would be the many opportunities for informal learning. Yet for many people, learning at work is still synonymous with 'being trained'.

This need not be the case, as the range of imaginative ideas and techniques in the first part of this chapter show.

Informal learning includes many different approaches, as the table on the next page indicates. It is a version of work undertaken by Michael Eraut, one of the UK's leading thinkers about informal learning at work.

'Anyone who stops learning is old, whether at twenty or eighty. Anyone who keeps learning stays young. The greatest thing in life is to keep your mind young.'

Henry Ford

Different kinds of informal learning

Here are some examples:

	Implicit	Reactive	Deliberate
Past	Drawing on an experience in a meeting a year ago to help you now	As you are being interviewed you recall half-formed observations about previous events	Keeping a learning log
Present	As you are speaking you remember a story which illustrates the point you are trying to make	Scribbling some notes during a meeting	Making a list of learning points at the start of every meeting
Future	Unconsciously choosing a way of doing something because of past memories	Using a learning method you like when an opportunity arises, for example making a Mind Map™	Using a Personal Development Plan and setting personal goals

Learning and working are, in many people's views, a virtuous cycle (as opposed to a vicious circle); a series of events which continue to reinforce themselves positively, as in the diagram below.

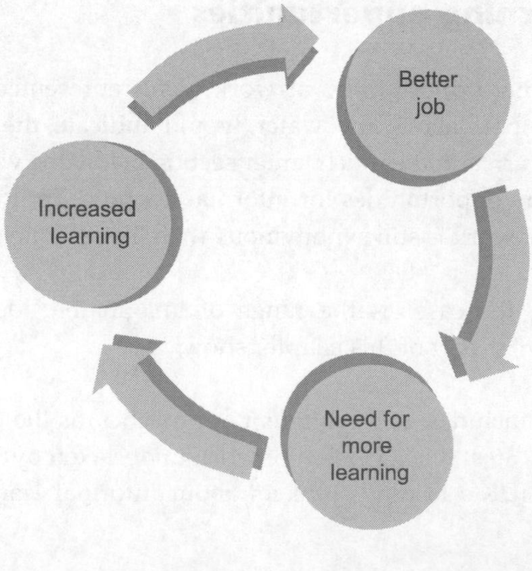

As you have already discovered, context – where you are, who is with you and how you are feeling – matters enormously in learning. For some, the environment of work is not very conducive to much planned learning. You might feel confident, for example, of your ability to develop an argument when chatting with friends, but go to pieces when put in front of your teacher or manager. Some people prefer informal learning, while others like more formal experiences.

> Curiosity is one of the most permanent and certain characteristics of a vigorous intellect.
>
> Samuel Johnson

In the workplace it is often a matter of finding out 'WIIFM' or 'What's in it for me?'

Historically, there have been two essentially different approaches to learning:

Just in case learning This is the kind of learning that has long been part of education systems the world over. You learn a range of subjects which you may or may not ever need to use, and

Just in time learning This is the kind of learning which is growing in importance in a fast-changing world and which is most common in the workplace. You learn what you need to know just before you need to know it.

Two other expressions which you may hear in the workplace describing learning are soft skills and hard skills. Soft skills, sometimes called people skills, are all the interpersonal skills you need to work effectively with others. Hard skills are the technical skills relating to a job. To be effective in today's working environment you need both hard and soft skills.

At work, as in the home or in your broader life, what you get out of your learning largely comes down to you and your own motivation.

The Pygmalion effect

Pygmalion was, in Greek mythology, a sculptor who fell in love with his own creation. In the play *Pygmalion* by George Bernard Shaw, Eliza Doolittle is taught how to lose her cockney accent and speak 'proper' English, but always knows that she is not a lady because of the way Professor Higgins treats her – as the flower girl that she was.

The Pygmalion effect is another way of describing the self-fulfilling prophecy. This theory has it that if you really believe you can do something (or if your teacher believes that you can do something) then you can do it. The effect works in reverse, of course, as in the play.

The implication for any parent is clear. The way you display your expectations of your children is really important. If they think that you have low confidence in their ability, they will perform less well. The same is true for managers and their staff.

You are, to a certain extent, what you want to be, although naturally there will be many barriers in your way to overcome. Ironically one of the most potent of these may be your own line manager who may not yet be convinced of the benefits of learning. (You could try showing them a copy of *Discover Your Hidden Talents* and suggesting the many ways in which your own performance might improve as a result of learning at work!) Also, there is the enduring problem of lower paid and part-time workers not having their learning needs adequately recognized.

The Hawthorne effect

Discovered at the Hawthorne Works of the Western Electric Company in the 1930s, where there was much interest in improving productivity, the Hawthorne effect describes the following phenomenon.

If you show particular interest in a process the process tends to improve regardless of whether your interest is, of itself, particularly helpful. Parents and managers take note! This gives you the green light to show interest in aspects of your child's learning whether or not you are confident that you have all the solutions.

However, the most likely objection your manager will have is that learning at work takes you away from your job. So, in the next section, there are a range of ideas and techniques which can be applied at work with minimal disruption.

An A–Z of non-intrusive methods of learning at work

In life, if you do not put anything in you are unlikely to get much out. The same is true of learning at work. So, while these methods are all far less unobtrusive than the traditional day's training course, they nevertheless require effort, planning and commitment. But because they are either very work-focused or short or part of working life they tend to be easier to fit into a busy work environment.

We know that learning pays at work, both for individuals and for organizations. It is, as many commentators have said, arguably the only source of sustainable competitive advantage available to contemporary organizations.

Action learning

Invented by Reg Revans in the 1980s for use in the coal industry in the UK, action learning is becoming increasingly popular with organizations, but the approach it suggests is also relevant for individuals in their private lives. Action learning is a process of inquiry. It starts with the identification of a real problem or issue and then a group of learners come together to find solutions through a process of enquiry.

Typically, this is how it works. A small group of individuals, often from different organizations and possibly with different professional backgrounds, come together for the specific purpose of learning together. This group is often known as a 'set'. Sometimes, one person acts as facilitator/adviser. The group establishes a trusting and confidential atmosphere in which it is safe to share difficult issues. Individuals take it in turn to describe one or more real business or organizational issues that they are currently struggling with. The group then decides which one (or more) of these they would like to tackle. In some cases the combined group expertise will be enough to provide useful answers to individual issues. But often a process of collaborative enquiry is called for. Normally action learning sets last over a period of months.

> "Why" said the Dodo, "the best way to explain it is to do it."
>
> Lewis Carroll, *Alice in Wonderland*

Action learning is profoundly different from other forms of organizational learning in the degree to which it is self-directed and relevant to real issues. It appeals to many managers because it is so work and issue focused that it hardly seems like learning.

If you are interested in putting action learning into practice, you might like to:

1. Identify a group of colleagues at work or who are your friends.
2. Make a commitment to spending a number of sessions together, say somewhere between three and 12.
3. Take it in turns to identify and describe real issues that are facing you
4. In the first session, decide whose issues you are going to explore first and agree a way of making sure that everyone in the group is happy that their needs will be met over the course of the time you plan to spend together.
5. In each session, see what ideas the group has to help solve each of the issues. Sometimes simply asking open-ended questions about the problem will get discussion going. Spend a few minutes before the end of each session agreeing what further research each person will do before meeting again.

Bite-size learning

First coined in the 1990s, this phrase describes very short episodes of learning. Unlike a course, which can last for a term or a year, bite-size learning can take as little as 15 minutes. The aim of bite-size learning is to make learning as accessible as possible to those who live busy lives.

Brainstorming

Created by Alex Osborn when working for a New York advertising agency in the 1950s, brainstorming involves a group of people generating ideas about a given topic. As ideas are generated they are written down, without anyone judging them and without stopping to explore them. The aim is to create as many ideas as possible in as free an atmosphere as possible on the assumption that some of the ideas will be worthwhile.

Brainstorming has possibly become the world's most used creative tool for thinking up ideas. While it can be helpful to defer evaluation (which can kill creativity stone dead) brainstorming tends to induce a sort of frenzy of talking which quieter and more reflective participants do not enjoy. Evidence suggests that the frame of mind of the participants and the culture in which the brainstorming takes place are critically important factors in determining the quality of the ideas produced.

Coaching

Coaching is one of the fastest growing kinds of learning at work. It involves two people – call them the coach and coachee – working together over an agreed length of time to identify issues which the coachee would like to explore or areas where s/he would like to improve and, with the help of the coach, plan ways of learning and behaving which will help. A coaching session lasts, typically, between 45 minutes and two hours.

There are a number of common models used in coaching. One of the more popular is the GROW model.

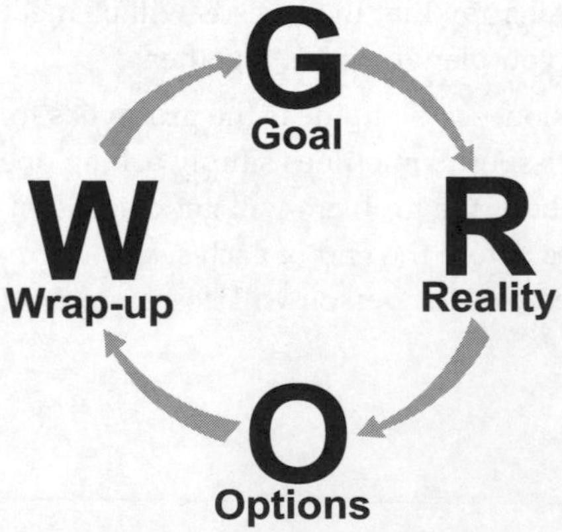

In a GROW session, the pattern of conversation follows these broad headings; The coach ensures that a clear goal for the session is agreed; The reality of the current situation is then explored; Why is it necessary? Who is involved? What are the issues? How many? How long? When does it need to be resolved by? and so on.

Other models include:

Story-telling This encourages the 'coachee' to see their life as an unfolding story over which they have control. It involves the use of stories, myths and metaphors to encourage the coachees to reflect on their situation.

Transformational This borrows an idea from Chris Argyris – double-loop thinking – and invents one on the back of this – triple-loop learning. The emphasis of the third loop is in engaging the motivation of the coachee to want to change. It is one thing to have shortcomings identified, quite another to want to do something about them.

Inner exploration This broad group of approaches involves a number of different, often psychologically grounded, techniques to focus inwards, exploring the coachee's self-belief, encouraging affirmations, visualization and so on.

Within these approaches there are many other possible variations, largely dependent on the character of the coach (for example, how directive s/he is) and the situation in which the coaching takes place.

Feed forward

Feed forward is a way of solving recurring problems.

It goes like this. You start by clearly describing your problem or issue in a single sentence, for example 'My problem is ...'. You then gather a small group of people around you, somewhere between two and six is ideal. They take it in turns to offer suggestions using this format: 'You might like to ....' After each suggestion you say 'thank you'.

When your 'advisory group' runs out of ideas, you stop and turn to helping someone else in the group with one of their issues.

If you would like to put feed forward into practice you might like to:

1. Gather a small group of friends or colleagues.
2. Take it in turns to think of issues.
3. Give it a try.

Force field analysis

Force field analysis is a useful technique, invented by Kurt Lewin, to explore the relative strengths of the impulses which make you want to act (driving forces) and those which prevent learning (restraining forces). In any situation you need to have more driving forces than restraining forces if you want to move forward. This theory is very helpful when dealing with change in life or in work and also when seeking to analyse your own learning, as can be seen by the example in the margin of how a person might analyse the value of accepting promotion.

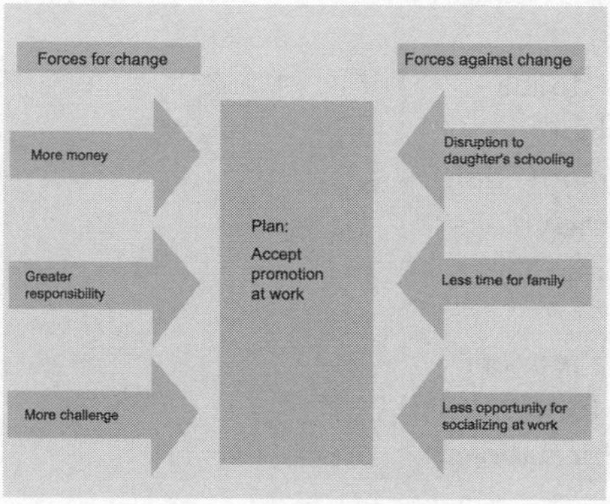

If you are interested in putting this into practice you might like to:

1. Identify the problem to be analysed.
2. List the key forces at work with one column for drivers and one for restrainers.
3. Prioritize the forces.
4. Decide on a course of action which maximizes the driving forces and minimizes the restraining ones.

Job swapping

As its name suggests, a job swap involves one employee changing places with another for a period of time, often as little as a day or so. The swap can be:

- with someone else in the organization at the same level;
- with someone else in the organization at a different level (the BBC showed how effective it can be to change places with someone who is much less senior than you in *Back to the Floor*);
- with someone from another organization.

Job swapping, when carefully prepared and when taken seriously, can give real insights into another person's job and be valuable for learning.

If you want to organize a job swap, you could:

1. Ask your manager if s/he might consider allowing you to try one. (Make sure that you are well-prepared about what the benefits would be for the organization as well as for yourself, for example increased flexibility, better performance, greater knowledge about what others do and so on).

2. Identify some possible job swap partners. If they are at roughly your level within the organization, then sound them out. If they are much higher or lower, get outline approval first.
3. Once you have identified your partner, arrange to meet them. Share each of your hopes and agree the practicalities. It sometimes works best to start with a short time, for example half a day 'being the other person' followed by some time together.
4. Once you have done the swap then meet up again. Review how it went. If you have any kind of internal magazine, a report of what you both learned would make an ideal article. Make sure that you share the benefits with your boss and with other colleagues.

Be careful that your job swap is not really a glorified job shadow (see below) as it is really important for you actually to do some of the things your partner does rather than just observe them.

Job shadow

A job shadow has one person shadowing another, sitting and walking alongside them to get a feel for the job. It is a good way of breaking someone into a new role or as part of an induction process.

Job rotation

Job rotation involves moving employees through a range of jobs so that they gain experience, become more flexible and understand more about their organization.

Some companies are beginning to explore job rotation as a legitimate alternative to giving someone one job, instead giving them a number of rotating roles. In such situations it is important to be clear about responsibilities. Job rotation is also helpful in allowing individuals brief experience of a role in order for them to clarify their career path.

Mentor

A mentor is a kind of coach, normally someone with experience of a specific subject or walk of life or type of work. Like a coach, s/he can offer you support and advice in your work or your life or both. Mentoring has a long and distinguished past, starting with the Ancient Greeks and taking in the idea of the master craftsman and the apprentice along the way.

Many organizations are beginning to see the value of mentoring. If you are offered the opportunity of having a mentor, then you may want to accept it. (You also may want to make sure that you and your mentor are compatible by asking whether you can have an initial trial meeting together before deciding on your mentor.)

Modern apprenticeships

An apprentice is someone who learns a skill by watching an expert and then practising with their guidance. In the sixteenth century a law was passed in England that made it illegal for anyone to enter a trade without having passed their apprenticeship, normally lasting seven years. The word comes from the French word *apprendre*, which means 'to learn'.

Watching someone else who is skilled and then practising what you observed is a powerful way of learning. Although originally used in the development of trades, such as carpentry or printing, apprenticeship is still relevant today in a range of professions, such as health, education and social work.

Recently the government has introduced something called a modern apprenticeship. There are two levels, one for apprentices and the other for advanced apprentices:

> Apprenticeships usually last at least a year and apprentices work towards a National Vocational Qualification at Level 2, Key Skills and, in most cases, a technical certificate. Advanced apprenticeships usually last at least two years and apprentices work towards a National Vocational Qualification at Level 3, Key Skills and a technical certificate. Apprenticeships offer a large range of training in 80 different sectors of industry, covering a huge range of subjects from health and social care to business administration.

On the job learning

Also known as sitting by Nellie (see next page), this remains a really valuable way of learning at work. This kind of learning works best when the employee is well prepared, the person being observed is willing and prepared and there is time for discussion and reflection on what is being learned.

Open learning

This is another term for flexible learning – learning which allows you to decide where and when much of it takes place.

Peer review

In many professions assessment by other colleagues is widely used. It is an effective means of ensuring high standards by sharing good practice and learning from others.

Self-managed learning

This approach, advocated by Ian Cunningham and others, assumes that, because learning is an entirely voluntary activity, we should know more about how you can manage your own learning. This means having control over what, how, when, where and, most importantly, why you learn.

Sitting by Nellie

A phrase to describe the informal learning alongside someone which goes on in organizations as an employee learns how a particular job is done by watching someone doing it. This approach can be very effective – 'Nellie' being a competent and communicative employee – much less so if not!

Six hat thinking

Six hat thinking is a classic lateral thinking technique created by Edward de Bono. The approach is an excellent way of getting the most out of creative teams and a gentle play with the saying 'putting on your thinking cap'. It recognizes that there are many different roles in the creative process and that it is sometimes helpful to be more explicit about this.

De Bono assumed that when a team is grappling with a problem, it may be helpful to be really clear about the different roles you can play. So he suggests that you wear six differently coloured hats and act according to the role that each one suggests.

White	=	You introduce neutral facts, figures and information
Red	=	You put forward hunches, feelings and intuitions
Black	=	You are logical and negative
Yellow	=	You are logical and positive
Green	=	You constantly come up with creative ideas for taking things forward
Blue	=	You act as the conductor of the orchestra, concentrating on managing the process of coming up with ideas successfully

There are all sorts of ways in which this can be used, but the simplest is just to play the roles that each hat suggests. You could add other colours and other roles.

You might like to try this technique using it in a social setting or as a warm-up item to a more serious meeting.

SWOT analysis

A SWOT analysis is not an extra keen learner but a method of analysing data. It takes its name from these four words: strengths, weaknesses, opportunities and threats. It is a very useful tool for analysing possible courses of action. Although it is often used in the workplace to help to determine future strategy, it is equally useful at home as a way of exploring possible decisions, for example moving home, changing school and so on.

Strengths	Weaknesses
Opportunities	**Threats**

If you are interested in using this technique, then you might like to:

1. Identify an area of interest, for example a new product you are thinking of developing.
2. Then share ideas on each of the four boxes.
3. Using this data, reflect on what you have learned and conclude on a best way forward.

Synectics

Created by William Gordon, synectics is a form of brainstorming that uses metaphors and analogies to help you to see the relationship between seemingly unrelated ideas. Unlike brainstorming, it seeks to evaluate as well as generate ideas.

Three approaches are commonly used:

1. Direct analogy – seeing how something is similar to something you are familiar with.
2. Personal analogy – pretending you are the object of the comparison, in other words using role play.
3. Symbolic analogy – developing a keyword or image to provoke ideas.

An essential difference between synectics and brainstorming is that critical comments are encouraged throughout the process.

If you are interested in trying this technique, then you might like to:

1. Define the problem: how it is experienced, the background, what has been tried and the possible scope of action.
2. Then express the problem as a wish or aspiration: 'It would be great if we could … .'
3. The group uses different creative techniques, for example direct, personal and symbolic analogies, as above: 'This is just like a …', If this were me I would …' 'This reminds me of a … .'
4. The group now focuses in on one or more solution areas and checks with the person who introduced the problem what they think about the different options.
5. The problem owner then paraphrases the idea he or she favours to check understanding of it.
6. The group identifies every possible positive feature of the idea and only after this process is exhausted are remaining problems listed and solved: 'What you need to do is … .'
7. Keep going until either time runs out or the person who identified the issue is happy.

Knowing what you do not know you know

In any organization there are different kinds of knowledge: first is explicit knowledge – the ideas and processes which have been written down or described. Often it is recorded in guides, manuals, directories and reports. Then there is tacit or implicit knowledge. Tacit knowledge, which cannot easily be stored or described, is the know-how which sits in people's heads. Some of the most important knowledge is tacit.

The traditional definition of knowledge used to be the remembering of previously learned material such as facts and opinions about the world. For most people there is an implied scale of knowledge which looks like this:

Data — Information — Experience — Intuition — Judgement — Values — Wisdom

Knowledge itself exists in a number of forms. These can be simplified as: know what, know how, know why and care why. Take the example of making an omelette:

Know what	It takes eggs, milk and butter
Know how	You have to whip up some eggs with milk and then cook them in butter in a pan without turning the mixture over until the last moment when you fold it in half
Know why	Eggs are good for us and an omelette is a light way of eating them
Care why	You can ruin the taste if you do not take care to …

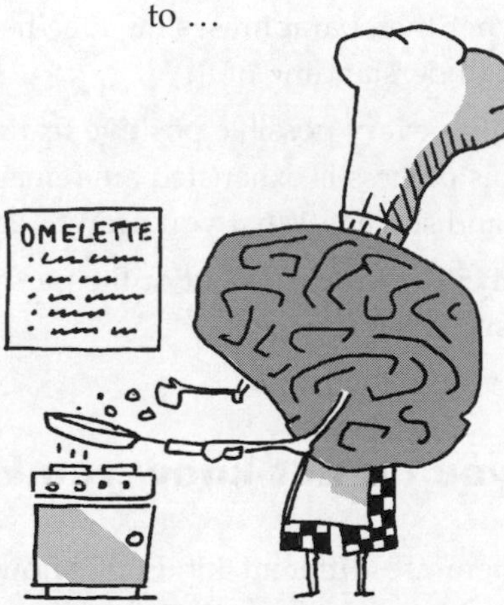

There are very few elements of knowledge which exist in isolation from the people who create or use them.

> Facts are generally over-esteemed. For most practical purposes, a thing is what men think it is. When they judged the Earth flat, it was flat. As long as men thought slavery tolerable, tolerable it was.
>
> John Updike

Somewhere in all of this are facts, although in a fast-moving world many of these change regularly. A fact is the true reality of something and is normally contrasted with a 'belief'. Much formal education is concerned with facts or 'know what'. Increasingly we are realizing that it is often difficult to be sure what is a fact and what is a 'best-we-can-do-at-the-moment' fact. Effective learners will be suspicious of people who tell them something is a fact and may want to find out more for themselves.

Knowledge management is the phrase that has been coined to describe what happens to knowledge in an organization. It has been developed at the same time as extraordinary developments in computer technology. Many people believe that, strictly speaking, knowledge cannot be managed only shared. The more you can do this effectively in an organization, the more your organization is going to be a learning one.

The learning curve

A learning curve is the graph that can be drawn to describe the speed at which a learner masters a new task. If it is steep, progress is fast; if flat, progress is slower. Different kinds of learning tend to proceed at different speeds. For example, changing a deeply held opinion may take a long time, while learning a small aspect of a computer program may be a quick task.

What kind of knowledge you need and which method of learning you choose in the workplace will be influenced by the likely learning curve of those who need to learn it.

Wherever you work, you have a right to expect a period of induction whenever you change jobs. This period of getting to know – induction – should be designed to help you settle in and, if new to the organization, find out about its history and values. If you have recently changed jobs and not been offered any induction it would be perfectly reasonable to ask your manager if you could arrange your own. You might like to shadow a small number of colleagues doing jobs in your area of work, as well as arranging to get to know how things are organized.

An important skill to acquire in any organization is being able to deal with interviews. Many things, from job appointments to entry onto courses, are determined by interviews – formal sessions where you are asked questions by one or more people.

How to get better at interviews

Here are some things to think about:

Beforehand

Think carefully why you want the job/course or whatever.
Look at any information that is available, for example a job or course description.
Make a list of all the things you are good at and match them to the description.
Find out more by searching the internet.
Think what to wear.
Arrive early.
Imagine that you are going to be successful.

At the interview
Make a positive first impression.
Have any notes you need ready.
Try and answer the questions.
If you do not understand the question ask the questioner to repeat it.
Ask questions.
Stick to what is true about you.
Come across as someone who is prepared and motivated to learn.

Afterwards
What went well?
What could have been better?
Make notes to remind you for next time.

In some workplaces it may be possible for you to become more involved as a workplace learning adviser and share some of your own passion for learning with others.

Learning representatives

Like heath and safety reps, a 'learning rep' has a voluntary role within a workforce to act as a promoter and supporter of learning and learners. First developed by the British trade unions' movement, learning reps have become reasonably common in the last few years.

Working in teams

Much learning and working takes place in teams. These teams may be groups of colleagues you work closely with or individuals gathered together for a specific project. For teams to work effectively, it helps if each member of the team has a clearly defined role. It may also be useful if someone takes on the role of facilitator.

> If a team is to reach its potential, each player must be willing to subordinate his personal goals to the good of the team.
>
> Bud Wilkinson

Although the role of a facilitator is largely associated with the workplace, the skills it involves are also extremely useful for parents. A facilitator is different from a teacher or a tutor or a coach or a mentor or even the chair. The job of a facilitator is to create a space for learning and exploration, to open things up and to engage individuals. Through a process of facilitation people can be enabled to take decisions which respect a wide variety of opinions. The job of a facilitator is not to tell people things or teach them or instruct them. There are many different styles of facilitating, some of which are very structured while others are more relaxed.

Why bother with facilitation?

It is very helpful when dealing with complex issues.

It ensures widespread participation in decision making.

You can reconcile different viewpoints.

It is good for getting the best out of people.

How to be an effective facilitator

Use the following suggestions as a starting point:

1. Make sure you know what the purpose of the session is and that you do your own preparation. This will involve understanding the topic to be covered and the likely perspectives of those who are going to be involved.
2. Lay down some simple ground rules, for example listening to others, speaking in a respectful way, looking for solutions and so on.
3. Outline your agenda or approach, including the time when the session will end and what you hope will have been achieved by then.
4. Make sure participants have a chance to introduce themselves.
5. If you are dealing with complex issues, give regular progress reports checking on what you think has been agreed. As you approach the end, start to give more regular time checks (for example, '50 minutes to go, let's see if you can move on to ...'), build in regular breaks but be clear about their timings.
6. Ensure that you use a variety of groupings and methods so that individuals, all of whom will have different preferred learning and working styles, feel that they have had a chance to be involved.
7. Make sure that the outcomes of the session are recorded in some way.
8. Ask for feedback on how it went and what you could do better next time.

Two ideas may be of interest to you as you observe those around you: both concern communication and its effect on others.

Transactional analysis

Transactional analysis a way of understanding the communication between people which can help you to know more about the kind of automatic responses which you give in certain situations. For example, you will 'transact' your communication very differently if you are talking colleague to colleague or parent to parent or parent to child.

You might like to 'listen' to yourself as you speak to different colleagues. Do you sound the same? If not, why not?

How much of what you say you believe in do you actually put into practice?

The theory in use

Chris Argyris developed a theory that suggests that people have a mental map as to how they act in certain situations. As a result of this he developed a helpful way of distinguishing between the theories we say we believe in and the ones we actually use in our lives. (He calls these the espoused theory and the theory in use.) He suggests that while it is common in organizations for individuals to say one thing and do another, if the gap between what people say and what they do gets too big it can be difficult.

For example, if you say that you believe in allowing your child to develop his or her own view of the world but spend your whole time telling him or her what to think, it may be problematic. Or in the workplace environment, where much of Arygyris's research was undertaken, you might explain your habit of interrupting a meeting by saying that an emergency had arisen. But the truth might be that you are very impatient and actually see your work as always taking priority over other people's.

Mental maps are important in a more general sense. For your map or outlook will largely influence your attitude to any learning that you undertake.

E-learning

Short for electronic learning, e-learning is much in vogue these days. It covers a range of learning involving computers, mobile phones and other hand-held electronic devices, often in tandem with the internet or an organization's intranet. The advantages of e-learning include its flexibility (anytime, anyplace and almost anywhere), the learner's control over content, method and pacing and the possibility to connect learners who live miles apart. These days, many employees have a computer on their desk connected to both the internet and an intranet.

You can learn with your colleagues online both asynchronously or synchronously. Asynchronous learning takes place when two or more learners are working together but not at the same time. An example of this kind of learning is distance learning, where correspondence takes place between a tutor and learners over a period of time. Asynchronous learning is a particular feature of e-learning using the internet. It occurs routinely when learners are using email (but are not online at the same time) or a discussion forum, whereas synchronous learning is actually happening at the same time, for example if you are having a teleconference and are online at the same time drafting a document.

The cybernetic approach to learning

Cybernetics is the science of studying the principles of how complex organizations work. Applied to learning it has increasingly borrowed from its association with the idea of cyberspace – the virtual space created by the internet. An interesting aspect of this approach is its emphasis on feedback and systems. Like computers, it is capable of continuously updating itself and learning from its experiences.

A phrase increasingly used to describe the mixture of e-learning and face to face learning which characterizes much of what goes on in organizations today is blended learning. This term began to be used in the 1990s when the word e-learning was first being used. It implies that e-learning – largely the use of online learning – is not sufficient for most learners. Blended learning is used to describe the range of methods – for example using computers, coaching, lectures and so on – which are used when delivering learning in the workplace.

Computers make one particular learning method – the simulation – increasingly effective. This is an activity which mimics a real life situation so that you can explore what it is like, possibly in a virtual (online) environment. (One of the earliest uses for this approach was in the eighteenth century when armies used it for military training.) Simulations are widely used by emergency services to practise their responses and most people will have encountered a special kind of simulation called a fire practice. With the development of online technology it is now possible to simulate almost anything in virtual reality.

Many organizations also have learning centres, a room or set of rooms with networked computers and other learning resources where people can go to learn, often within a workplace, but also in the wider community. Some libraries have begun to refer to themselves as learning centres. Although many learning centres are associated with internet access, as high street internet cafés have shown, there are many other ways in which they can support learners, including, for example, the provision of childcare.

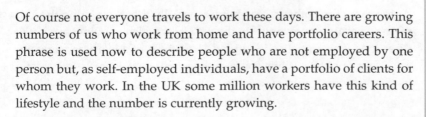

Of course not everyone travels to work these days. There are growing numbers of us who work from home and have portfolio careers. This phrase is used now to describe people who are not employed by one person but, as self-employed individuals, have a portfolio of clients for whom they work. In the UK some million workers have this kind of lifestyle and the number is currently growing.

The idea of the 'learning organization'

In the last 30 years it has become clearer that there are certain ways in which organizations can organize themselves so that the learning is shared around more effectively.

Many people have contributed to thinking about the learning organization. Arguably the first was Reg Revans. Working in the coal industry in the 1980s, Revans invented action learning, a powerful way of combining learning and doing which lies at the heart of the idea of the learning organization. It was Reg Revans who also noticed two crucial things about learning.

First, if the speed of external change is faster than the speed at which an organization learns, then that organization is doomed. Second, you cannot separate thinking or learning from doing. The two need to go hand in hand. Not surprisingly, his approach has a particular appeal to busy managers who need to see the immediate practical benefits of learning.

At about the same time, Chris Argyris with his colleague Donald Schon was developing an interesting theory in the USA. Argyris noticed that there are two kinds of learning that go on in organizations, double loop and single loop (see page 171).

Although Peter Senge is largely credited with first using the term 'learning organization' it had in fact been widely used by Bob Garratt a few years earlier, in 1988. Garratt concentrated on the top and the bottom of organizations. Senior managers, he argued, need to be able to learn all the time and be strong direction givers. Conversely, he recognized that the detailed learning in organizations is mainly done at the lower levels. For it is here that the needs of customers are expressed and met. Garratt suggests that it is the job of senior managers to make a reality of the mantra that 'people are our greatest resource' by really listening to their people and putting in place systems to share what has been learned.

At the same time other researchers, especially those exploring the idea of the 'learning company' in the UK, were also moving in similar directions. This initiative identified 11 features of a learning company, as set out opposite. While some of the vocabulary is fairly jargonistic, its concepts are sound.

Features of a learning company

1. A learning approach to strategy, with experimentation and feedback.
2. Participative policy making.
3. Informating, where IT is used to empower front-line staff (not automate them).
4. Formative accounting and control, financial systems that encourage staff to see how money works in the organization.
5. Internal exchange, all departments see themselves as servants of the customer.
6. Reward flexibility, with rewards that are not just about money (for example time and learning).
7. Enabling structures, where structures change in response to innovation.
8. Boundary workers as environmental scanners, everyone seeing themselves as bringing back useful insights to the organization.
9. Inter-company learning, lots of cross-departmental working and projects.
10. A learning climate.
11. Self-development opportunities for all.

In the USA, Peter Senge brought a more detailed analysis of how organizations learn. He made a strong case that they need to develop five areas of their thinking.

The first of these is *personal mastery*. This means involving all individuals in a process of continuous development. It is really a variation of what is described earlier as lifelong learning.

The second is *mental models*. Mental models are the assumptions and beliefs on which an organization operates. Mind set matters hugely, as does organizational culture for which this is really another description.

The third is *building a shared vision*. While organizations have always needed a vision, the keyword here is 'shared'. In a learning organization the emphasis is on ensuring that all employees, especially those who are less senior, have a clear role in creating the vision. A key approach here is the use of dialogue as part of the process of internal communications.

The fourth is *team learning*. Senge describes teams in which the individuals are very intelligent, but which fail to work effectively together. Team learning assumes that an organization values differences, seeks real interaction between team members and encourages the kinds of behaviours that establish genuine collaborative work.

And the fifth is *systems thinking*. In other words, organizations need to see how the parts relate to the whole and get better at sharing knowledge. This is really what Argyris meant by double-loop learning.

One more bit of jargon. You may find yourself described as an intangible asset! This phrase was introduced recently to describe the people in any organization (as opposed to the fixed assets like computers and buildings).

Formal learning opportunities

According to the National Adult Learning Survey in 2001, 48 per cent of all formal learning is provided by employers. This is more than universities and colleges combined, reminding us that workplaces are very significant providers of formal learning opportunities. According to the same survey, 74 per cent of all employees will receive some kind of training in any one year.

> I find it rather easy to portray a businessman. Being bland, rather cruel and incompetent comes naturally to me.
>
> John Cleese

Most large organizations have human resource or training departments which lay on a range of formal activities and courses. Much of this tends to be based around competencies. A competency is a combination of knowledge, skill, and attributes which can be described clearly enough that it can be observed and measured. This could be something like 'dealing with customer complaints' or 'running a team meeting' or 'changing a nappy'. If you can show certain competencies then you are likely to be competent for a particular task. In many walks of life it is the opposite of competence – incompetence – which is more openly (and unhelpfully) talked about.

Competencies are most often spoken about with regard to work life. For example, an employer might list the competencies required for a particular role or job. These might include descriptions of aspects of communication, managing people, working in teams, planning, using technology and so on.

However, competencies also have a use in the home and wider community where getting on with people, interpersonal skills and problem solving might be just as important.

The focus of what training departments offer will inevitably be largely vocational, in other words learning that is to do with and relevant to the world of work. Increasingly, smart employers are realizing that if there is no such thing as a job for life any more, then there is a bargain to be struck between employees and themselves. This involves equipping people with life skills which will continue to ensure an employee's employability.

Two formal methods still widely used include:

Demonstration A demonstration is a showing of a skill or process by someone who is an expert. So a chef might demonstrate how to make a soufflé, for example. Being able to demonstrate expertise is a key skill of managers in the workplace and parents in the home. It involves breaking a process down into its component parts.

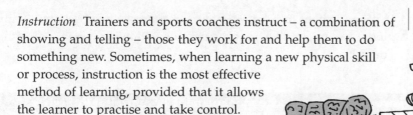

Instruction Trainers and sports coaches instruct – a combination of showing and telling – those they work for and help them to do something new. Sometimes, when learning a new physical skill or process, instruction is the most effective method of learning, provided that it allows the learner to practise and take control.

In some professions, formal and certified learning is compulsory (doctors and lawyers for example). Most professions assume that those who practise them will need to keep up to date and continue to improve by ensuring that they continue to develop. In some cases, continuous professional development is a requirement for the individual to continue to be licensed to practise.

Formalizing learning

There are many ways in which learning can be formalized at work. The following are three of them – learning contracts, performance management and personal development plans.

Learning contract

Some organizations provide employees with a learning contract. A learning contract is a written agreement normally between an employee and someone else, often their manager. It describes learning goals, what learning will be offered, what resources are available – time, money and materials – and the evaluation process which may be used to monitor the progress of learning. Especially for low-paid workers, a clear statement of entitlement can be very useful. Some colleges and universities also establish contracts with learners. The home/school agreement between schools and parents is also a kind of learning contract.

Performance management

Then there is performance management, also known as performance appraisal. Many employees have regular (or at least annual) meetings with their manager to determine how they are getting on and the extent to which they are meeting their targets. These meetings or interviews can be very stressful and are often done very poorly, with managers paying scant regard to the actual situation in which the employee finds him or herself. In many cases the stakes are high as an element of your pay is tied to your performance.

If you are about to have a performance management session of any kind, you might like to consider the following when preparing yourself.

How to prepare for a performance management or appraisal interview

1. Ask for a pre-meeting well before the date of the actual one and find out how your manager proposes to conduct the session and what you can do to prepare for it. (Often you will be asked to carry out some kind of self-assessment beforehand.)
2. Gather together all necessary information to help you prepare. This might include:
   - your job description/profile
   - a note of any positive comments you have received from other staff, clients, customers or service users
   - examples of any work you are especially pleased with.

3. Review the last period. What was your main goal? Did you achieve it? If so, why? If not, why not?
4. Go through your job description line by line (or create an outline for your job if you do not have one). Think of specific examples for each aspect of your job where you have performed well. Make a note of each one.
5. Now think of specific examples of where you know you could have performed better. Were there good reasons why you were unable to do as well as you wanted, for example lack of clout, unclear directions, poor systems or equipment and so on)? Be prepared to be honest about your own role in this. No one likes to hear a long story about how it was always someone else's fault.
6. Rehearse your interview. Are you going just to let yourself be interviewed? In which case prepare and practise. Or are there some things that you want to say? In which case, write them down and take your notes in with you. You might like to get a colleague or family member to role-play the interview.
7. Do not be afraid to ask questions and make reasonable demands, for example:

   How can you help me to do my job more effectively?

   What learning do I need to do my job in the next period?

   What do you see as my strengths?
8. It will be a matter of your judgement (and trust in your manager) as to whether you choose to share your own career plans. Ideally this should always be possible, but in some organizations it might not be a wise approach!

Personal development plan

Lastly, a personal development plan, or PDP for short, is an annual plan for your own learning at work. It identifies your strengths and weaknesses and identifies learning which will help you to develop to be able to do your job better. Most PDPs also encourage the development of a more general set of skills which you may find just as helpful in your daily life, for example 'getting on with people', communication', 'listening' and so on.

Many organizations expect all employees to have a PDP and to use it from time to time in discussions with their manager. If you do not have one, you might like to:

- make one for yourself anyway
- ask your manager if you could create one
- start a campaign at work for you and your colleagues to have one.

Given the importance of learning today, a request for a PDP is a perfectly reasonable one in any organization for any person.

Part Three

Quick reference

In this section you can read summaries of information contained in Part Two and look up other fascinating new material.

three PART

three PART

An A–Z of techniques

Chapter 13

Here are all of the techniques and 'how-to' suggestions from Part Two in alphabetical order for ease of reference:

M

N

O

P

Q

R

S

U

W

Chapter 14

Frequently asked questions

True or false? Myth or reality? Yes or no?

Here are some commonly asked questions which suggest certain beliefs about learning. You might like to see how many of them you feel sure of. They have been loosely grouped together by the alphabetical order of the main keyword in each question.

Do **A**ffirmations really work?

Yes. Affirmations – positive statements that you repeat to yourself – do work. They help to engage all of your mind (or body) on the task in hand.

Does **A**lcohol help you to relax and learn better?

A limited amount of alcohol does help you to relax, but more than this and it may adversely affect your learning and ability to remember.

Is it true that your **A**bility is fixed at birth?

Scientists have been debating the respective influence of nature or nurture for many years and the evidence is inconclusive. The answer to this question is that your ability is partly fixed at birth but that it is possible to increase it during your lifetime. Interestingly, identical twins do not have identical brains.

Can you change the way you **B**ehave?

Yes. For some while behaviourists thought that we were victims of our environment. But we now know that this is not the case. The more engrained a behaviour is the more difficult it may be to change.

Is it true that only some people are **C**reative?

No. This is a myth. While not all of us will turn into a Mozart or a Darwin, we all have the capacity to be creative.

Is it true that we all learn in **D**ifferent ways?

Yes. We all have different personalities and we acquire different habits. However, as it is possible to change and grow, just because you prefer to learn in one way now does not mean that you cannot learn to prefer other ways.

Is it true that **E**motions are more important than thoughts for learners?

Emotions are very important. Thoughts are important, too. Increasingly we are learning about the complex connections that exist between thinking and feeling.

Is it true that you are what you **E**at?

Not strictly! Our diet has a huge impact on us and undoubtedly affects our performance as learners. Most of us need to drink more water and less coffee and alcohol. We also need to eat a more balanced diet with more fresh fruit and less fatty food.

Is **F**ormal learning better than informal?

No. Scientists are unsure as to how much of our learning is formal and how much is informal. Some put the amount of informal learning as high as 90 per cent and are clear that informal learning is more important precisely because it happens more often. You need both to be effective.

Is it true that we only use a **F**raction of our brain?

There is a myth about that we use only 10 per cent of our brain. Where this comes from is not clear; there is no scientific justification for the assertion. As we learn more about the brain, it is clear that we use huge amounts of it much of the time, that when we are using all of our senses we use more of our brain and that there is plenty of spare capacity in most brains.

Does **G**ender matter? Do men and women learn differently?

Men and women do learn differently, but not quite in the simplistic way that the men are from Mars and women from Venus industry assumes.

There are some differences between male and female brains, but these differences are less than the differences that exist between various individuals of the same gender.

Is it true that your **L**eft brain is different from your right brain?

Only a bit. But nothing like as much as popular myth would have us believe. It is not true to say that the right-hand side of your brain deals with creative matters and the left-hand one is logical. Most activities involve areas of your brain in both left and right sides.

Does **M**usic help you learn?

It can do. Music affects your mood and this can help. There is some evidence that music can help you to get into a relaxed/alert state for learning. But just playing music will not make you more intelligent!

Is it true that some people are born **P**essimists?

Probably not. Although people definitely learn to interpret events in ways which tend towards being either pessimistic or optimistic. It is definitely possible to 're-programme' your outlook.

Can you increase the **S**peed of your learning?

There are some differences between male and female brains, but these differences are less than the differences that exist between different individuals of the same gender. So, yes, some of the techniques in this book will help you to learn faster (and many of them will help you to learn better).

Is it true that you **U**se it or lose it?

Technically yes, but practically no! Your neural networks decay throughout your life and using your brain does encourage new connections to be made. But to suggest that you cannot learn in later life if you have not used your brain is simply not true. Lots of adult learners have shown this not to be the case.

15

Chapter 15

Who's who in learning

The following is a list of just some of the thinkers who have helped to shape what we know about learning. It is inevitably incomplete and reflects my view of who and what are important.

Argyris, Chris Born in the USA, Chris Argyris is often seen as the real inventor of the idea of the learning organization, mainly on account of his theory of single-loop and double-loop thinking. This theory helps to explain the different ways in which we deal with mistakes.

Bandura, Albert Created a social theory of learning that challenged conventional behaviourist views by showing that you did not just learn by imitating but also by observing.

Bateson, Gregory Researcher who was interested in how both animals and human beings behave. Bateson thought that learning involved change of a delicate and subtle kind. He also believed that it was helpful to understand these levels more. See 'Levels of learning' on page 141 for an explanation of Bateson's thinking and also models of learning

Bloom, Benjamin An American educational psychologist who, in 1956, developed a taxonomy or model of learning that is still helpful today. In Bloom's view there were three overlapping domains or areas of knowledge–cognitive (mental), psychomotor (physical) and affective (emotional).

Bruner, John Influential constructivist thinker who argued that any theory of teaching should address four major areas:

1. The learner's predisposition towards learning.
2. The ways in which a body of knowledge can be structured so that it can be most readily grasped by the learner.
3. The most effective sequences in which to present material.
4. The nature and pacing of rewards and punishments.

Buzan, Tony Thinker and memory expert, Tony Buzan is the inventor of a revolutionary method of organizing, remembering and thinking about information called mind mapping. See Mind Maps™, on page 97, to find out what is involved.

Claxton, Guy Guy Claxton, psychologist and educationalist, is the originator of the term 'learnacy' (learning about learning, like 'literacy' is learning about reading), an advocate of soft thinking and a challenging contemporary thinker about lifelong learning. See also learnacy on page 72.

Clinton, Bill American president who was one of the first politicians to make lifelong learning a serious issue.

Clutterbuck, David David Clutterbuck is one of a group of experts who has consistently championed the value of mentoring in workplace learning. See also mentor on page 233.

Covey, Stephen American writer about leadership and learning, Stephen Covey created the idea that people were effective because of their habits. He described seven: be proactive; begin with the end in mind; put first things first; think 'win:win'; seek first to understand, then to be understood; synergize and sharpen the saw. See also emotional bank account on page 196 and pause button on page 81.

Cunningham, Ian Ian Cunningham's particular contribution has been the idea of self-managed learning.

Csikszentmihalyi, Mihali American psychologist, Csikszentmihalyi, (pronounced 'Chick-sent-me-high-ee') has developed new thinking about learning and creativity, in particular his discovery of the state of flow.

Dawkins, Richard Biologist and thinker who writes about the way our genes are selfish (we are programmed for survival) and invented the idea of the meme, the smallest unit of an idea, which he argues evolves just as genes do.

De Bono, Edward One of the most radical thinkers about thinking. De Bono invented the idea of lateral thinking and many other thinking tools, for example six hats (on page 235), and plus, minus, interesting (page 95).

Delors, Jacques Along with Bill Clinton, one of the first politicians to make lifelong learning a serious issue.

Dewey, John American philosopher and educator who stressed the need of hands-on learning and was very much against the prevailing authoritarian culture in education of his day.

Freire, Paulo Brazilian educator, Freire showed the importance of informal learning in real-life situations. He demonstrated the ways in which informed action arising out of learning could transform the lives of individuals and their communities.

Freud, Sigmund Freud was a hugely influential thinker about the unconscious mind, personality and motivation (he thought there were two dominating forces – sex and aggression).

Fryer, Bob Chair of the first UK committee to explore all aspects of lifelong learning and make public policy recommendations.

Gagne, Robert American experimental psychologist who believed that learning takes place in the head (rather than in the heart).

Gardner, Howard Harvard psychologist and educator who invented the theory of multiple intelligences (see pages 136–140).

Gibbs, Graham Thinker about learning who created the MUD model of learning – memorizing, understanding, doing.

Golay, Keith American educator who has developed the thinking of the MBTI® by suggesting four basic learning styles for young people: actual–routine, actual–spontaneous, conceptual–global and conceptual–specific.

Goleman, Daniel American author and thinker who is credited with developing and popularizing the idea of emotional intelligence or EQ.

Greenfield, Susan A world respected neuroscientist, Susan Greenfield has done much to popularize the mind through her books and television appearances.

Hermann, Ned American physicist who applied some of the early thinking about brain hemispheres and developed a way of assessing perceptions of your brain so that it indicated personality – the Hermann Brain Dominance Inventory.

Herzberg, Frederick Frederick Herzberg's theory of motivation is particularly relevant to learning. He argued that there are two forces at work. One set is necessary (but not sufficient). He called these hygiene factors. The other is a more powerful set which he called motivators.

Holt, John American educator who talked about the importance of learners enjoying learning and knowing how to learn effectively well before this was a serious subject of general enquiry.

Honey, Peter Co-inventor, with Alan Mumford, of the Honey and Mumford Learning Styles Questionnaire.

Jung, Carl One of the founding fathers of modern psychology, Yung's theory of personality (see MBTI®, pages 143–144), exploration of the idea of the 'collective unconscious' and development of thinking about archetypes have hugely influenced all who have followed him.

Kirkpatrick, Don Thinker about the impact of learning in the workplace. Kirkpatrick suggested that there were four levels at which this could be measured: 1. Reaction; 2. Learning; 3. Behaviour; 4. Results.

Knowles, Malcolm American educator whose work on 'andragogy' has helped us to understand adult learning (see page 13).

Kolb, David American educator who is widely credited with the invention of the idea of experiential learning and of much thinking about learning styles.

Langer, Ellen American thinker about learning, specifically the theory of mindfulness, the creation of an open and effective state for learning.

Lewin, Kurt One of the founders of modern psychology, Lewin helped us to understand how groups work together, explaining that human interactions are driven by both the people involved and their environment.

Lozanov, Georgi Credited with the idea of accelerated learning (then called suggestology) and much useful thinking about the best mind set in which to learn – a state of relaxed alertness.

MacLean, Paul Work on the evolution of the brain.

Maslow, Abraham Psychologist who showed that there is a hierarchy of needs when it comes to learning. These include physical, emotional and intellectual needs. Maslow argued that unless your physical and emotional needs are met, you are not ready to engage your intellect fully (see page 28).

Mezirow, Jack Credited with creating the theory of transformational learning. For learners to change their beliefs, attitudes and emotional reactions they must engage in critical reflection on their experiences and this will lead to changing their perspective, becoming more aware of how and why their assumptions have been formed and how they can choose to behave differently.

Mumford, Alan With Peter Honey, the inventor of the Honey and Mumford Learning Styles Questionnaire.

Pavlov, Ivan Nobel prize winning Russian best remembered for his discovery of the conditioned reflex. See behaviourist theory of learning (page 278) for how he proved this by using his dog!

Pert, Candace American neuroscientist who discovered the molecular basis of our emotions, the way certain chemicals – called peptides – link body and brain together as we experience emotions.

Piaget, Jean Hugely influential psychologist whose theories about the ways children develop (in stages, each of which allows them to develop knowledge in different ways) and intelligence have influenced learning and education throughout the world. Piaget's thinking has contributed greatly to two of the five major theories of learning – the cognitivist and constructivist approaches – although many now see his stages for child development as being much more fluid than he had imagined (see page 194).

Pinker, Steven Radical American scientist whose views about the mind and language challenge many current beliefs. For example, Pinker leans heavily towards those who believe that nature rather than nurture is the more powerful force.

Resnick, Lauren American educationalist whose work has sought to connect school learning with the wider world and develop understanding about the way pupils learn and think.

Revans, Reg Reg Revans invented the concept of action learning, now increasingly used in organizations throughout the world (see page 229).

Rogers, Carl Thinker whose work on understanding between learners and those who help them learn stresses the quality of their relationship. Rogers believed that everyone wants to learn and improve and that if they do not do so it is likely to be the fault of the system rather than of the learner.

Schön, Donald Thinker who stressed the important contribution of reflective practice by professional people – reflection in action.

Seligman, Martin American psychologist who through his concepts of learned helplessness and learned optimism has shown how we can change the way we view the world. See also learned optimism (page 180).

Senge, Peter American thinker about learning at work who created the idea of the learning organization which is now widely used all over the world.

Skinner, Burrhus Frederic One of the most influential advocates of the behaviourist theory of learning, Skinner believed that you can shape people's behaviours by administering rewards or punishments.

Sperry, Roger Work on brain hemispheres .

Sternberg, Robert American thinker about creativity and intelligence.

Thorndike, Edward Psychologist whose definition of intelligence predates much of the current debate about emotional intelligence. Thorndike specified three conditions for effective learning:

1. The law of effect. The likely recurrence of a response depends on the consequence or effect, in other words reward or punishment.
2. The law of recency. What you did last matters most.
3. The law of exercise. Repetition and reinforcement matter.

Usher, Robin Australian educator who in his work on adult learning has narrowed the gap between theory and practice by showing how skilled practitioners are able to engage in practical theorizing.

Vygotsky, Lev Russian psychologist whose theory of the zone of proximal development is important in understanding how we learn (see page 41).

Wenger, Etienne Etienne Wenger is an expert in an aspect of learning theory – communities of practice – in other words, groups of professional who learn together.

Zohar, Danah With Ian Marshall, the creator of the idea of spiritual intelligence. See also multiple intelligence and emotional intelligence on pages 136–140.

16

Big ideas

Chapter 16

Throughout *Discover Your Hidden Talents* you have encountered many interesting ideas (indicated by the icon).

Some of them are big. When they were first suggested they rocked the learning world, including Jean Piaget's views of child development and Howard Gardner's radical alternative to IQ: multiple intelligences.

Some are less big, but have nevertheless had or are beginning to make an impact.

In this chapter you can find all the ideas in this book collected together and a few more as well. You will need to be the judge of how big they are and if you choose to apply them to your own learning life.

‘Learning theory is an evil-smelling bog.’

Frank Coffield

‘There's nothing so practical as a good theory.’

Kurt Lewin

The idea	The thinkers behind it	So what?
Double-loop learning (fixing the system – more powerful than single – dealing with the immediate problem)	Chris Argyris	Work out the underlying reason why a system fails rather than relying on what appears at the surface
The theory in use and the espoused theory (if the gap between what you say you believe and what you do is too great, this causes problems to others)	Chris Argyris	Constantly try to ensure your behaviour is aligned with your beliefs (easy to say, harder to do)
Observation and imitation is powerful	Albert Bandura	Choose your friends carefully as you will be influenced by what they do
Levels of learning	Gregory Bateson	If you want to achieve the highest level of learning you are likely to end up changing your life
Parent types (closeness, degree of optimism, scope of focus, degree of relaxedness, view of routines, emotional display, acceptance, praise/blame, coaching, view of adults, tolerance of conflict)	Diana Baumrind, Bill Lucas and others	The more you know about the different kinds of roles you may play, the more choice you have
Transactional analysis (a theory of personality and a systematic psychotherapy for personal growth and change involving understanding how you 'transact' your communication with others)	Eric Berne	You might like to listen to your different 'voices' as you speak to different people. Are they consistent?
Assessment for learning (types of assessment that help learners learn)	Paul Black and Dylan Wiliam	Involve young people in the assessment of their own progress by giving them specific helpful feedback

The idea	The thinkers behind it	So what?
Taxonomy of learning (six levels of learning)	Benjamin Bloom and others	Really effective learners can customize other people's thinking and make it their own
Domains or fundamental types of learning (cognitive, affective and psychomotor)	Benjamin Bloom	How you learn a physical skill is very different from how you might seek to change a deeply held view about something
Lateral thinking (approaching a problem more creatively)	Edward de Bono	Seeing problems as challenges and from fresh angles helps you to solve them
Concept of learnacy (learning to learn)	Guy Claxton	Learning is learnable
Emotional bank account (like a real bank account, human beings need to keep their emotional one in credit)	Stephen Covey	Remember to show support and love for those close to you more than you demand theirs for yourself
State of flow (a condition of total and rapt absorption in a task)	Mihali Csikszentmihalyi	You are at your most creative if you can get yourself into a state of flow
Self-managed learning	Ian Cunningham	It is the individual's commitment to getting the best out of their learning that matters
Deep and surface learning (engagement in learning depends on the attitude of learners)	Noel Entwhistle	It is important to engage with your learning, reorganizing ideas to make them your own
Theory of multiple intelligences (linguistic, logical–mathematical, spatial, bodily–kinesthetic, musical, intrapersonal, interpersonal, naturalist)	Howard Gardner	We all have a broad range of potential and there is much more to life than IQ

The idea	The thinkers behind it	So what?
Memorizing-understanding-doing model (MUD)	Graham Gibbs	These are three essential ingredients of most learning that we all need to master
Model of emotional intelligence (being able to recognize and manage emotions is a key part of intelligence)	Daniel Goleman	There is 'thought smart' and 'feeling smart' and you need to develop both
Goodhart's law (when a measure becomes a target it ceases to be a good measure)	Charles Goodhart	Beware of 'teaching to the test'
Neuro Linguistic Programming (NLP)	John Grinder and Richard Bandler	There's no such thing as failure, only feedback
Brain dominance model (based on the two hemispheres in your brain)	Ned Herrmann	It is helpful to be aware of your patterns of thought
Model of motivation (satisfiers which motivate and hygiene factors which are not enough)	Frederick Herzberg	The opposite of being turned off from learning is not being turned on; it's a more neutral mid-point
Activist-reflector-theorist-pragmatist learning styles	Peter Honey and Alan Mumford	The more we know about our instinctive preferences, the more we can try and develop other areas
Paradigm shift (when a fundamental way of seeing the world is changed)	Thomas Huhn	Be alert to the way you are feeling about change in your life and learn to manage the inevitable feelings of discomfort
Tip of the tongue phenomenon (when a memory for a name or fact just eludes you)	William James and others	Find personal ways of triggering elusive memories, for example retracing your steps

The idea	The thinkers behind it	So what?
Experiential learning cycle (concrete experience, reflective observation, abstract conceptualization, active experimentation)	David Kolb	Experience is an essential part of the learning cycle, so is reflection
Accelerated learning	Georgi Lozanov and others	You can learn more quickly if you use all of your senses
LP or learning practitioner (a buddy or critical friend with whom we can diagnose and solve learning issues)	Bill Lucas	We all need one or more LPs to ensure that we explore and resolve the many issues which need the support of other minds
Primacy–recency effect (you tend to remember and be influenced by the first and the last things in any one period)	F.H. Lund, Edward Thorndike and others	To aid memory, break your learning up into chunks so that there are lots of beginnings and endings
Hierarchy of needs model (physiological, safety, love, esteem, self-actualization)	Abraham Maslow	It is very difficult to learn effectively if you are tired, hungry, stressed or feeling un-loved
Nature v. nurture (are you who you are because of your genes or because of your environment?)	Margaret Mead, Derek Freeman and others	Believe in the power of nurture then you can use learning to help you
Sleeper–adventurer–warrior –sage model (for learners dealing with planned and unplanned learning)	David Megginson	You need to be prepared to plan your learning and make the effort to extract meaning from your unplanned learning experiences
Pygmalion effect or self-fulfilling prophecy (once an expectation is set, we tend to do what is expected)	Robert Merton and others	Let your children and colleagues think that you are confident that they will be able to do whatever you ask them (they may begin to believe they can too)

The idea	The thinkers behind it	So what?
Model of transformational kinds of learning (life-changing experience, critical reflection, rational discourse)	Jack Mezirow	To be able to make fundamental change you need to reflect critically on the things you are taking for granted in your current view of the world
Theory of personality types (extravert/introvert; sensing/intuitive; thinking/feeling; judging/perceiving)	The Myers–Briggs sisters, based on Carl Jung	If you want to get the best out of people it really helps to understand how there are fundamentally different kinds of people
Behaviour conditioning (stimulus-response model)	Ivan Pavlov	Certain things stimulate predictable responses in you, so learn to recognize this
Learning by assimilation (absorbing into your world view) **and by accommodation** (adapting your previous thinking)	Jean Piaget	You learn by adapting. Sometimes this involves re-thinking the way you see the world and not just fitting it in to your existing view
Stages of child development (zero to two sensory-motor, two to seven pre-operational, seven to eleven concrete operational, 11+ formal operational)	Jean Piaget	Taking account of the broad stages of child development is helpful when working out what children may be able to do at certain stages
Action learning (issues based and enquiry based small sets of learners solving real-life problems)	Reg Revans	Learning is a combination of thinking and doing. It works very well when it results from real issues to which people are committed to finding workable solutions
Person-centred approach to learning (best conditions for facilitating learning involve realness, acceptance and empathy)	Carl Rogers	Trust and empathy are essential in any learning relationship

The idea	The thinkers behind it	So what?
Model of online learning (motivate-socialize-information exchange-create knowledge-true responsibility)	Gilly Salmon	You need to become engaged with the process of online learning to be good at it
Learned optimism (you can become positive if you change the way you see events – seeing them as less personal, less pervasive and less permanent)	Martin Seligman	You need not be helpless or negative. You can change your mind set
Learning organization (organizations as well as individuals can learn if the conditions and systems are right)	Peter Senge	You need adaptive systems in organizations to ensure that learning is shared around
Behaviourist view of learning (the environment is a stronger force than individual will)	Burrhus Frederic Skinner	Reinforce the actions that you want rather than punishing the ones you dislike
Law of effect (actions which lead to pleasant consequences tend to be repeated and those which lead to unpleasant effects tend to be diminished)	Edward Thorndike	Reward behaviours you want to encourage immediately after the event
Practical theorizing (how practical experiences can be turned into theories and usefully compared with existing ones)	Robin Usher	Stop and think about the theories that guide your actions – why you do things the way you do

The idea	The thinkers behind it	So what?
Zone of proximal development (we learn best when we are able to move out of our comfort zone, provided there is scaffolding (support))	Lev Vygotsky	Seek out people who can help to stretch you beyond your comfort zone and support you while they do so
Gestalt theory (seeing the whole picture and its structure helps)	Max Wertheimer and others	Seeing the whole picture and getting an idea of its structure can lead to better thinking and learning
Zeigarnik effect (you tend to remember uncompleted tasks more than completed ones)	Bluma Zeigarnik	Create your own personal 'cliff-hangers' (uncompleted activities where the next step is not known) to help you to stay involved in a task even when you are not able to be working on it
Spiritual intelligence	Danah Zohar and Ian Marshall	You may wish to give more time to your own spiritual development
Skills model (unconscious incompetence, conscious incompetence, conscious competence, unconscious competence)	Unknown	You tend to respond to learning opportunities when you are aware of your own needs
Impact of role models	Various	We are influenced by those around us and we can decide who we spend most time with
Left and right handedness	Various	It's a right-handed world, so extra support will sometimes be necessary for left handers (especially children)
Use it or lose it (neural decay means that we lose brain cells throughout our life)	Various	Keep as active as you can and learn throughout your later life to help you to stay healthy

The idea	The thinkers behind it	So what?
Rote learning (learning by heart)	Various	Some skills (times tables for example) are well reinforced by rote learning; more complex skills tend not to be
Accreditation of prior experience and learning (APEL)	Various	Keep various records of your learning – diaries, testimonials, pictures and so on
Hawthorne effect (show interest in people and their performance improves regardless of what you actually do to help)	Various	Have confidence to show interest even in those aspects of your children's learning which you do not understand
Learning curve (the speed at which a learner masters a new task)	Various	Expect different speeds, even temporary backwards movement, in your learning
Learning representatives (individuals with a role to support the learning of their colleagues at work)	Various, including the TUC (Trades Union Congress)	You could consider becoming some kind of workplace learning adviser yourself
Cybernetics (the principles of how complex organizations work)	Norbert Wiener and others	This may help you if you are trying to understand complex organizations

In addition to these ideas there are generally accepted to be five main schools of thought about learning. These are inter-related and overlapping, but each nevertheless has some distinctive features.

Behaviourist theory of learning

The behaviourist theory of learning is founded on the belief that learning takes place in response to changes in the learner's environment. One of the most famous examples of this is Russian scientist Ivan Pavlov, who discovered that when dogs encounter food they begin to produce saliva or drool. Pavlov discovered that dogs would also drool if they heard a sound which they associated with feeding time, for example the ringing of a bell, whether or not there actually was food on offer.

In other words, the behaviour of the dogs with regard to drooling could be controlled by changing the environment (ringing a bell). B.F. Skinner and Edward Thorndike are also important names who have contributed to this thinking.

Cognitivist theory of learning

The cognitive theory of learning is mainly interested in the internal thought processes that we acquire through learning, the insights and perceptions we gain in our heads. Key thinkers in this area are Jean Piaget, Kurt Lewin and Robert Gagne. Also part of this view of learning is Gestalt theory. This sees the importance of looking at wholes rather than parts. Gestalt theorists see the individual mind at the centre of it all, as opposed to the behaviourist theory of learning, which sees the environment as more important.

The cognitive domain is also one of three domains (fundamental aspects) of learning along with affective and psychomotor domains.

Constructivist theory of learning

Constructivism is one of a small number of important theories about how we learn. It assumes that learners construct their own knowledge based on the way that they personally extract meaning from their experiences and beliefs (rather than, for example, being told what it is by someone else). According to constructivists, learning is a process by which learners make sense of the world. This process is hugely shaped by previous experience. There is no such thing as absolute knowledge; knowledge is relative to the perspective of the learner.

There are two particular implications for the learner of this theory. The first is that learners move to the centre of the stage; they are more important than subjects, for people construct their own meaning and their perspective matters.

The second is that learning involves doing. As with experiential learning, involvement is key.

This theory was first suggested by John Dewey, but has subsequently been adopted and adapted by many other thinkers. Not surprisingly, constructivist theories are much cited by more progressive educators as they put the child rather than the school or school subjects at the centre of things.

Humanist theory of learning

The humanist view is that learning is the key to self-fulfilment and growth. Each person in this theory has an unlimited potential for growth. Humanists do not accept that either the environment or your innate nature determines success in learning. Humanists believe that we learn best when we are safe, confident, respected and empowered.

Key advocates of this view include Abraham Maslow and Carl Rogers.

Social theory of learning

Social theory values contact with other people. It assumes that learning happens through interaction with others and explores the different relationships in which this can happen. Social theory complements the other four major theories. The degree to which you enjoy the social aspect of learning is likely to be related to the extent to which you are extrovert by nature.

17

Chapter 17

How your brain works

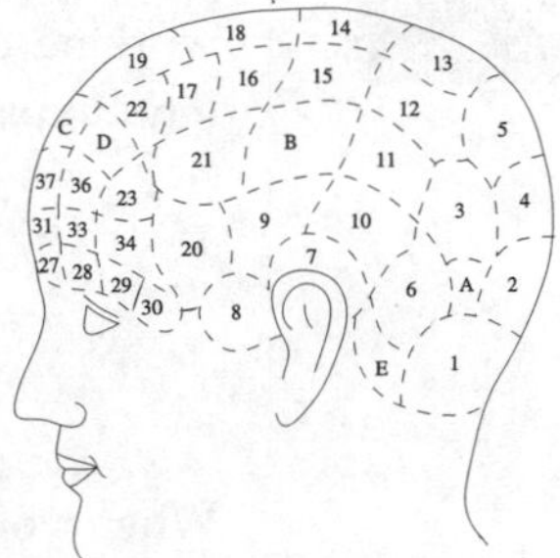

Your brain is at the 'heart' of your learning. The illustration above is what we used to think the brain looked like.

The illustration below is a cross-section showing some of the main features that we now know the brain possesses.

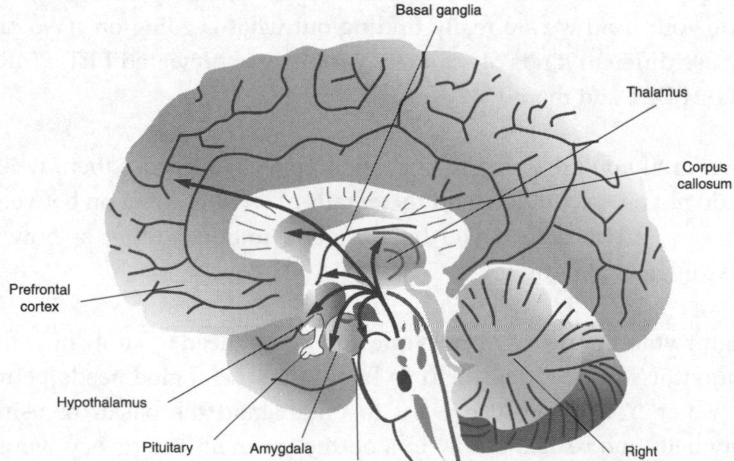

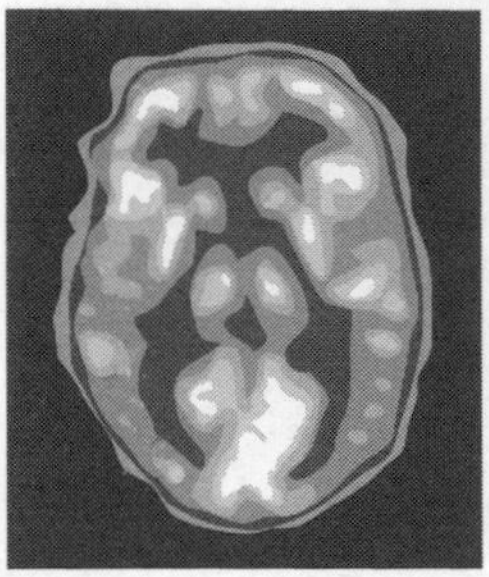

This is what your brain looks like when it is 'thinking'.

One of the paradoxes of the brain is that the more we learn about what specific bits of it do, the more scientists realize that it is incredibly flexible or plastic, able to call on different 'areas' to fulfil new functions.

Of course, when it comes to learning we are really dealing with the mind not the brain. For you are much more than your brain when you are living and learning. Psychologists (who mainly specialize in the working of the mind) and neuroscientists (who deal with the brain) tend to put it like this:

Mind = Brain + Personality

When you look at those archetypal images of a brain in a jar, you would not think of calling it a mind. You would instead call it a brain because its owner is dead and gone. By the same token, neuroscientists can tell us a lot about the brain but may need to confer with a psychologist when it comes to talking about the mind and related personality issues.

Did you know that your brain has some 100 billion nerve cells called neurons in it? No? Don't worry! Lots of people do not and yet they manage very well in life. Or that now we can see what is going on inside your head we are really finding out what is going on? (We can now use different kinds of scanners variously abbreviated PET, FMRI, MEG, SPECT and more.)

However, if you are going to become an effective learner then, while you do not need to understand the details of what is going on between your ears, it will help if you have a good understanding of how it works in general terms.

Imagine your brain was a car. While you do not need to know how the carburettor works, it does help to know that the engine needs petrol and water. You might also want to understand the basics of using safety belts and realizing how to stop the car in an emergency would be essential.

It is the same with your brain, the key organ when it comes to your learning. You do not need to know the details (fascinating as these are) but it does help to understand the main operating principles.

Five key principles of the brain's operation

Emerging research into the myriad and complex ways the brain works is refining our knowledge on a daily basis. In an attempt to provide you with a model of what is going on, I have simplified this into five broad principles. These principles may help to explain why things happen in certain ways.

Principle one: the brain loves to explore and make sense of the world

The 100 billion neurons in your brain are on a mission to communicate with each other. Each one has the potential to connect with thousands of others, reaching out a 'tentacle' called an axon. Each neuron has other tentacles called dendrites which it uses to receive incoming signals from another neuron's axon. The minute gap between axons is called a synapse.

Your dendrites 'learn' from other cells by receiving messages and the cell then, in turn, 'teaches' other cells by passing on information through its axon. It is the number of connections not the number of cells that are important.

We learn by experience, by interacting with the world using our senses. The connections or pathways develop between neurons which become the routes through which we access our experiences. These connections are the important thing.

Just as its individual neurons are, so your brain is endlessly seeking to make sense of what it experiences. Your brain is constantly searching for new data and new experiences. Like your dendrites and axons, it is a very determined explorer.

Principle two: the brain likes to make connections

The way that the brain learns is by making connections; axons and dendrites link together to enable meaning and learning to 'flow' from one neuron to another.

In fact, your brain is so good at making connections that it will often try to fill in the gaps even when it is missing information. You see a cat moving along behind a fence and although part of the cat's body is obscured by the posts of the fence, your mind fills in the rest and thinks it is seeing a complete cat. Or another obvious practical effect of this is our tendency to fill in missing information. So when someone tells us a half truth or only gives us part of the information we need, our mind immediately starts to make up the missing bits. If you are trying to solve a problem, this tendency is a positive one. But if you are trying to communicate to your colleagues or family and only give part of the story, it can lead to suspicion, gossip and unease as their brain tries to fill in the gaps for itself.

Principle three: the brain thrives on patterns

As your neurons establish the same or similar connections with each other over time, so patterns are established. Pattern-making is at the heart of you mind's filing system: its ability to make sense of what it has learned. If you have never seen a lion, the first time it rushes at you you may think it is some kind of horse. Assuming you survive this ordeal, the next time one attacks, you will make yourself scarce. Your mind has noticed, for the second time, that a creature with a tawny mane and a roar is not going to be friendly. A pattern has been established. All lions which appear in future will be 'filed' in the part of the mind which is labelled 'dangerous animals'.

Our ability to make patterns is at the heart of our civilization. We organize ourselves into houses, streets and towns. We lay out road networks. We create languages and number systems. Interestingly, this very positive attribute can also limit our potential when certain patterns become engrained and we consequently become resistant to change.

Principle four: the brain loves to imitate

Allied to pattern-making is the brain's extraordinary capacity for imitation. Until a synaptic connection has been made there is no 'knowledge', except what we are born with. One way for connections to be established is by watching what others do and copying them. So we learn to speak and talk when we are young by watching and listening to others. We learn many of our social customs by observation.

Effective learners are very aware of who they spend their time with, conscious of the influence that such relationships will have on them and their behaviours. The capacity of the brain to mimic others is an important one to use. Learning by watching an expert can be a really useful way to learn. In most families much of the learning takes the form of copying other family members. And the use of role models and the modelling of certain behaviours at home and at work are powerful methods of passing on learning.

Of course, you do not only copy. Sometimes you observe and deliberately do it differently. So, if you see a car skidding on ice in front of you, you do not try and copy it; you take evasive action instead.

Principle five: the brain does not perform well under too much stress

Your brain has evolved from the 'bottom' upwards. The most primitive functions are at the bottom of your brain near the brain stem. It is here that rapid decisions of life and death are taken. These are normally referred to as your 'fight or flight' instincts. If you perceive a major threat to your survival, you have to act fast. In practice this means the release of chemicals which put your body into a state of heightened arousal. Either your arms and legs begin to fight your attacker or your legs start to move rapidly as you flee from the scene. When your brain is under severe stress, it can only think of survival. Blood and energy, which would otherwise be available for higher-order thinking, is simply diverted into ensuring that you live to fight another day.

This is not the same thing as saying that all stress is bad for you. On the contrary, without the challenge that your mind also thrives on, you simply would not grow and evolve. But few find it easy to think about complex issues when they are staring disaster in the face. For effective learning to take place there needs to be a balance between high challenge and low threat.

A guided mini-tour of your brain

If you are interested in finding out more about what different parts of your brain do and about some issues directly related to your brain functioning, then read on.

Organized in a simple A–Z fashion, please be aware that these are only very brief summaries and are, of necessity, simplified accounts of some of the most complex scientific processes. In many cases, new research is emerging as fast as we can write about it.

Adrenalin Adrenalin is a hormone produced by the adrenal gland particularly during intense emotional states such as fear and rage. It increases the heart rate and increases certain metabolic processes, while relaxing bronchial and intestinal muscles.

Amygdala The amygdala is a small, almond-shaped cluster of nerves in the limbic system of the brain which plays a role in processing, 'tagging' and responding to emotions and helping to regulate your state of arousal.

Arousal Arousal is a state of heightened activity in the brain caused by external or internal factors. To undertake any activity human beings need to be aroused. Indeed a certain amount of arousal is essential in everyday living. But for effective learning to take place we know that the state of arousal needs to be managed. Get too aroused and you are unlikely to be able to function effectively. The ideal state of arousal is to be alert but relaxed, challenged and engaged but not threatened.

Hopefully you are seldom, if ever, under any direct threat to your well-being. But strong emotions like fear or anger may cause you to be aroused to such a degree that you are unable to concentrate or remember properly. See also *hypothalamus* and *amygdala* if you are interested in finding out more about what is going on in your brain.

Axon Each nerve cell (neuron) in your brain has an extended branch coming off it called an axon which connects with the dendrites – similar branch-like growths – from other neurons. It is through these connections, nerve cell to nerve cell, that data is electronically and chemically exchanged within your brain. When people talk of your brain being 'wired' they have in mind the network of connections made by axons and dendrites.

Basal ganglia These are a series of connected nerve cells in the middle of the brain which seem to have a role in controlling eye and limb movement.

Biorhythms The theory of biorhythms suggests that our daily lives are affected by cycles or rhythms over which we have little or no control. While there is little or no scientific evidence to support the general theory, there is increasing evidence to suggest that human beings perform differently according to certain obvious rhythms, such as night and day. Certain very real biological events – menstruation or pregnancy, for example – will clearly affect the bodily and mental rhythms of women, accounting for a range of symptoms from loss of concentration to tiredness.

Some researchers believe that your memory is more efficient in the morning and have concluded that mornings are the best time to present new information. Others have shown that learning takes place best in 'waves' – you have a period of intense concentration followed by a period of more relaxed sensing. These waves are sometimes referred to as pulses.

Common sense (and recently some research) suggests that some learners are 'morning people' while others prefer to stay up late. Clearly, as we go through the day, our brains become fuller and fuller with new data. We need to sleep on this to help us process it. It follows that many people experience gradual mental fatigue over the day and, consequently, become less efficient as learners.

Brain gym® Brain Gym® was created by Paul and Gail Dennison, in the USA, to help young people with learning difficulties, especially dyslexia. Brain Gym®, as its name suggests, consists of physical activities that enhance the performance of the brain and so improve learning. Proponents of Brain Gym® claim that it leads to improvements in areas like concentration, memory, reading, personal organization, language and number skills, writing and speaking. Increasingly used in the UK, many of its claims have, as yet, to be proved conclusively. But it is certainly a harmless and possibly a beneficial learning activity.

Brain wave Not your latest great idea but, in fact, a phrase referring to the different waves or pulses of activity which can be recorded in your brain. Essentially your brain 'runs' at four different speeds (waves), depending on what you are doing. Think of this as four different gears in a car. These can be measured by something called an electroencephalograph or EEG machine. These different waves have been given letters from the Greek alphabet as their names. Beta waves are the fastest and gamma the slowest.

Beta waves: 13–25 cycles per minute. During much of the normal activity of your day, this is the speed at which your brain runs. It now appears that this may not be the most creative state to be in and is more suited to the basics of surviving life.

Alpha waves: eight–12 cycles per minute. This is the state you are in when you are in a state of relaxed alertness, arguably the best state to be in for your learning. There is some evidence that this is the state – sometimes also called the 'alpha state' or the state of 'flow' (see Mihali Csikszentmihalyi) – during which you have your best ideas. Certain kinds of baroque music, for example by Bach or Handel, with its distinctive rhythms seem to help you relax into this state. Some experiments suggest that, during this state, both halves of your brain are working in a fully integrated way. Other ways of inducing this state include yoga, jogging and various relaxation techniques. In this state it appears that the brain secretes a chemical called GABA (gamma-aminobutyric acid) which aids concentration by ensuring that our brain cells only respond to certain kinds of stimuli.

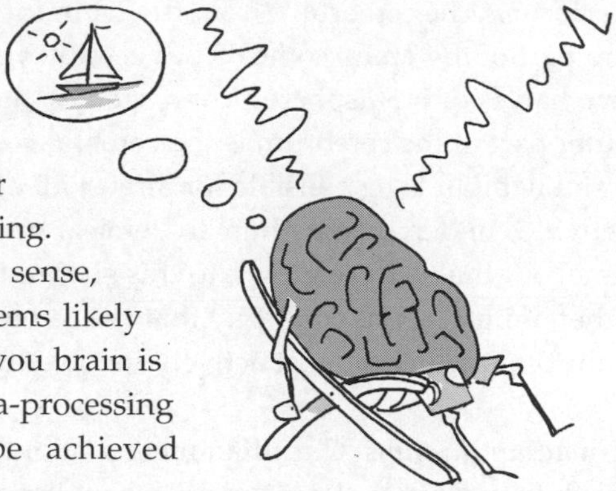

Theta waves: four–seven cycles per minute. Theta waves typically occur just before you fall asleep or when you are day-dreaming. Your body has, in a real sense, slowed right down. It seems likely that, at periods like this, you brain is engaged in complex data-processing tasks. This state can be achieved through meditation.

Gamma waves: fewer than three cycles per minute. Gamma waves signal the fact that you are in a deep, dreamless sleep of the kind that all effective learners need in order to somehow organize and consolidate the learning of the day.

Broca's area Discovered by Paul Broca in 1861, Broca's area is a part of the left frontal cortex of the brain which plays an important role in speech, especially, it seems, the processing of words and syntax. See also *Wernicke's area*.

Cerebellum Shaped like a cauliflower and literally meaning 'little brain' the cerebellum is a part of your brain, near the brain stem, which acts as a sort of co-ordinator of much brain activity, especially to do with physical skills using the input from your senses. Along with the basal ganglia, the cerebellum has a key role in co-ordinating movement.

Cerebrum The cerebrum (from the Latin for 'brain') is the largest and top part of the brain, some 85 per cent by volume. It is divided into two halves or hemispheres, connected by the corpus callosum. The outer part of the cerebrum is the cerebral cortex, the familiar grey wrinkly bit. It is responsible for almost all of the more complex activities undertaken by human beings (which explains why, over time, our brains have grown to this size and are much bigger than other animals). You could say that the cerebral cortex is the part of your brain which is most actively involved in your learning.

Circadian rhythms Circadian means 'about a day' and circadian rhythms are any biological rhythms which occur in a predictable cycle like that of days and nights. For learners, the rhythms of life are all around us. We are affected by sunshine in the summer months (in the northern hemisphere), by patterns of light and dark, by patterns of sleep and so on. In a typical day our temperature fluctuates by about two degrees Fahrenheit, being lowest in the early morning and highest in the evening.

Our circadian rhythms affect our ability to think and learn, making us more or less sleepy or alert. A healthy brain produces a chemical called melatonin during the night when it is dark, and this, in turn, makes you feel sleepy. Disruptions to our normal patterns of life, such as those produced by travel across time zones or patterns of shift work, can be very disruptive to our ability to learn.

Corpus callosum A bundle of nerves, some ten by two centimetres in size, that connect the left hemisphere of the brain with the right hemisphere. The corpus callosum acts as a connector, relaying information from one half of the brain to the other in complex ways which we are only just beginning to understand.

Cortex The outer part of the brain. See also *cerebrum*.

Cortisol Cortisol is a hormone produced by the adrenal gland to help the body cope with stress by raising blood sugar levels. In evolutionary terms, cortisol provided the necessary get up and go either to fight or flee in the face of an attack. Too much cortisol puts your mind in a state which is not conducive to learning. See also *adrenalin*.

Cross-lateral Cross-lateral means 'of the other side', so a cross-lateral movement would involve your right arm and your left leg, for example. Ever since we noticed that some people were right handed and others left handed there has been interest in cross-laterality. But this interest intensified when Roger Sperry discovered that there are two hemispheres or sides to the brain, in the 1960s. It was discovered early on that the right-hand side of the brain controls the left-hand side of the body, so in the example involving your right arm and left leg, both sides of your brain would be involved.

Engaged by the idea of 'whole-brain' working, various groups have become more interested in this area. These include those interested in dyslexia (some dyslexics use their right foot for kicking a ball but their left hand for writing, for example), advocates of Brain Gym® and many others. Much of this is, in fact, supposition, and the one thing we can be sure of is that cross-laterality and the use of different brain hemispheres is much more complex than was first thought.

Dendrite Each nerve cell or neuron in your brain has branch-like growths growing out from it which connect with other similar growths called axons, from other neurons. It is through these connections, nerve cell to nerve cell, that data is electronically and chemically exchanged within your brain. When people talk of your brain being 'wired' they have in mind the network of connections between the synapses made by axons and dendrites.

FMRI *(functional magnetic resonance imaging)* FMRI is a scanning technique for determining which parts of the brain are activated by different types of physical sensation or activity.

Hemisphere In the 1960s, Roger Sperry first discovered that our brain has two halves or hemispheres, connected by the corpus callosum, each of which seemed to be associated with different activities. For example, the right hemisphere controls the left-hand side of the body and vice versa. Another scientist, Roger Ornstein, went further and began to explore the ways in which the right-hand side tends to deal with more complex overall meaning.

The danger of great scientific breakthroughs is that they can all too easily become oversimplified. This is exactly what has happened, with a whole industry of people saying that the left-hand side of the brain is logical and sequential and the right-hand side is associative and creative.

While there is some truth in this, the real picture is so much more complex that it is very easy to end up more confused than ever.

Hippocampus The hippocampus is a part of the brain which is shaped like a sea-horse (hence its name) and which plays an important role in memory, along with the amygdala and the cortex. The hippocampus seems to be especially important in long-term and spatial memory. (A study has shown that many London taxi drivers have larger hippocampuses – especially the bit at the back – than the average person.) The hippocampus is in the limbic system of the brain and is vulnerable to stress, which explains why, during stressful periods, your memory becomes less effective.

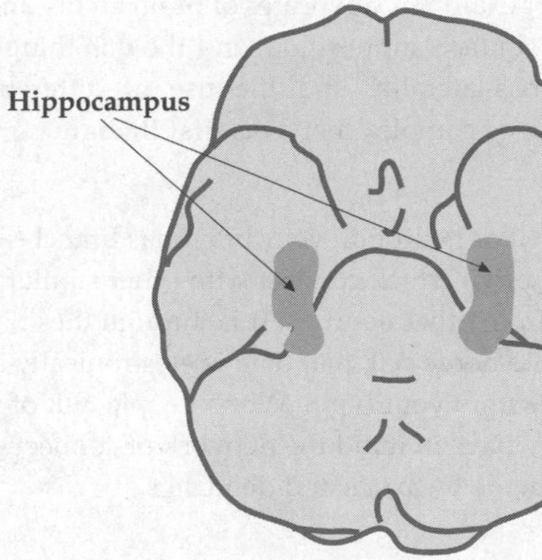

Hypothalamus The hypothalamus is located close to the pituitary gland and monitors basic bodily functions like the intake of food and water. The hypothalamus has often been compared to a kind of thermostat, controlling the body's intake of food to match its energy needs. The hypothalamus is a gland which links the nervous system to the endocrine system by releasing hormones.

Left brain Used to describe the left hemisphere (see *hemisphere*) of your brain. Also used in a popular sense to describe the more sequential and logical activities of the brain. In fact many brain activities involve both hemispheres. See also *right brain*.

Left hemisphere See *left brain* and *hemisphere*. See also *right brain*.

Limbic system The limbic system sits in the middle of your brain. In it are, among other key brain parts, the amygdala and the hippocampus. The limbic system contains many key elements which play a part in your emotional responses, states of arousal, perception, motivation and memory.

MEG *(Magnetoencephalography) scans* These work by detecting the magnetic fields created by the brain's electrical signals. These fields are a billion times smaller than the Earth's magnetic field, so MEG has to be carried out in a heavily shielded room, often at night when other electrical devices are switched off. You sit inside a 'helmet' of special sensors that detect the tiny magnetic signals produced by the brain.

Myelination A process whereby axons are coated with a fatty substance – myelin – which improves the flow of information between neurons.

Neocortex The neocortex is the outer part or surface of the brain, the crinkly bit that looks like a cauliflower. This bit of the brain is proportionately bigger in humans than in any other mammals, especially the front part. Consequently, scientists have naturally deduced that it is responsible for much of the higher thinking, learning and creating functions that are only present in humans.

Nerve cell See *neuron*.

Neural pruning Throughout your life your brain is changing, with brain cells being lost or 'pruned' depending on a range of factors, including use and age.

Neuron Neuron is the name for the special brain cells in your brain, of which you have some 100 billion. Discovered by Camillo Golgi and Santiago Ramon y Cajal a century ago, each one has the potential to connect with another, reaching out a 'tentacle' called an axon. Each neuron has other tentacles called dendrites which it uses to receive incoming signals from another neuron's axon. The minute gap between axons is called a synapse.

It is at this detailed level that the brain is operating when you learn, have a thought, remember something, feel aroused or undertake any of the other brain functions. One cell connects chemically and electrically with another and a neural pathway or synaptic connection is made. Your dendrites 'learn' from other cells by receiving messages and the cell then, in turn, 'teaches' other cells by passing on information through its axon. It is the number of connections not the number of cells which are important. Just as any electrical appliance has wires bringing the current in and wires which go out to complete the circuit, so your nerve cells are connected.

We learn by experience, by interacting with the world using our senses. The connections or pathways develop between neurons which become the routes through which we access our experiences. These connections are the important thing. When we think or learn, the neural networking that is taking place is at a micro-chemical level: our brain learning from our experiences.

When stimulated, neurons grow lots of dendrites. These look like twigs from a branch and connect with an axon from another neuron or group of neurons. In fact the dendrites and axons can connect with each other at various points along their length. When they connect, they are literally exchanging a small electrical charge and also releasing minute amounts of different chemicals, depending on the nature of the experience.

The first time we learn something we are comparatively slow. The next time it is easier because there is already a route 'laid out'. In fact scientists think that this may involve a chemical called myelin which coats and insulates axons ensuring much faster transmission of impulses.

Neuroscience Neuroscience is the study of the growth, development and function of the nervous system. Given the huge importance in the brain, it has almost come to mean the study of the science of the brain.

Oestrogen A hormone secreted by the ovary and responsible for female characteristics. At the menopause, women stop producing this hormone. Oestrogen levels can affect women's abilities to learn effectively, with some researchers suggesting that it can help to guard against memory loss and may improve the functioning of the brain.

Oxygen One of the brain's essential foods. So if you are feeling unable to concentrate, stand up and move around for a while to get some oxygenated blood into your brain!

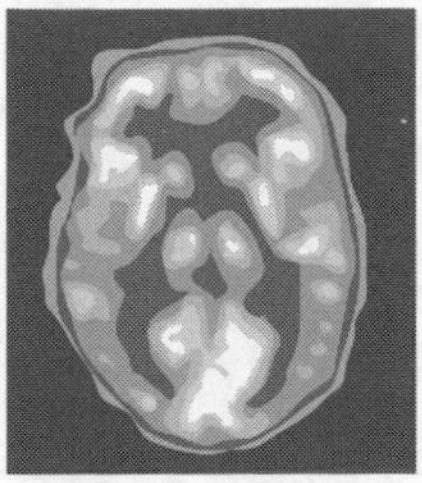

PET *(positron emission tomography)* Positron emission tomography scanning uses a number of stationary detectors around the patient. The name tomography refers to the fact that the scanner computes a 'slice' of the scanned object, not just a flat image (as shown in this picture).

Plasticity Plasticity is the word used to describe the amazing way in which the 'circuits' of the brain change in response to experience or sensory stimulation. This happens when:

- the very young brain is first beginning to process sensory information;
- changes in the body, for example with eyesight, alter the way data is received by the brain;
- we change our behaviour as we learn and use our memory (neurons make more connections);
- the brain is damaged in some way and has to adjust the way it processes data.

Psychology Psychology is the science of the mind and, along with neuroscience and educational research, is one of the key areas of interest for anyone in becoming a more effective learner.

Psychometrics Psychometrics is a branch of psychology dealing with measurable aspects of the way the mind works, of particular interest to employers, sports coaches and anyone interested in improving their own performance. An enormous range of tests exists which purport to measure intelligence, emotional intelligence, creativity, personality, thinking, motivation, and attitudes to life and work.

Rapid eye movement Rapid eye movement or REM is just what it seems and occurs when you are deeply asleep. Researchers are still seeking to find out more about what is going on, but it seems that this type of sleep is especially important and restorative to us.

Right hemisphere Your brain has two hemispheres or halves, connected together by the corpus callosum. See also *left brain* and *hemisphere*.

Sleep Although we do not yet fully understand the function of sleep in learning and memory, we are beginning to get some clues. Generally speaking, we tend not to get enough of it; many people need seven or seven and a half hours and often run on at least an hour short every night.

We know that there are two kinds of sleep: REM (rapid eye movement) and non-REM. REM sleep comes late in the sleep cycle and is a period when brain and body are active although you are still asleep. There is emerging evidence that sleep plays an important role in processing memory and is, consequently, especially important during examination periods.

It is also widely accepted that sleep has a critical role in early brain development. So, if you are a parent, keep sticking to bedtimes for your child!

SPECT *(single-photon emission computed tomography) scan* A procedure in which a gamma ray camera rotates around you and takes pictures from many angles, which a computer then uses to form a tomographic (cross-sectional) image.

Synapse The gap between neurons. It is the number of synaptic connections rather than the number of neurons which matters!

Testosterone Testosterone is a steroid hormone produced in men by the testes and adrenal glands. It is a very important hormone providing energy and motivation, having a key role in puberty, promoting muscle definition and driving sexual libido.

Thalamus The thalamus is the area around the brain stem and acts as a kind of relay station for information. It plays a role in regulating sleep and wakefulness and in responding to extremes of pain or temperature.

Triune brain theory In 1978, Paul MacLean proposed the idea that we had three brains not one:

1. A primitive or reptilian brain governing your most basic survival instincts, for example whether, if threatened, you will stay to fight or run away. It seems also to control other basic functions, such as the circulation of your blood, your breathing and your digestion.
2. Your middle or mammalian brain, sometimes called the limbic system, after the Latin word *limbus* meaning collar. This is the part of your brain that you share with most mammals.
3. Your outer, third, 'brain', the cortex. This is the part that sits behind your forehead and wraps around the whole of your mammalian brain. It is the bit that only humans have.

There is no doubt that, in evolutionary terms, your small 'reptilian' brain is the oldest and the outer, 'learning' brain, is the most recently acquired. However, scientists are increasingly clear that MacLean's theories are an over-simplification of the way that the way brain works. The brain is much more flexible and plastic.

Wernicke's area Wernicke's area, first discovered in 1874, is an important area of the brain involved in understanding language. It seems that speech and sound information are processed both by Wernicke's area for the significance of its content and by Broca's area for its syntax. In speech production, content words seem to be selected by systems in Wernicke's area, while grammar is a role of Broca's area. Of course, given the plasticity of the brain, many other parts are also involved.

Whole brain There is something of a 'whole brain' and 'brain-based' industry at the moment. Ever since the discovery of two hemispheres in the brain, there has been an understandable wish to ensure that both halves are being used as much as possible. This has led to some gross over-simplifications of the science involved and some very doubtful conclusions being drawn. For much of learning you are, in any case, using most of your brain.

It would, nevertheless, be a reasonable assertion to make that to be an effective learner you need to be confident in using the largest possible range of approaches and methods. This would seem likely to involve lots of your cranial capacity.

A positive benefit from the whole brain approaches is an acceptance that we need to nurture our heads *and* our hearts *and* our bodies, each of which is intimately connected to the others.

Chapter 18

Common conditions

Here are a few of the more common conditions, some more distressing and challenging than others. In many cases these conditions present themselves during childhood, so you may well be reading this from the perspective of a concerned parent.

If you have jumped to this part of the book, please be very wary of these brief descriptions and seek out more information from some of the websites listed.

Each of the conditions mentioned here has had many books written about it. And there will be many experts to whom you can turn if you are concerned.

Only use these entries as signposts to further investigation.

Alzheimer's Alzheimer's disease is the most common kind of dementia. Sufferers endure a gradual degeneration of brain cells which causes memory loss, impairment of reasoning and general lack of concentration, among other symptoms. It normally occurs in older people.

Not enough is known about either the causes or the cure for this disease. It is almost inevitable that patients will eventually require full-time care.

Helpful websites include:

www.alzheimers.org.uk
www.alz.org

Asperger's syndrome Like autism, Asperger's syndrome involves severely impaired capacity for social interaction. The syndrome means that individuals find it difficult to empathize with others and have great trouble in 'reading' what is going on in different situations. The condition seems to be more common in men and is often diagnosed in boys between the ages of five and nine.

Helpful websites include:

www.aspergers-syndrome.org.uk
www.nas.org.uk

Attention deficit hyperactivity disorder *(ADHD)* To survive, human beings have had to learn how to remain alert or, over the centuries, they would have dozed off to sleep and been eaten by predators. Today, in some people, the alert state is so strong that they find it difficult to pay attention for any period of time and are hyperactive. Initially in the USA and, more recently, in Europe, ADHD is being diagnosed in children as a condition which prevents them from learning effectively. There are many symptoms of ADHD, including:

- poor concentration, including apparently not listening and being easily distracted
- failure to follow instructions
- difficulty in organizing tasks
- losing things
- forgetfulness
- fidgeting
- being excessively talkative
- interrupting.

Of course many of these symptoms are displayed by perfectly healthy children (and adults). If you think that your child is suffering from ADHD, the first thing to do is contact your child's teacher to discuss it with them. This will enable you to see if the behaviour you are seeing at home is similar to what goes on at school. In many cases it is likely that your child is being perfectly normal, if a little high-spirited. There is some emerging evidence that food colourings, additives and excessive amounts of sugary food and drink can contribute to the symptoms of ADHD.

As with most learning 'conditions', consistency and clearly structured organization are key factors in making progress. Any child needs to grow up in a learning environment in which rules are consistently applied and in which s/he is helped to break down any task into manageable chunks.

Helpful websites include:

www.addiss.co.uk

Autism Autism was first defined in the 1940s and since then our understanding of what is involved has grown enormously. Autism is a learning disability which normally appears in the first three years of life. It is a neurological disorder that affects the way the brain works. It affects an individual's ability to communicate and to interact socially. People with autism tend to be resistant to change, preferring patterns of activity with which they are familiar. They show emotions for no apparent reason. They have tantrums and are unresponsive to many normal teaching or learning methods. They have great difficulty in fitting into a typical class of children. The film *Rain Man* gives a classic account of one man's life with autism.

Each person with autism is an individual capable of giving and receiving love and affection, and some may exhibit only very slight symptoms. If you are concerned about your own child, then you should seek help initially through your child's doctor or teacher, or both.

Helpful websites include:

www.nas.org.uk

Dyscalculia Less well known than dyslexia, dyscalculia is a learning condition that affects mathematical calculations. It seems likely that it is caused by the brain's inability to visualize numbers and mathematical relationships which leads them to make many apparently simple mistakes, for example reading a list of numbers out of sequence. Dyscalculia may also cause great difficulty with time, directions and name recognition.

If you think that your child may be showing dyscalculia, talk to his or her teacher and, if necessary, see an educational psychologist.

Helpful websites include:

www.bda-dyslexia.org.uk

Dyslexia Dyslexia has now been established as a condition which, while not fully understood, creates anomalies in the way the brain works. People with dyslexia have difficulties with reading, writing and spelling. Dyslexia affects people of all abilities and is not the result of low concentration. While there is no such thing as a total cure, many of its effects can be overcome with specialist help.

If you think that your child may be showing signs of dyslexia, talk to his or her teacher and, if necessary, see an educational psychologist. Most schools will have codes of practice which can be used to help those with the condition. They will also be able to show how computers can help children.

Helpful websites include:

www.bda-dyslexia.org.uk

Dyspraxia Dyspraxia is a learning condition affecting the organization of movement. We do not yet understand its causes. Dyspraxia leads to difficulty in interpreting the messages you receive from your senses. This, in turn, tends to produce poor co-ordination of movement. The condition affects boys more then girls.

If you think that your child may be showing dyspraxia, talk to his or her teacher and, if necessary, see an educational psychologist.

Helpful websites include:

www.dyspraxiafoundation.org.uk

Reading difficulties Reading involves recognizing which letters are which, knowing which sounds letters make individually and when turned into words, and understanding what words and sentences mean. You also have to enjoy reading or the whole process can be a terrible chore.

Some children and adults find reading difficult. If you are a parent with a child experiencing difficulties, it is really important that you do two things: spot it as early as possible, getting help to support your child, and do your best not to communicate your own anxieties to your child. Reading is so important to all aspects of life that, whether or not your child ends up enjoying reading out of choice, it is essential that you persist in helping him or her.

See also *dyslexia* and *dyspraxia*.

Stammering Stammering is having difficulty with pronouncing certain sounds. Many children go through a phase when they have difficulty saying certain words, but this soon passes. For some, however, stammering becomes part of their lives. If you are a parent with a child who seems to be stammering or stuttering, then get specialist advice from an educational psychologist as early as you can.

Helpful websites include:

www.stammering.org

Visual impairment Many people have a visual problem at some stage in their life, most commonly either being long-sighted or short-sighted. Regular eye checks are the simple precaution. Young people's eyes are particularly sensitive, especially in the early years, so if you are a parent you need to take particular care as vision is such an important sense.

There are about one million people in the UK whose vision is such that they could be registered as 'blind' or 'partially sighted'. About three-quarters of these people are over retirement age and over half live alone. About 75 per cent have sufficient vision to read a newspaper headline with appropriate correction (for example, with spectacles) and good illumination.

Conditions include:

Myopia or short-sightedness, when the image is focused in front of the retina. This can be corrected by concave lenses.

Hypermetropia, or long-sightedness, when the image is focused behind the retina. This can be corrected with convex lenses.

Astigmatism, in which case the image is elongated or distorted.

This is corrected with cylindrical lenses.

Macula degeneration affects about half of those who are visually impaired in the UK. It is particularly common among older people. The macula is at the centre of the retina and is used for detailed activities such as reading and recognizing faces, and is also used to detect colours. Magnification and high levels of illumination will help.

Cataracts create a dirty windscreen effect. If the sun is behind you the view is reasonably good, but if the sun is in front then it can be seriously impaired. Cataracts can form at any age, but most often develop as people get older. Correction by surgery is normally easy.

About 2 per cent of the population in the UK are affected by diabetes and diabetes sufferers are more likely to have visual impairments.

'Tunnel vision' and colour blindness are two more conditions.

Helpful websites include:

www.rnib.org.uk
www.moorfields.org.uk

Further reading

Blakemore, Susan (1999) *The Meme Machine*, Oxford University Press.

Bransford, John D. (ed.) (2000) *How People Learn, Brain, Mind, Experience and School*, US National Academic Press.

Butler, Gillian and Hope, Tony (1995) *Manage Your Mind: The Mental Fitness Guide*, Oxford University Press.

Buzan, Tony (2003) *Use Your Head*, Oxford University Press.

Clark, Andy (2003) *Natural-born Cyborgs: Minds, Technologies and the Future of Human Intelligence*, Oxford University Press.

Claxton, Guy (1998) *Hare Brain, Tortoise Mind: Why Intelligence Increases When You Think Less*, Fourth Estate.

Claxton, Guy (2000) *Wise Up: The Challenge of Lifelong Learning*, Bloomsbury.

Claxton, Guy (2005) *The Wayward Mind*, Little Brown.

Claxton, Guy and Lucas, Bill (2004) *Be Creative: Essential Steps to Revitalise Your Life and Work*, BBC Books.

Covey, Stephen R. (1999) *The 7 Habits of Highly Effective Families*, Simon & Schuster.

Csikszentmihalyi, Mihali (1997) *Creativity: Flow and the Psychology of Discovery and Invention*, HarperCollins.

Dawkins, Richard (1989) *The Selfish Gene*, Oxford University Press.

Dryden, Gordon and Voss, Jeanette (2001) *The Learning Revolution*, Network Educational Press.

Gardner, Howard (1993) *Frames of Mind: Theory of Multiple Intelligences*, Fontana.

Gerhardt, Sue (2004) *Why Love Matters: How Affection Shapes a Baby's Brain*, Brunner-Routledge.

De Geus, Arie (2002) *The Living Company: Habits for Survival in a Turbulent Business Environment*, Harvard Business School Press.

Goleman, Daniel (1996) *Emotional Intelligence: Why it can Matter More than IQ*, Bloomsbury.

Greenfield, Susan (2000) *Brain Story: Why Do We Think and Feel as We Do?*, BBC Books.

Handy, Charles (1998) *The Hungry Spirit: Beyond Capitalism – A Quest for Purpose in the Modern World*, Arrow.

Handy, Charles (2002) *The Elephant and the Flea: Looking Backwards to the Future*, Arrow.

Hargreaves, David (2004) *Learning for Life: The Foundations for Lifelong Learning*, The Policy Press.

Harris, Judith Rich (1999) *The Nurture Assumption*, Bloomsbury.

Holford, Patrick (2003) *Optimum Nutrition for the Mind*, Piatkus Books.

Honey, Peter and Mumford, Alan (2000) *The Learning Styles Questionnaire – 80 Item Version*, Peter Honey Publications.

Howard, Pierce (1994) *The Owner's Manual for the Brain: Everyday Applications for Mind–Brain Research*, Gilmour Drummond Publishing.

Illeris, Knud (2000) *The Three Dimensions of Learning: Contemporary Learning Theory in the Tension Field Between the Cognitive, the Emotional, and the Social*, Krieger.

Knasel, Eddy, Meed, John and Rossetti, Anna (2000) *Learn for Your Life: A Blueprint for Continuous Learning*, Financial Times/Prentice Hall.

Knight, Sue (1999) *Introducing NLP*, Chartered Institute of Personnel and Development.

Kroeger, Otto and Thuesen, Jane (1989) *Type Talk: The 16 Personality Types that Determine How We Live, Love, and Work*, Bantam, Doubleday, Dell Publishing.

Langer, Ellen J. (1998) *The Power of Mindful Learning*, Da Capo Press.

Leibling, Mike and Prior, Robin (2004) *The A–Z of Learning: Tips and Techniques for Teachers*, RoutledgeFalmer.

Lucas, Bill (2001) *Power Up Your Mind: Learn Faster, Work Smarter*, BBC Books.

Lucas, Bill and Smith, Alistair (2002) *Help Your Child to Succeed: The Essential Guide for Parents*, Network Educational Press.

Malone, Samuel A. (2003) *Learning About Learning: An A–Z of Training and Development Tools and Techniques*, Chartered Institute of Personnel and Development.

Mind Gym, The (2005) *Wake Up Your Mind*, Time Warner Books.

Mithen, Steven (1999) *The Prehistory of the Mind: The Cognitive Origins of Art, Religion and Science*, Phoenix.

Pert, Candace (1999) *Molecules of Emotion: Why You Feel the Way You Do*, Pocket Books.

Pinker, Stephen (2003) *The Blank Slate: The Modern Denial of Human Nature*, Penguin.

Pinker, Stephen (2004) *How the Mind Works*, Penguin.

Prashnig, Barbara (2004) *The Power of Diversity*, Network Educational Press.

Ratey, John (2003) *A User's Guide to the Brain*, Abacus.

Restak, Richard (2004) *The New Brain: How the Modern Age is Rewiring Your Mind*, Rodale.

Robinson, Ken (2002) *Out of Our Minds: Learning to be Creative*, Capstone.

Rose, Colin and Nicholl, Malcolm J. (1998) *Accelerated Learning for the 21st Century: The Six-Step Plan to Unlock Your Master-Mind*, DTP.

Seligman, Martin E.P. (1998) *Learned Optimism*, Pocket Books.

Senge, Peter (1993) *The Fifth Discipline: Art and Practice of the Learning Organization*, Random House Business Books.

Smith, Alistair (2004) *The Brain's Behind It: New Knowledge About the Brain and Learning*, Network Educational Press.

Smith, Alistair, Lovatt, Mark and Wise, Derek (2003) *Accelerated Learning: A User's Guide*, Network Educational Press.

Smith, Jim and Spurling, Andrea (1999) *Lifelong Learning: Riding the Tiger*, Continuum.

Sternberg, Robert (1996) *Successful Intelligence*, Simon & Schuster.

Stoll, Louise, Fink, Dean and Earl, Lorna (2003) *It's About Learning and It's About Time*, RoutledgeFalmer.

Toffler, Alvin (1984) *Future Shock: The Third Wave*, Bantam.

Vaill, Peter B. (1996) *Learning as a Way of Being: Keeping Afloat in Permanent Whitewater*, Jossey Bass Wiley.

Zohar, Danah and Marshall, Ian (2001) *Spiritual Intelligence: The Ultimate Intelligence*, Bloomsbury.

Index

Other titles from Bill Lucas

Help Your Child To Succeed by Bill Lucas & Alistair Smith
Help Your Child To Succeed – Toolkit by Bill Lucas & Alistair Smith
Power Up Your Mind by Bill Lucas
Be Creative by Guy Claxton & Bill Lucas

Other titles from Network Educational Press

VISIONS OF EDUCATION SERIES

The Power of Diversity by Barbara Prashnig
The Brain's Behind It by Alistair Smith
Wise Up by Guy Claxton
The Unfinished Revolution by John Abbott & Terry Ryan
The Learning Revolution by Gordon Dryden & Jeannette Vos

LEARNING TO LEARN

Let's Learn How to Learn: Workshops for Key Stage 2 by UFA National Team
Brain Friendly Revision by UFA National Team
Creating a Learning to Learn School by Toby Greany & Jill Rodd
Teaching Pupils How to Learn by Bill Lucas, Toby Greany, Jill Rodd & Ray Wicks

CREATIVE THINKING

Think it–Map it! by Ian Harris & Oliver Caviglioli
Thinking Skills & Eye Q by Oliver Caviglioli, Ian Harris & Bill Tindall
Reaching out to all thinkers by Ian Harris & Oliver Caviglioli
With Drama in Mind by Patrice Baldwin
Imagine That... by Stephen Bowkett
Self-Intelligence by Stephen Bowkett
StoryMaker Catch Pack by Stephen Bowkett

ACCELERATED LEARNING SERIES

Accelerated Learning: A User's Guide by Alistair Smith, Mark Lovatt & Derek Wise
Accelerated Learning in the Classroom by Alistair Smith
Accelerated Learning in Practice by Alistair Smith
The ALPS Approach: Accelerated Learning in Primary Schools by Alistair Smith & Nicola Call
The ALPS Approach Resource Book by Alistair Smith & Nicola Call
MapWise by Oliver Caviglioli & Ian Harris
Creating an Accelerated Learning School by Mark Lovatt & Derek Wise
Thinking for Learning by Mel Rockett & Simon Percival
Reaching out to all learners by Cheshire LEA
Move It: Physical movement and learning by Alistair Smith
Coaching Solutions by Will Thomas & Alistair Smith

ABLE AND TALENTED CHILDREN COLLECTION

Effective Provision for Able and Talented Children by Barry Teare
Effective Resources for Able and Talented Children by Barry Teare
More Effective Resources for Able and Talented Children by Barry Teare
Challenging Resources for Able and Talented Children by Barry Teare
Enrichment Activities for Able and Talented Children by Barry Teare
Parents' and Carers' Guide for Able and Talented Children by Barry Teare

PRIMARY RESOURCES

Promoting Children's Well-Being in the Primary Years: The Right from the Start Handbook edited by Andrew Burrell and Jeni Riley
But Why? Developing philosophical thinking in the classroom by Sara Stanley with Steve Bowkett
Foundations of Literacy by Sue Palmer & Ros Bayley
That's English! Learning English through song by Tim Harding
That's Maths! Learning Maths through song by Tim Harding
That's Science! Learning Science through song by Tim Harding
The Thinking Child by Nicola Call with Sally Featherstone
The Thinking Child Resource Book by Nicola Call with Sally Featherstone

EXCITING ICT

New Tools for Learning: Accelerated Learning meets ICT by John Davitt
Exciting ICT in Maths by Alison Clark-Jeavons
Exciting ICT in English by Tony Archdeacon
Exciting ICT in History by Ben Walsh

EFFECTIVE LEARNING & LEADERSHIP

Leading the Learning School by Colin Weatherley
Closing the Learning Gap by Mike Hughes
Strategies for Closing the Learning Gap by Mike Hughes with Andy Vass
Transforming Teaching & Learning by Colin Weatherley with Bruce Bonney, John Kerr & Jo Morrison
Effective Learning Activities by Chris Dickinson
Tweak to Transform by Mike Hughes
Making Pupil Data Powerful by Maggie Pringle & Tony Cobb
Raising Boys' Achievement by Jon Pickering
Effective Teachers by Tony Swainston
Effective Teachers in Primary Schools by Tony Swainston

EMOTIONAL INTELLIGENCE

Becoming Emotionally Intelligent by Catherine Corrie
Lend Us Your Ears by Rosemary Sage
Class Talk by Rosemary Sage
A World of Difference by Rosemary Sage
Best behaviour and Best behaviour FIRST AID by Peter Relf, Rod Hirst, Jan Richardson & Georgina Youdell

For more information and ordering details, please consult our website: www.networkpress.co.uk

Network Educational Press – much more than publishing...

NEP Conferences – Invigorate your teaching

Each term NEP runs a wide range of conferences on cutting edge issues in teaching and learning at venues around the UK. The emphasis is always highly practical. Regular presenters include some of our top-selling authors such as Steve Bowkett, Bill Lucas, Sue Palmer and Barry Teare. Dates and venues for our current programme of conferences can be found on our website www.networkpress.co.uk.

NEP online Learning Style Analysis – Find out how you and your students prefer to learn

Discovering what makes your students tick is the key to personalizing learning. NEP's Learning Style Analysis is a 50-question online evaluation that can give an immediate and thorough learning profile for every student in your class. It reveals how, when and where they learn best, whether they are right brain or left brain dominant, analytic or holistic, whether they are strongly auditory, visual, kinaesthetic or tactile ... and a great deal more. And for teachers who'd like to take the next step, LSA enables you to create a whole-class profile for precision lesson planning.

Developed by The Creative Learning Company in New Zealand and based on the work of Learning Styles expert Barbara Prashnig, this powerful tool allows you to analyse and your students' learning preferences in a more detailed way than any other product we have ever seen. To find out more about Learning Style Analysis or to order profiles visit www.networkpress.co.uk/lsa.

Also available:
Teaching Style Analysis and ***Working Style Analysis***.